The Fragile Entente

Westview Replica Editions

The concept of Westview Replica Editions is a response to the continuing crisis in academic and informational publishing. Library budgets for books have been severely curtailed. Ever larger portions of general library budgets are being diverted from the purchase of books and used for data banks, computers, micromedia, and other methods of information retrieval. Interlibrary loan structures further reduce the edition sizes required to satisfy the needs of the scholarly community. Economic pressures on the university presses and the few private scholarly publishing companies have severely limited the capacity of the industry to properly serve the academic and research communities. As a result, many manuscripts dealing with important subjects, often representing the highest level of scholarship, are no longer economically viable publishing projects--or, if accepted for publication, are typically subject to lead times ranging from one to three years.

Westview Replica Editions are our practical solution to the problem. We accept a manuscript in camera-ready form, typed according to our specifications, and move it immediately into the production process. As always, the selection criteria include the importance of the subject, the work's contribution to scholarship, and its insight, originality of thought, and excellence of exposition. The responsibility for editing and proofreading lies with the author or sponsoring institution. We prepare chapter headings and display pages, file for copyright, and obtain Library of Congress Cataloging in Publication Data. A detailed manual contains simple instructions for preparing the final typescript, and our editorial staff is always available to answer questions.

The end result is a book printed on acid-free paper and bound in sturdy library-quality soft covers. We manufacture these books ourselves using equipment that does not require a lengthy make-ready process and that allows us to publish first editions of 300 to 600 copies and to reprint even smaller quantities as needed. Thus, we can produce Replica Editions quickly and can keep even very specialized books in print as long as there is a demand for them.

About the Book and Author

The Fragile Entente:
The 1978 Japan-China Peace Treaty
in a Global Context
Robert E. Bedeski

Between early 1978 and late 1980, power relationships in the Pacific region underwent historic transformation. Deng-Xiaoping, re-emerging as a key leader in
the People's Republic of China, demonstrated pragmatism
in domestic and foreign policy. Beijing negotiated a
Peace and Friendship Treaty with Japan, apparently
opening an era of Sino-Japanese economic cooperation.
Moscow viewed this development with alarm, fearing it
would lead to a three-way alliance including the United
States. Meanwhile, Japan foreswore any military significance in closer links with the PRC, but by succumbing
to the Chinese demand for inclusion of a treaty clause
denouncing Soviet hegemony, became an involuntary participant in the Sino-Soviet conflict.

In this environment, the Sino-Japanese treaty--
which might have been an innocuous footnote to postwar
history--became an event marking a new phase in East
Asian affairs. Dr. Bedeski draws on Chinese, Soviet,
and Japanese sources to clarify the relationships among
the wide range of events ensuing from the treaty and
points to its relevance to a new era of Sino-Soviet
relations. The irony of the Peace and Friendship Treaty,
he concludes, is that it probably was a catalyst of
insecurity and hostility in the region and that it
became an important event leading to the participation
of non-Communist actors--Japan, the U.S., and NATO--
in the Sino-Soviet conflict.

Robert E. Bedeski studied Chinese in Taiwan and
received a Ph.D. in political science at the University
of California, Berkeley. This book was written while
Professor Bedeski was a research fellow of the Japan
Foundation at the National Defense College in Tokyo.
Currently a professor of political science at Carleton
University in Ottawa, he is the author of *State-Building
in Modern China: The Kuomintang in the Prewar Period*.

The Fragile Entente
The 1978 Japan-China
Peace Treaty in a Global Context

Robert E. Bedeski

Westview Press / Boulder, Colorado

A Westview Replica Edition

Copyright © 1983 by Westview Press, Inc.

Published in 1983 in the United States of America by
    Westview Press, Inc.
    5500 Central Avenue
    Boulder, Colorado 80301
    Frederick A. Praeger, President and Publisher

Library of Congress Cataloging in Publications Data
Bedeski, Robert E.
    The fragile entente.
    (A Westview replica edition)
    Bibliography: p.
    1. Japan--Foreign relations--China   2. China--
Foreign relations--Japan.   3. World politics--1975-1985.
I. Title II. Title: Japan-China Peace Treaty in a
global context.
DS849.C6B42 1983   327'.095   82-21990
ISBN 0-86531-944-8

Printed and bound in the United States of America.

10 9 8 7 6 5 4 3 2 1

To Kathleen

Contents

Acknowledgments

Research and writing for this study was made possible by a research grant from the Japan Foundation. Other assistance was provided by the Social Science and Humanities Research Council of Canada. The author wishes to express appreciation to Carleton University, the Faculty of Social Sciences, and the Department of Political Science for support. In Tokyo, the National Defense College provided access to library resources and a pleasant environment, and the author is grateful to the faculty and staff of the College. Mr. Kitahara Iwao, Embassy of Japan, Ottawa, Mihara Asahiko in Tokyo, and the staff at the International House Library were helpful in making the time fruitful in accomplishing my research.

The author also wishes to thank various Diet members, officials at the Defense Agency and Foreign Ministry, and Keidanren, and General Kurisu Hiromi. In Ottawa, special thanks is due to Professor Henry Mayo, Mrs. Betty Weiss and Caroline Caiger. International Journal and Issues and Studies have given permission to include previously published material in this book.

Finally, my wife Kathleen helped in numerous aspects of the project and provided indispensable moral support in its completion. The author alone is responsible for conclusions and materials herein.

Robert E. Bedeski

1
Introduction

The Peace Treaty between Japan and China was signed nearly a third of a century after the end of hostilities. It was concluded after nearly six years of normalization, but had been expected much sooner. By 1978, the global situation, regional alignments, and post-Mao government in China had changed significantly. China under the leadership of Deng Xiaoping was seeking allies against the USSR, and insisted that the Japanese align themselves against "hegemony" - the code word for Soviet expansionism. US President Carter was planning to withdraw all ground forces from Asia in the aftermath of the Vietnam war. The Soviets were building up their military forces in East Asia.

In this environment, the Sino-Japan Treaty - which might have been an innocuous footnote to postwar history - became an event marking a new phase in East Asian affairs. By acquiescing to the Chinese demand for inclusion of the hegemony clause, Japan became an involuntary participant in the Sino-Soviet conflict and was followed by the more enthusiastic Americans within a few months. Possibly heartened by these diplomatic successes, which were to bring billions of dollars in trade and credits, Beijing attacked Vietnam in 1979, risking that the USSR would not counterattack to save its ally.

The Japanese were brought into the power politics of the region very quickly. The Soviets interpreted the Treaty as evidence of a growing China-US-Japan entente against the USSR, although Tokyo denied any such significance. To convince Japan that a pro-China alignment was unwise, the Soviets reinforced the military garrisons on the islands of the northern territories which were claimed by Japan. These forces, the augmentation of air, land and naval forces in the Soviet Far East, and the growing Soviet presence in Vietnam have caused growing concern over national security in Japan. The credibility of US guarantees to Japan's security has been eroded by perception of increasing Soviet military capacity in the region, American priorities in Europe

1

and the Mideast, and the self-doubts which clouded American resolve in the post-Vietnam years. These factors, more than any residue of militarism, could cause the rearming of Japan if constitutional and opinion barriers are broken down.

The irony of the Peace and Friendship Treaty was that it was probably a catalyst in a new stage of insecurity and hostility in the region. Détente between the US and USSR may be largely unmourned in the aftermath of Soviet invasion of Afghanistan. Perhaps one of the most significant developments of the final quarter of this century in international affairs is that previously neutral spectators in the Sino-Soviet dispute - including Japan, the US, and NATO - have become pro-China participants, and have taken considerable pressure off the Chinese. It is this development which the present book explores and analyzes.

2
The Regional Environment: America's New Asian Strategy

The Peace and Friendship Treaty (PFT) symbolized the end of nearly a century of suspicion and hostility between the two Asian neighbors. Although relations had been normalized in 1972, it was not until 12 August 1978 that the formal treaty of peace was signed between the People's Republic of China (PRC) and Japan. This was to usher in a new era of stability and cooperation in the region. Earlier in the year, Japan promised capital and technology to assist in China's four modernizations, and China had agreed to supply Japan with millions of tons of crude oil. The possibilities of cooperation appeared most promising.

During subsequent years, Japan's expectations of economic benefits were scaled down as China reduced the pact of industrial development. The earlier "China fever" in Japan subsided. But more important, the 1978 treaty not only failed to stabilize the region but also may have contributed indirectly to new confrontations and insecurities. It was a strictly bilateral agreement, but it affected complex relations among the US, USSR, Vietnam and Korea, as well as the original signatories.

The origins of the treaty go back to 1972, when the Zhou-Tanaka Joint Communiqué called for the PFT to be concluded, [1] but nearly six years passed before it was successfully negotiated. Continued leadership struggles in Beijing and disagreements within the Japanese Liberal Democratic Party (LDP) contributed to the delay. China's insistence on including a hegemony clause also created difficulties for Japan. Hegemony had become a term linked to anti-Soviet polemics, so that Japan could incur USSR wrath by accepting the PRC phrasing. Japan had little reason to join in China's anti-Soviet united front, and demurred for years before signing a treaty containing such a clause.

By 1978, changes in the international environment and in the PRC combined to overcome Japan's reluctance. Among these changes were:

(1)   The   Americans   were   disengaging   from   previous
levels of military commitment in East Asia.   The removal
of U.S. troops from Southeast Asia, and Carter's pledge
to withdraw ground forces from South Korea, raised
doubts about the future of US involvement in the region.
The Japan-China Treaty could conceivably contribute to
stabilizing the region as the American military presence
declined.
       (2)   China needed foreign assistance and technology
to repair damages to the economy caused by the Cultural
Revolution.   China also needed to modernize all aspects
of society and economy to raise living standards and
improve military security. Japan had signed a Long Term
Trade Agreement (LTTA) with China in February 1978, and
the PFT would further strengthen bonds between the two
countries.
       (3)   The Soviet military buildup in East Asia had
been in progress for a number of years, directed largely
against the PRC.   There had been no lessening of the impasse over the northern territories, and some persons
thought that a treaty with China could nudge Moscow to
take a softer line.
       (4)   Prime Minister Fukuda Takeo saw the PFT as
important in restoring the LDP's sagging fortunes.
Japan's economy was stagnating, and the trade surplus
with the US was stirring American business hostility.
Fukuda hoped that expansion of the China market would
provide major relief to both problems.
       These four factors emerged as critical in the tim-
ing of the treaty.   Under other circumstances, the PFT
probably would have had little impact on international
relations. In the midst of new international conditions,
however, the treaty may have been a trigger for a new
round of military buildups and confrontations in the
East Asian region, especially as the USSR viewed the
Sino-Japan cooperation and Sino-US normalization as
steps towards an entente with anti-Soviet implications.

THE CARTER FACTOR

       With the existence of the US-Japan Security Treaty,
these new moves appeared to strike at Soviet positions
in Asia.   After the US withdrawal from South Vietnam in
1975, the American public mood shifted towards pacifism.
The election of Jimmy Carter to the presidency was partly due to a growing reluctance to pursue national interests abroad where involvement of US forces was required.
Many Americans, including the new administration in
Washington, wanted to avoid any more Vietnams.
       The new mood played a role in subsequent events in
East Asia, and prompted some Japanese to call for greater diplomatic autonomy vis-à-vis the US. During the Carter years, US foreign policy in Korea, Japan, and China
was to seek stability at lower cost, in contrast to the

policy of halting communist aggression taken by previous postwar administrations.

President Carter sought to create a new international sense of justice by insisting that America's allies - and adversaries - observe basic human rights. The moralist stand of the administration minimized the pursuit of US interests through military force. However, noble sentiments are rarely translated into effective foreign policy. United Nations Ambassador Andrew Young became a major administration spokesman for the new idealism in foreign policy, and there was criticism that international power realities were ignored.

To American allies, the Carter vision of peace through justice and moderation was deja vu. In previous postwar periods of modern American history, overseas commitments and involvements were seen as sources of conflict. This widely-held view led to years of relative isolation after world war one, and delayed US entry into the second war. After the end of the second world war, the brief disengagement from Europe and Asia was ended by confrontations with the USSR. Containment of Soviet expansion - either by direct military means or through allies - became the cornerstone of American foreign and defense policy.

Vietnam was the end of a policy which had begun in the Korean war - dispatching US combat troops to stop communist aggression. The failure of the US to attain its ends, despite massive deployment of men and equipment, stimulated debate over the effectiveness and necessity of anti-communist foreign policy. As a limited war, Vietnam had less domestic support than the Korean conflict of 1950-53. Moreover, American doubts were fueled by portrayal of Vietnam guerrillas as nationalist partisans fighting for independence. In the eyes of sympathethic journalists and intellectuals, Ho Chi Minh and his followers could not be considered the Soviet puppets of aggrandizement as portrayed by Washington.

To an increasingly larger number of Americans, the war against the National Liberation Front appeared not only unnecessary, but also unwinnable. The denouement in Saigon in April 1975 was seen as an inevitable end to unpopular military involvement. Coupled with Nixon's Watergate affair, and Ford's stoic but unpopular pardon for the ex-President, the agony of Vietnam smoothed the way for the ascendency of Jimmy Carter, as many Americans looked for less conflictual foreign policy and some moral leadership for the country.

During the 1976 presidential campaign, Carter translated the perceived American antipathy against future ground wars in Asia into his election promise to withdraw US ground forces from South Korea. Once elected, he took steps to implement the promise, despite misgivings by allies and officials at home. During his first year in office, Carter conveyed an image of a president who was edging towards a new isolationism - at least in Asia.[2] The post-Vietnam reduction of US forces in Asia indicated an impending psychological and material disengagement from the region. If such disengagement were realized, and if the USSR pursued outward expansion, there was danger that a power vacuum would be created and the Soviet Union would seek new opportunities. It would be ironic if the result of America's Vietnam intervention became Soviet expansion in Asia.

This was the international environment in which the Japan-China PFT was negotiated and concluded. To these two giants - one in economic and technological strength, and the other in population, territorial and resource quantity - an Asia with decreased American presence was an unknown future, and possibly an unstable region. This was more crucial to Japan, because of the three and a half decades of intimate political, military, economic, and cultural relations with the US. The PRC, which lost Mao Zedong as leader in September 1976, was undergoing its own transformation. Some Chinese leaders were not certain that American withdrawal from Asia was a desirable development. Without the US to counterbalance the USSR, China would be vulnerable to Moscow intimidation.

The presence of US ground forces in South Korea was insurance that an attack from the north would immediately involve the US in a war. It was a circumstance which assured US attention to the region. It reassured the Seoul government, and doubtlessly reduced Japanese anxieties about stability in the peninsula. The US forces were hostages, to be sure, and they might become involved again in "the wrong war, in the wrong place." But from Seoul's perspective, the likelihood of war occurring was significantly reduced by the American presence.

This was a disagreeable possibility to the US, but it was a source of comfort to Japan that American commitment to the security of the Republic of Korea (ROK) was expressed in the physical presence of American forces. Since the Korean peninsula for centuries had been considered vital to Japanese security, its occupation by hostile forces, or becoming a theater of war again, were matters of grave concern to Japanese defense planners.

While the PRC could hardly be expected to embrace the presence of US forces with enthusiasm, the implications of withdrawal were that the balance of power in the tense East Asian region could be altered. The draconian regime of North Korea's Kim Il Song maintained a tenuous independence from Moscow and Beijing. The PRC had intervened in the peninsular war in late 1950 to support Pyongyang. By early 1977 the Chinese leadership was moving to a pragmatic post-Mao regime, and needed to avoid conflict with the US and USSR. The Carter-planned withdrawal of US forces conformed to Chinese ideological demands against US imperialism, but it could also signal destabilization of the peninsula if Pyongyang (or Seoul) sought to settle the reunification issue by force.

In Southeast Asia, the communist victory in Vietnam was creating new distractions for the PRC. Hanoi quickly consolidated control over all Vietnam, and the neighboring states of Laos and Kampuchea appeared to be the next targets in Vietnamese expansion. With captured American weapons, and a momentum borne from years of struggle against French and US armies, Hanoi raised Chinese fears of a reunified Indochina growing into a regional rival in the south. The extension of Soviet influence into Vietnam heightened Chinese anxiety towards allies they once described as being as "close as lips and teeth."

From the Japanese perspective, America's post-Vietnam strategy in East Asia after Carter's election pointed to decreased involvement. Washington assured its allies that the US would honor its treaty commitments. What Asians questioned, however, was the American will to use military force where security interests were involved.

Vietnam had demonstrated the limited efficacy of military force, although critics on the right argue that political restraints made the war unwinnable. Among some countries, there was anticipation of reduced US interest in security problems of the region. ASEAN* countries sought assurances from Vietnam that its postwar policies would be limited to economic reconstruction, rather than to expanding its territorial sway.

AMERICA'S NEW STRATEGY IN ASIA

The president's policy to withdraw ground forces from the ROK disturbed allies in East Asia, especially when interpreted as part of American separation from Asia. Japanese newspapers saw other evidence that the US was to change strategy toward East Asia.[3] It was suggested that Carter was prepared to tolerate a tilt in the balance of power in the Soviet's favor, at least in East Asia.

Amid these growing doubts, Secretary of Defense Harold Brown attempted to define the US government's new Asian strategy. According to him, the US faced a highly favorable istuation because of the confrontation between the PRC and USSR. Their respective reinforcement of military power was directed against each other, and therefore reduced the likelihood of attacks against third countries. The ongoing Sino-Soviet dispute decreased the possibility of either China or the USSR going to war against the US and its allies in the East Asian region.

Brown pointed out that rapprochement between the US and the PRC was helping to stabilize China as well as

*The Association of Southeast Asian Nations which includes Malaysia, Thailand, Singapore, the Philippines and Indonesia.

the rest of East Asia. A stable China would be less
likely to engage in or support adventures against South
Korea or elsewhere. As Japan's economy became stronger,
that country could take more responsibility for its own
defense. The thrust of administration thinking was that
the US should reduce its presence and obligations in the
region.

The East Asian situation had changed since the
1950s and 1960s, when the presence of US military forces
was considered the major deterrent to aggression. By
the late 1970s, the PRC was a counterweight to the USSR
and its client, Vietnam. South Korea had developed
military and economic strength, and decreased earlier
dependence on the US. Japan had emerged as an economic
superpower, while ASEAN countries progressed in political stability and economic viability. To the Carter administration, the region appeared to be an area where
military presence could be reduced without endangering
peace and stability.

This favorable assessment of the Asian strategic
situation was tempered by recognition of some destabilizing factors: The USSR had been reinforcing Far Eastern
forces in the previous decade, while the US countered
with deployment of its own advanced weapons. There was
also the possibility of a peaceful resolution of the
Sino-Soviet quarrel, which would threaten the foundation
of America's new Asian strategy.

It is not an exaggeration to say that, from the
standpoint of realpolitik, the task of American strategy
is to tolerate and avoid discouraging Sino-Soviet differences. Any acts which appear, or could be interpreted,
as actual encouragement or stimulation of the dispute,
would constitute dangerous involvement. Such involvement
on one side or the other could undermine any advantages
gained from continuation of the dispute, as well as
create difficulties for the US.

However, the Carter administration may not have recognized the delicacy of the balance, and moved to the
side of the PRC in 1978 to redress perceived inadequacies in previous foreign policy. The government of Japan
also dangerously tilted towards China, and became an in-
advertent participant in the Sino-Soviet conflict. It
is possible that the US and Japanese warming to China
during 1978 played a major role in heightening Soviet
belligerence in East Asia in 1978-79.

This is not to hold the USSR blameless, nor to ignore its heavyhanded intervention and occupation of
neighboring Afghanistan. However, the American and Japanese experiences of the Carter years must be examined
from the perspective of these two industrial democracies
leaning towards the PRC and antagonizing the USSR. In
effect, China has been able to divert some of the pressure from the USSR onto the US and Japan. This allows
Beijing to reduce its own military spending, and to push
ahead with civilian economic rehabilitation.

During the first year of the Carter administration, these considerations were not of primary importance. In the 1979 National Defense Report the US Defense Secretary stressed Europe as the main arena of security preparation.[4] Troops were to be transferred from the ROK to Western Europe. The USSR was simultaneously increasing military strength in East Asia, and some Japanese feared a tipping of the regional balance of forces. If the American withdrawal went ahead, it was speculated that Japan might rearm on a large scale. The US complained about Japan's "free ride" in defense, but few wanted a remilitarized Japan.

US diplomatic normalization and rapprochement with China became an underlying premise of the new Asian strategy. The 1979 National Defense Report stated that the US was no longer planning deployment of armed forces based on a hypothetical conflict with the PRC.[5] Beijing, under the post-Mao group led by Deng Xiaoping, reciprocated the American desire for improved relations - but only if the US ended relations with Taiwan. The US administration also explored the possibility of relations with the Democratic People's Republic of Korea (DPRK) in Pyongyang, but no progress was made. Without concrete assurances from the Kim Il Song regime, US unilateral withdrawal from the ROK was a dangerous risk - leaving Seoul to carry the consequences of failure.

The Japanese raised concern over US plans in the region in several meetings and in summit talks. In April 1978, the Foreign Ministry prepared agenda items for the May 3 summit talks between Carter and Fukuda, announcing that the Prime Minister would emphasize "that the US is necessary for Asian peace and security, request its continued fulfilling of its important political, economic and military roles, seek the US side's confirmation of these points, and have it show clearly that the US is not 'separating itself from Asia'."[6]

The administration insisted that no "separation" was considered. Vice-President Mondale visited ASEAN,[7] and various American officials stressed the continued commitment to East Asian security. The large volume of trade between the US and the region long-standing close relations with Japan, and the need for Southeast Asia as a source of strategic materials were among factors which tied US national interests to East Asia. Private American investment amounted to sixteen billion dollars.[8] The lessons of world war two and the Korean war demonstrated the importance of preserving the security of nations on the Asian perimeter. Whatever isolationist impulses were stimulated by the Vietnam conflict, the US could not withdraw from its wide range of diplomatic, security and economic involvements in the East Asian region.

The Japanese stressed the symbolic importance of the US presence in the ROK. The US administration argued that reduction was logical because of a stable

international situation, and also because the ROK was
now strong enough to take care of its own security
needs, at least in the initial phase of conflict. Defense analysts could demonstrate that, under existing
assessments of regional military strengths, some reduction of US ground forces would not adversely affect ROK
security.

Liberal circles in the US also argued for reduction
of forces in the ROK as an appropriate sanction against
the government of Park Chung Hee for South Korean reluctance to implement reforms in human rights. Some members
of Congress expressed displeasure over the Park Tong Son
bribery allegations. The Unification Church of Rev. Sun
Myung Moon was an object of Congressional investigation
and was linked to the Korean Central Intelligence Agency. The projected withdrawal of US forces from the ROK
was argued to be rational from the viewpoint of regional
security, and as a means of disciplining an ally whose
moral performance did not live up to administration
criteria.

Along with the pullback of ground forces, the US
government formulated its new Asian strategy. It was a
strategy which relied more heavily on naval and air
force firepower and mobility, and less on ground forces
already in place. The navy was to deploy F-14 fighters
and would modernize the Pacific fleet over a five-year
period. Cruise missiles were to be installed in B-52
bombers of the Strategic Air Command in Guam.[9] These and
other moves were intended to quiet East Asian (especially Japanese) concerns that the US was disengaging
from the region, but there was anxiety that the introduction of new weapon systems could bring about a new
round of American-Soviet confrontations in the Pacific
area.[10]

The administration initiated its "optional presence" in the region. American forces had departed from
Vietnam and Thailand, and were scheduled to leave South
Korea. The notion that the US army would not fight again
on the Asian continent was implicit in the new doctrine.
In military terms, this doctrine was expressed as ob-
taining maximum results with a minimum of armed forces.
This included: avoiding intervention with US ground forces, the modernization and computerization of the navy
and air force, and increased accuracy of bombs and missiles with laser and television guidance systems. US officials maintained that the removal of ground forces (in
1978 down to their lowest number since 1945) did not
mean retreat of the US or any decrease in overall security. (Withdrawal of forces from Vietnam accounted for a
major portion of the decrease.)

Whatever efficacy the new strategy had as a substitute presence of US ground forces, it was partially undercut by doubts about American will and leadership.
President Carter's irresolution over the neutron bomb

did not seem to reflect decisiveness.[11] Japanese concern
over the administration's lack of continuity in East
Asian policy was again noted when Carter indicated new
revisions of the ROK withdrawal plan.[12]

The optional presence of US forces in East Asia was
to mean that they would be based in Japan (including
Okinawa), various Pacific islands, and the continental
US. In emergency, these forces would move to trouble
spots, but only by a Presidential Order. From the American standpoint, this decreased the automatic involvement of the US in any future Asian war, and gave the
President greater discretion in choosing when and where
to fight. The government of the ROK, and the Japan Defense Agency (JDA) considered Presidential discretion as
a less effective substitute for the "trip wire" and
"hostage" American forces in South Korea.

Another problem with the new Asian strategy of optional presence was that the military importance of Japan and of US bases in Japan and Okinawa* was sharply increased. In testimony before the US House of Representatives Foreign Relations Committee, Defense Secretary
Brown stated that if war broke out in the Korean peninsula, the US would commit Okinawa-based marines within
two days.[13] This may have reassured Congress and Japanese defense officials, but it led to another controversy
in Japan. The prefectural government of Okinawa reiterated opposition to the US-Japan Security Treaty, as well
as to further expansion of US military activities on the
island.[14]

Through early 1978, the administration continued
plans for winding down the American presence in the ROK.
In joint-military operations dubbed "Team Spirit '78",
the US and South Korea deployed 110,000 men on the peninsula. The object of the maneuvers was to practice
coordinated actions in a hypothetical second Korean war,
and demonstrate how US forces would be deployed. In addition to using air forces already in Korea, the US relied heavily on marine, air, and naval reinforcements
from Kadena, Yokota, Yokosuka, and Iwakuni bases in
Japan.[15]

Because of Japanese constitutional restrictions,
the maneuvers involved no Self Defense Forces. Nevertheless, Team Spirit '78 had implications for Japan's
security. As Secretary Brown had stated in a report to
Congress, Japan was the "front line of the defense of
the US" and the "anchor in the north," referring to its
importance as a naval base in the norther Pacific.[16] The
new Asian strategy was to allot greater geopolitical importance to Japan, and especially to Okinawa, as US
bases after withdrawal from the ROK. Europe and the

*Although Okinawa is an integral prefecture of Japan the
presence of sizeable US forces merits separate treat-
ment.

Middle East were higher priorities, and Washington
wanted maximum flexibility. Japanese anticipated that
the US would be calling for greater support, and for
stronger self-defense efforts from the "anchor in the
north."[17]

Carter's plan called for phased withdrawal of US
ground forces during a give year period. In 1978, 2400
combat and 2600 non-combat personnel were to be withdrawn from the 42,000-man ground forces in the ROK.[18]
This was later revised to a reduction by 3400 men during
1978, and 2600 the following year, mostly from the Second Infantry Division.[19]

The potential effects of the administration plan to
withdraw US ground forces from South Korea can be summarized as follows:

(1) The US would gain some flexibility as to where
and when to deploy forces in an emergency, such as an
attack on South Korea. But in the "Europe-first" framework which was perceived by many Japanese, the optional
presence in Asia appeared as a prelude to the transfer
of more US forces to the North Atlantic region. Both
Japan and the US recognized the need to avoid a second
Vietnam-type war, but there were differences as to the
appropriate steps.

(2) American credibility in defense commitments
was placed in doubt, especially as the Vietnam trauma
appeared to weaken American will to strengthen or util-
ize its military forces. Because Japanese security
depended heavily on the efficacy of a US deterrent,
questions arose as to how great an emergency would be
necessary for the president to commit American forces to
a conflict. Another flurry of doubts occurred in June
1978 when it was reported that the administration was to
study the effect of abrogating the security treaty.[20]

(3) Had the above trends continued, and if the
administration had not frozen the projected withdrawal,
it is possible that powerful arguments would have been
heard within Japan advocating far stronger and autonomous defenses. The peace constitution, the security
treaty, and the deployment of US military forces in the
Far East have combined to relieve Japan of heavy defense
burdens. Major changes in any of these factors might
set Japan on the road to rearmament.

(4) In new security arrangements, Japan could become the US front line in the Pacific basin - a situation which caused Japanese anxiety as American-Soviet
high technology nuclear confrontations became more
likely. Team Spirit 78 had already demonstrated that
American bases in Japan would be used as logistical
bases to supply and consolidate forces in Korea in the
event of war.

Japan had played this role during the Korean war.
But in the present age of missiles and sophisticated air
warfare, there was greater likelihood of direct involve-

ment of the support bases. Japanese governments have
cultivated an international posture of quasi-neutrality
and omnidirectionality in foreign policy, although the
linkage to the US has been prominent. The country did
not want to return to the status of a subordinate support base of the US, as it was in the 1950's. At the
very least, many in Japan wanted assurances of prior
consultations with the US in the event of an emergency.
If these did not occur, Japan might automatically become
involved in an American war.[21] Furthermore, as the US
increased reliance on tactical nuclear weapons, their
transit through or around Japan would become inevitable
in an emergency. This state of affairs could violate
the country's non-nuclear posture.[22]

(5) Finally, the withdrawal of ground forces could
alter the balance of power in the region. Despite repeated US assurances to the contrary, many Japanese were
skeptical that increased weaponry and mobility of US air
and naval forces would be as effective as ground forces
in deterring attack. Also, as Sino-American normalization progressed, it appeared that the American commitment to Taiwan would be surrendered.[23] There was speculation that the Guomindang government in Taiwan might
seek rapprochement with the USSR but this was highly
unlikely. Such action would have permanently damaged
the claim of the Nationalists to speak for all Chinese.

If historical precedent is a guide, pre-1941 East
Asia demonstrated one possible arrangement (but not the
only one) of regional powers without the involvement of
the US. From the late nineteenth century until world
war two, Japan and Russia were the major contenders in
the area, with the US exercising an optional presence,
and China suffering international intervention. The
present regional system has been complicated since 1945
(or stabilized, depending upon one's perspective) by a
resurgent China, and a permanent American presence.
Should the US withdraw a major portion of forces from
the region, a new regional configuration could be expected to emerge.[24]

By the end of his second year in office, Carter was
reversing his plan to withdraw from South Korea, while
asserting that the plan was merely "frozen" for the
present. Officially, the administration stated that the
buildup of North Korean forces posed a threat to the
south, and therfore the US ground force deployment had
to be maintained. To critics, it was a convenient face-
saving device, but it served the purpose of halting a
difficult policy.

Domestic pressure played a part in reversing Carter's decision. He underlined the importance of Asian
security in a speech of 17 March 1978 - the day on which
Team Spirit '78 concluded.[25] The maneuvers were intended
to communicate US readiness to intervene if South Korea
were invaded. US and ROK troops were deployed to the

north of Seoul - the invasion route of 1950. The maneuvers also applied psychological pressure on Pyongyang and Moscow.[26]

But if Team Spirit '78 was a signal of US commitment to ROK security, it also transmitted the message of preparations for a new American relationship in Northeast Asia. ROK forces played the leading combat role, while US forces were subordinate. These were the third joint exercises. After the 1969 and 1971 maneuvers, a total of 20,000 men had been withdrawan from Korea.[27] In this sense the maneuvers were also a form of preparation for the future circumstances of American "optional intervention", which would take place strictly according to US choices.

If the US hoped to appease non-communist Asian countries by using the joint maneuvers as proof of commitment, it was not completely successful. Moreover, there was growing nervousness in Congress and among US military officers over the consequences of the pullout. There were complaints that Carter had not adequately consulted with the legislative branch and his commanders.

In April 1978 Carter announced reduction of the withdrawal schedule. Instead of 2400 combat troops, only 800 would be removed from the ROK that year. The official reason was that Congress had not yet passed the military supplements of $800 million to be paid to Seoul to help with military modernization. This reduction was considered significant in the light of Carter's speech, in which he referred to the "reduction" of US forces in Korea rather than "withdrawal."[28] From the Japanese perspective, political considerations, rather than strategic or economic factors, appeared most important in whatever final decision emerged. The withdrawal plan had been an election campaign pledge, and had to be treated delicately.

Within the US Army, there was considerable and even outspoken opposition to the withdrawal. Generals Singlaub and Stilwell expressed criticism of the plan, while in Congress, the House of Representatives Armed Services Committee adopted a resolution opposing withdrawal. A report by the Senate Armed Service Committee (March 1979) called for cancellation of the withdrawal because "the US must have its allies firmly believe that it is not withdrawing from Asia."[29] These sentiments coincided with some Japanese views, which had strongly urged the US to move cautiously in its proposed withdrawal.[30]

A major objective of the withdrawal plan had been to reduce tensions in Asia. The administration had hoped that a dialogue could be established with Pyongyang. However, by undertaking unilateral withdrawal, Washington may have discarded an important bargaining lever with North Korea. It was even suggested that the Team Spirit maneuvers were a provocation to the north, and

became a source of insecurity which caused an arms increase.[31]
    In any event, North Korea did not respond posi-
tively as hoped, and set out to expand its armed forces.
When the President declared the freeze on US withdrawals
in July 1979, two reasons were mentioned.[32] One was that
the North Koreans were expanding their combat forces by
committing approximately 30 percent of their GNP to military spending. Second, there was the increasing buildup
of Soviet forces in East Asia, and increasing tensions
in the region which required continued US strength in
the region.
    Prior to the freeze announcement, a Senate group
headed by Samuel Nunn submitted a report after its fact-
finding mission to East Asia. Its recommendation was
that the US suspend withdrawal of any forces until the
degree of North Korean buildup was clear.[33] The Nunn
report revised upward the previous estimates of North
Korea divisions from twenty-nine to forty, indicating
there were more than a 100,000 more troops than previously estimated. The Nunn group also estimated that
there were six hundred more tanks in North Korea than
earlier believed.[34]
    The Nunn report mentioned other reasons to suspend
withdrawal: (1) Instead of saving money, the plan would
require $1.5 billion to $2.5 billion for implementation;
(2) even with withdrawal, the American forces might
still become involved in future conflicts in the Korean
peninsula; (3) it would not be easy to transfer the
forces from Korea to other areas; (4) the withdrawal
plan could force the ROK to develop nuclear weapons; and
(5) there would be a decline in East Asian trust in the
US.
    When Carter visited Seoul in late June 1979, the
South Korean government hoped the president would announce the freeze on US withdrawals at that time. However, President Park was disappointed when the Carter
visit did not produce a communiqué on the freeze.[35] The
decision had already been made in Washington, but perhaps Carter wanted to use the freeze as leverage to
extract concessions on human rights. If true, it meant
that the administration was shrewder in bargaining with
an ally (ROK) than with an adversary (DPRK).
    Despite the freeze on withdrawals from Korea, the
decline of US forces in Asia was evidence of decreasing
military involvement in the region. From 600,000 men in
1970, American forces in the Asia/West Pacific region
decreased to 134,000 men by the end of 1976. US forces
in Japan decreased from 98,000 to 46,000 during the same
same period - in contrast to a much slighter decrease in
Europe-based forces, from 298,000 to 284,000.[36] Pro-US
countries in Asia recognized that Vietnam war levels
could not be maintained, but they expressed concern that
the Korean reductions were a part of general withdrawal

16

from the region. The US appeared to reverse its postwar role in the region after the Vietnam war. During 1977-78, it was not certain where that disengagement would stop.

Japan had at least two major options to assist in readjusting to decreased US presence in the region. The first option was to build up military strength so as to fill the security gap left by American withdrawal. But as long as the security treaty was dependable, the incentive for Japan's remilitarization was slight. Domestic opposition and constitutional obstacles also minimized the possibility of rapid increases in Japan's defense capacity.

The second option was to embark on diplomatic initiatives which would cushion the shocks of decreasing US military reliability and deterrence in East Asia. Japan had to prepare for the possibility of more autonomous diplomacy, which, under American patronage, was not easily realized. As with West Europe, the United States was the senior ally to Japan. In both cases, the strength of the alliance depended in part upon the physical presence of American forces in the respective region. If the "Carter shocks" were allowed to accumulate into a general decline of US-Japan cooperation, then Japan might be forced to pursue policies that were based on narrower national interests, as opposed to the mutual interests of the two countries.

These considerations were part of the diplomatic environment which surrounded the negotiations and conclusion of the 1978 Japan-China PFT. Japanese leaders and officials did not believe the US was considering a total disengagement from the region. However, the expectation of a reduced American military presence probably led some to hope that a firmer relationship with the increasingly moderate and pragmatic PRC would influence and correct whatever imbalances emerged in the future. The treaty may have been inevitable, but its timing was linked to specific international circumstances - including the new American strategy.

Footnotes

1. Lee Chae-Jin, Japan Faces China (Baltimore: John Hopkins University, 1976), pp. 210-212.
2. See, for example, his speech at Notre Dame University, 22 May 1977.
3. Mainichi Shimbun, 16 January 1978, p. 5 (Hereinafter MS).
4. US Department of Defense. Annual Report Fiscal Year 1979 (2 February 1978), p. 23.
5. Nihon Keizai, (Hereinafter NK), 23 March 1978, p. 2.
6. Asahi Shimbun, 23 April 1978, p. 1 (Hereinafter AS).

17

7.   Ibid.
8.   Yomiuri Shimbun, 7 May 1978, p. 3 (Hereinafter YS).
9.   YS, 25 February 1978, p. 7.
10. Ibid.
11. Sankei, 17 May 1978, p. 4 (Hereinafter SK).
12. NK, 27 March 1979, p. 2.
13. YS, 28 February 1978, p. 7.
14. Ibid.
15. AS, 11 March 1978, p. 3.
16. YS, 25 February 1978, p. 7.
17. Ibid.
18. Tokyo Shimbun (Hereinafter TS) 30 April 1978, p. 5.
19. SK, 24 January 1979, p. 1.
20. YS. 24 June 1978, p. 2.
21. YS, 4 March 1978, p. 5.
22. NK, 23 March 1978, p. 2.
23. SK, 17 May 1978, p. 4.
24. Ibid.
25. NK, 23 March 1978, p. 2.
26. Ibid.
27. TS, 17 March 1978, p. 5.
28. SK, 27 April 1978, p. 6.
29. AS, 7 April 1979, p. 2.
30. SK, 27 April 1978, p. 6.
31. YS, 28 April 1978, p. 5.
32. MS, 22 July 1979, p. 5.
33. SK, 24 January 1979, p. 1.
34. The Japanese monthly Sentaku reported that the information that led the US to reassess North Korea's military strength and to freeze the planned troop withdrawal was provided by China, which had received the reports from Pyongyang itself. Korea Herald, 5 September 1979, p. 1.
35. YS, 13 June 1979, p. 2.
36. SK, 22 May 1978, p. 4.

3
The Japan-China Treaty
of Peace and Friendship

The prospect of decreasing US military presence in East Asia was an important background factor which encouraged Japan and China to conclude the PFT. Whatever the consequences of withdrawal, China and Japan would be forced to play more active roles in maintaining peace and stability in the region, as well as restraining Soviet pressures.

The post-Korean war structure of international relations in East Asia was predicated on US strategic domination. If the US displayed reluctance to exercise strategic leverage in maintaining the balance of power in the Pacific, or, if this dominance was supplanted by Soviet expansion into the Pacific region, Japan would have grounds for anxiety about security.[1] Both conditions were becoming apparent in 1977 and 1978. Tokyo translated some of this anxiety into resolution to improve diplomatic and economic relations with the PRC.

Relations with China had been normalized in 1972, and thereafter Japan's diplomacy between the PRC and USSR rested on more certain diplomatic foundations. These relations were predicated on the US military presence in East Asia while the relative weakness of Japan's military forces precluded armed rivalry with the two communist giants. If the US strategic position eroded, then Japan would become more vulnerable to threats from the continental powers to the west, and this vulnerability might revive a remilitarized Japan.

A change in US commitment was one factor which determined the direction of Sino-Japanese relations. There was mutual attraction between the two states--reinforced by geographical propinquity and common cultural roots. After the death of Mao Zedong, Japan became more attractive to China as a source of technology and investment in the ambitious modernization program. Japanese businessmen recognized the possibilities of resource development and project construction under the more legalistic, stable and pragmatic political order of Deng Xiaoping. From the standpoint of Asian international relations, a

stronger Sino-Japan connection could stabilize the region if parallel interests were pursued cooperatively.
If the US had completed the withdrawal from South Korea,
for example, China and Japan might have to take joint
measures to prevent outbreak of conflict in the peninsula, or at a minimum, clarify their parallel interests.

Japan's desire to move closer to China in diplomacy
and economic affairs was moderated by the existence of
the Sino-Soviet dispute. Such a move would further antagonize Moscow, with whom relations had long been cool.

The nineteenth century Russo-Japanese rivalry over
Korea and Manchuria culminated in the war of 1904-5.
Japan's Siberian intervention after the first world war,
and tensions between the two nations during the second
war, led to mutual suspicions in postwar relations. Representatives of the USSR participated in the postwar
occupation government of Japan, but their role was minimal.[2]

Against a background of rivalry and suspicion, it
was unlikely that Japanese diplomacy would move towards
reconciliation with the Soviet Union as enthusiastically
as with the PRC. Fishing disputes, Soviet retention of
the northern territories, frequent intrusion of air
space by Soviet planes, and a series of other aggrava-
tions have made the USSR the most unpopular nation in
Japanese public opinion polls.

In the 1970s, the USSR was an occasional nuisance
to Japan, rather than a military threat.[3] The prospects
of energy and other resources from Siberia, assisted by
Japanese capital and technology, necessitated mutual accommodation. China did not welcome Siberian development,
especially when it augmented Soviet military efforts on
the northern borders.[4] Thus, Chinese insistence on the
hegemony clause in the PFT could undermine some of the
cooperation between the USSR and Japan.[5]

Although opposition to hegemony was mentioned in
the 1972 Communique,[6] the Japanese government was reluctant to enter an agreement which could be interpreted
as an anti-Soviet entente. The hegemony clause had to
be inserted in the treaty, insisted the Chinese negotiators. A compromise was agreed on with an additional
clause disclaiming that the treaty affected relations
with third countries. The compromise may have salvaged
Tokyo-Moscow relations, but did not prevent a series of
events which directly related to the Sino-Soviet dispute: These include the Soviet increased fortification
of the northern territories and the Chinese attack
against Vietnam. These developments will be examined in
later chapters.

From the perspective of the PRC, the US and the
USSR had been locked in "hegemonistic" rivalry for world
domination since the end of the second world war. There
was the continued possibility that the two superpowers
would wage direct war against one another. At the same

time, the PRC posed as the protector and friend of revolutionary movements in the third world, and the leading
proponent of world peace. After 1960, the Chinese increasingly regarded the USSR as the more dangerous superpower, especially since it was the nearer threat.
    A new turn in this world view came after the US
withdrawal from Vietnam. As the Carter administration
sought peace and detente with the Soviet Union, a new
danger was presented to the Chinese. Soviet "socialist
imperialism" had not changed, but now it appeared that
American "hegemonism" was reluctant to "hegemonize". If
American post-Vietnam trauma turned into isolationism,
then opportunities for Soviet expansionism would multi-
ply, and China would become even more vulnerable. The
choice for Beijing after 1975 was narrowing to two options - either negotiate an accomodation with Moscow
from a position of strategic weakness, or, convince the
US leadership that it was dangerous to ignore the Soviet
threat to world peace. In the interim, China sought to
strengthen defenses as well as to promote closer relations with the "second world" of capitalist industrial
countries.
    The Chinese have used a tripartite classification
of the world (superpowers, advanced industrial nations,
and the developing nations) as their guide to international relations. The third world, which included China,
could have decisive influence only as long as the two
superpowers vied for supremacy. If the US or the USSR
surrendered, or refused to struggle with the opposite
superpower, an equally dangerous situation would emerge
giving the other a free hand to expand. Under these
conditions, the third world would be unable to halt a
single hegemonistic superpower, although the combined
forces of the third and second worlds might be effective
in slowing expansion.
    Therefore, the second world had to be brought into
the struggle against Soviet hegemonism, Beijing proalim-
ed. Under the North Atlantic Treaty Organization (NATO),
Western Europe, the US and Canada were already committed
to an anti-Soviet alliance on one Soviet flank. The declining presence of the US in Asia, however, and especially the withdrawal from South Korea, were symptoms of
US weariness in playing the part of superpower in that
part of the world.
    Next to China, Japan was the strongest potential
adversary of the USSR in Asia, and moreover a prominent
member of the second world. Japan was linked by the security treaty to the US, but the defensive capabilities
of this economic superpower were hamstrung by the peace
constitution, and Self Defense Forces (SDF) which were
under constant scrutiny and criticism. It was in China's
interests for Japan to realize the magnitude of the
Soviet threat, and to translate that realization into a
positive declaration opposing hegemony. The hegemony

clause which the Chinese insisted on inserting in the
treaty was thus rooted in a strategic and historical
world view which sought to enlist Japan in an anti-
Soviet united front.

If China could not stiffen Japan against the USSR
with arguments of international law and the necessities
of defense, then economic inducements could be used.
Japan, a major manufacturing and trading nation, had few
natural resources in the home islands. The prewar Greater East Asian Co-Prosperity Sphere had been intended to
provide resources and markets for Japan at the expense
of China and other Asian nations. A view of regional
cooperation, which Japan had sought and lost in the
Pacific war, was now re-emerging as a more cooperative
and equitable arrangement. China's new program of modernization in 1977 offered Japan a privileged position
in rebuilding the PRC after its false start of the Great
Leap Foward and the disaster of the Great Proletarian
Cultural Revolution.

From the Japanese side, 1978 was the year of decision on the PFT. Soviet intransigence over the northern
territories indicated that there would be no retrocession of the islands, even if Japan refrained from concluding the treaty. After the treaty, Moscow's position
against Japan further hardened. Soviet countermoves
occurred, and Japan-Soviet tensions increased as a result of closer Japan-China relations. Although these
prospects were foreseen, the Japan Foreign Ministry had
pushed ahead with negotiations, as the government denied
the intention of any Sino-Japanese alliance.

A possible PRC-US-Japan entente against the USSR
was a formidable threat to the Soviet Far East. Japan
was most cautious, therefore, to deny that the treaty
with China had any third nation in mind. The Gaimusho,
(Japanese Foreign Ministry) however, could not speak for
the Chinese Waijiaobu (Foreign Ministry) in this respect. Beijing considered the treaty a victory over Soviet hegemonism, according to a 15 August 1978 People's
Daily commentary, "The Sad Drone of an Autumn Insect -
Refuting the Tass Attack on the Signing of the Sino-
Japanese Peace and Friendship Treaty."

The Japanese government may have been overly optimistic or disingenous in this regard. Faced with the
linkage of the economic and population giants of Asia,
Soviet leaders could hardly have been comforted by even
the most sincere of Japanese disclaimers. A few months
later on 1 January 1979, the PRC and the US normalized
diplomatic relations in an atmosphere of growing anti-
Soviet sentiment. If the US was retreating from Asia in
1976 and 1977, the year 1978 marked a turnaround. From
the Soviet view, the Sino-Japanese PFT, and Sino-US
normalization indicated a dangerous development towards
a tripartite alliance. Perhaps both in anticipation and
in reaction to this trend, the USSR stepped up its own

diplomatic and military countermeasures.
None of this is to say that the USSR has been acting only defensively, or that Japan was responsible for
triggering a new cold war in the late 1970s by concluding the treaty with China. However, a combination of
events occurred in which the 1978 treaty appears to have
been a major catalyst in East Asian confrontations.
These have involved China, the US, the USSR, Japan,
Vietnam, and secondarily, Afghanistan and Pakistan.
Ironically, the Korean peninsula has been largely left
out of these developments - developments which can be
characterized as extending the Sino-Soviet conflict into
the diplomacy of non-communist countries.
The central question of the 1978 treaty remains:
Why did Japan pursue the treaty, even though Soviet
countermoves were anticipated? The simplest answer is
that Foreign Minister Sonoda Sunao and his colleagues
calculated all the risks, and then concluded that the
opportunities made the treaty worthwhile. There was also
the belief that Soviet suspicions could be overcome by
inserting the "third nation" clause (Article 4) in the
treaty, and proving by subsequent behavior that no Sino-
Japanese military alliance was intended. There was also
the precedent of the 1972 Sino-Japanese normalization
when a major diplomatic breakthrough was achieved at
little cost to Japan-USSR relations. Finally, the treaty
was seen as a major advantage for Fukuda in the election
for the LDP Presidency - a vain hope as it turned out.
The 1972 Sino-Japanese normalization occurred in a
simpler diplomatic environment than the PFT. Normalization had merely involved the establishment of bilateral
relations between China and Japan, while in 1978, both
the USSR and China were seeking a treaty and better economic relations with Japan. In addition, the structure
of Nixon-Kissinger diplomacy in 1972 treated the USSR
and the PRC in roughly equal terms. This had established
the equidistant structure within which the 1972 Japanese
initiative took place. By mid-1978, a pronounced pro-
China tilt was evident in US policy.
Japan urged China to abrogate the Sino-Soviet
treaty of 1950 prior to conclusion of the Japan-China
treaty because of the anti-Japanese clause in the former.[7] The signals received by Moscow in 1978 must have
raised fears of a growing encirclement, as Japan aligned
with China in diplomacy and economic relations.
Future historians may see the 1978 treaty as the
beginning of Japan's resumption of a larger regional
power role. But at the time, there seemed to be a degree
of innocence concerning the international ramifications
of its diplomatic acts. These ramifications were considered, but generally, Japan handled the treaty as a
strictly bilateral instrument, when in fact it marked a
new beginning in the region. The US government also may
not have given the treaty the importance it deserved,

and treated the negotiations as a formality involving
only Japan and China.

As will be examined later, the PFT was also intended to strengthen economic bonds. The US and PRC were
moving closer together during 1978, and Japanese leaders
feared loss of substantial trade and investment opportunities to the Americans if the PFT was not quickly
concluded. With the Japan-China Long Term Trade Agreement, American business interests saw expanding possibilities in the China market, and anticipated strong competition from their Japanese counterparts. Thus Japanese
and Americans quickened their efforts to conclude diplomatic and trade agreements. In part to retain the lead,
Tokyo pushed ahead with the treaty.

As the US moved forward in normalization with the
PRC, and the Carter administration drew back from plans
to withdraw from South Korea, Japanese concerns about US
disengagement from the region receded. Nevertheless,
peace and stability of Asia were among the key reasons
mentioned by Tokyo in concluding the treaty of 1978.
Japan was beginning to try on the new role as a regional
diplomatic power. The irony of the treaty was that it
was destabilizing, and indirectly, has stimulated a
greater Soviet presence in the Far East.

In the following pages, we shall examine the progress of the treaty negotiations in order to understand
the intentions, perceptions and circumstances of the
countries involved. It will be many years before diplomatic historians are able to accord the treaty the attention it deserves. But because the treaty played a
significant part in affecting Asian relations and
Japan's defense posture in the 1980s, it is vital that
we seek to understand the events surrounding the treaty
and its conclusion.

RELATIONS BEFORE 1978

Because of proximity to a continental mass, successful industrialization, and past maritime empire, Japan can be likened to Britain. Unlike Britain, however,
Japan was not overwhelmed by historical waves of migra-
tion or invasions from the mainland, nor did Japan involve itself with continental politics throughout most
of its history -- except for Hideyoshi's abortive invasion of Korea in the sixteenth century. Aside from the
unsuccessful assaults of the Mongol forces in the thir-
teenth century, Japan remained unthreatened until the
the mid-nineteenth century. Japan's pattern of interac-
tion with the continent has thus been largely by choice.
Flourishing trade with China and borrowing of Chinese

culture in the eighth century were matters of deliberate
choice by the Japanese court at Nara.[8] The Japanese
emperors did not accept the suzerainty of the Son of
Heaven, as did the Korean kings, and thus preserved
their political sovereignty from the Chinese dynasties.

During the late nineteenth century, China drifted
into dynastic collapse and regional fragmentation, while
Japan adapted to the new realities of modernization by
using the Euro-American industrial model. A pattern of
external expansion was also adopted by the Meiji modern-
izers who saw opportunities for territorial aggrandizement in the crumbling régimes in China and Korea. Unless Japanese influence and power on the mainland were
expanded, they argued, Russian, British, French, and
American control would freeze Japan out of potential
markets and colonies in East Asia. A successful war
against China in 1894-5, defeat of Russia in 1905[9], and
the annexation of Korea in 1910 assured Japan of recognition as a major regional power by the time of the outbreak of the first world war.

During the interwar years, Japanese expansion continued at the expense of China and resulted in the crea-
tion of the client-puppet régime of Manchukuo and the
occupation of much of eastern China.[10] But by attempting to conquer more territory and people than the Japanese empire could successfully administer, the imperial
army helped to strengthen its own nemesis -- the Chinese
communist guerrilla forces. The Japanese invasion and
the installation of puppet régimes ousted the moderate
nationalist government from Nanking, facilitating expansion of communist forces in the northwest. The civil
war between nationalist and communist forces after 1945
resulted in the installation of a government which had
come to power on the basis of agrarian reform and anti-
Japanese nationalism. War and the threat of war remained
a primary element in Beijing's ideological legitimacy.
The war and the fear of a revival of Japanese militarism
sponsored by the United States coloured much of the
PRC's perspective toward Japan.

Nevertheless trade between China and Japan developed on an informal basis and was handled through the
Japanese Memorandum Trade Office in Beijing. After the
Cultural Revolution, trade grew apace, facilitated by an
annual Memorandum Trade Agreement as well as by contracts signed at the Canton trade fair. Japan's continued recognition of the Guomindang régime in Taiwan remained the major obstacle to improved relations, but
this did not prevent Sino-Japanese trade from reaching
$650 million by the end of 1969.[11]

Other issues also inhibited closer relations. Chinese propaganda continued to portray revived Japanese
militarism as imminent, and Beijing required at least
one Japanese trade delegation to condemn its own country's activities. The Tokyo Foreign Ministry reacted

with calm pragmatism, recognizing that such political
statements were tolerable as long as trade flourished.
The havoc of the Cultural Revolution, the imprisonment
of Japanese citizens, the detonation of nuclear weapons,
and the existence of an anti-Japanese treaty with Moscow
prevented improvement of Sino-Japanese relations until
1971 when the logjam over the China seat at the United
Nations was broken.

The United Nations resolution to seat the PRC as
the rightful representative of China strengthened those
elements in Japan's Liberal Democratic party who favour-
ed recognition of Beijing. Opposing them was the pro-
Taiwan group, the <u>Seirankai</u>, or "Blue Lightning Society". The Nixon-Kissinger initiatives and the subsequent
Presidential visit to China broke the Sino-American
stalemate and made an improvement in Sino-Japanese relations not only feasible, but necessary. Taiwan was the
major hurdle, because Tokyo had carried on a profitable
trade with the island and had had diplomatic relations
with it for two decades. For its part, the PRC desired
normalization with Japan for several reasons, including
a reduction of threats to it in East Asia, the desire to
prevent Japan from drifting too far toward accomodation
with the USSR, and the need for Japan as a partner in
China's drive for modernization.

In January 1972, Soviet Foreign Minister Andrei
Gromyko arrived in Tokyo to persuade the Japanese not to
move toward Beijing.[12] To Japanese leaders and public
opinion, the Soviet return of the northern islands of
Shikotan, Habomai, Kunashiri, and Etorofu was a necessary condition for improved relations. The retrocession
of Okinawa from United States control was about to occur, and this strengthened Tokyo's demands that all the
northern islands also be restored. Under these conditions, the Russian offer of improved relations and more
investment opportunities did little to entice Japan away
from recognizing China.

The United States could hardly protest Japanese
recognition of the PRC, since Nixon had set the process
in motion with his own visit. The Nixon administration
hoped that Japan would not act too precipitously and en-
danger the delicate balance of power in East Asia. The
war in Vietnam continued to distract the United States,
so Sino-American normalization was unlikely as long as
the conflict continued. Moreover, the American treaty
commitment to Taiwan's defense allowed Washington less
flexibility than Japan, which had no such commitment.
The appeal of Sino-Japanese rapprochement was that it
could draw China out of its isolation from the United
States sphere of power and make a reforging of the Sino-
Soviet alliance less likely. From the United States
standpoint, Japan could thus act as a cultural and diplomatic bridge to China.

Prime Minister Sato had been linked to the pro-

Taiwan elements in his party. Beijing thus preferred to
wait for the installation of Tanaka Kakuei before con-
summating normalization. After the election, the new
Prime Minister held a press conference and announced
that the time was ripe for the establishment of relations with the PRC. Tanaka accepted the PRC as the only
"orthodox" government of China. Premier Zhou Enlai responded with words of encouragement, and on 12 August
1972 he invited Tanaka to visit China. Before going to
China, Tanaka met with President Nixon in Hawaii, and
the two issued a joint communiqué which expressed hope
that Asian tensions would be relieved by the normalization of Sino-Japanese relations.

The Tanaka visit took place from the 25 to 30 of
September and included an interview with Mao Zedong. A
round of banquets and speeches celebrated the occasion,
during which Foreign Minister Masayoshi Ohira (later
Prime Minister) declared the treaty between Japan and
Taiwan terminated. According to the People' Daily these
events were the death blow of the "Two-China fallacy".
The visit concluded with a joint statement which was to
be the basis of subsequent relations. It contained the
following points:

(1) The "abnormal state of affairs which has hitherto existed" between China and Japan was terminated.
(2) "The Government of Japan recognized the Government of the People's Republic of China as the sole
legal government of China."
(3) China reaffirmed that Taiwan was "an inalien-
able part of the territory of the People's Republic of
China," -- but the government of Japan gave less than
full support for this claim. Tokyo "fully understands
and respects this stand of the Government of China," the
statement read. The phrasing left open the possibility
of continued trade and other economic relations with
Taiwan.
(4) Diplomatic relations were established as of 29
September 1972.
(5) The PRC, "in the interest of friendship," renounced demands for war indemnities from Japan.
(6) Both countries would respect the sovereignty
and territorial integrity of the other.
(7) Normalization was not directed against any
third country. Neither state "should seek hegemony in
the Asia-Pacific region and each country is opposed to
efforts by any other country or group of countries to
establish such hegemony."
(8) China and Japan agreed to hold negotiations on
a treaty of peace and friendship.
(9) Both governments agreed to hold talks on other
matters, including trade, navigation, aviation, fisheries, and so on, aiming at agreements.

With the announcement of Sino-Japanese normalization, Taiwan broke off relations with Japan, although
Beijing was to tolerate non-diplomatic exchanges in
recognition of existing economic links. The USSR saw
the Sino-Japanese rapprochement as a threat to its East
Asian interests. For Japan, the new relationship offered
opportunities for trade and investment which had been
destroyed decades before by militarist adventures. The
proximity of the two countries, the complementarity of
their economies, and their historical and cultural affinities provided the basis for a relationship which
seemed long overdue. The next step was a treaty of
peace and friendship.

THE TREATY OF PEACE AND FRIENDSHIP

Following normalization, China and Japan settled a
number of outstanding issues. They concluded an air
traffic pact, continued negotiations on shippping and
established a cable link. China promised larger ship-
ments on oil in order to relieve Japan's dependence on
Soviet exports.[13] Official and private delegations were
exchanged. Trade grew from $2 billion in 1973 to nearly
$3.3 billion in 1974, and to $3.79 billion in 1975.
However, progress towards signing the PFT moved slowly
under the Tanaka, Miki, and Fukuda administrations.
Conversations on the treaty began in early 1974, and
negotiations were initiated in December 1976, but the
treaty was not signed until 12 August 1978.
Normalization had taken place within the context of
Japan's special relationship with the United States.
Because of mutual trade and defense interests, Tanaka
had first consulted with Nixon. LDP leaders had declared
their nation's psychological independence from the United States after the "Nixon shocks" of 1971, and out-
lined a foreign policy of "equidistance" or "omnidirec-
tion" which had hitherto been more evident in relations
with China and the Soviet Union. During the six years
after normalization of Sino-Japanese relations, Tokyo
policymakers walked a thin line to avoid precipitating
antagonism from neighboring continental powers.
After the Zhou-Tanaka communiqué of 1972, Beijing
pressed for a more explicit declaration of a Japanese
tilt towards China. From the Japanese standpoint, the
equidistance approach was most prudent. China offered
increased trade and investment opportunities. As oil
costs soared, Chinese supplies appeared more attractive.
But the Russian presence in northeast Asia could become
a hostile force if Japan succumbed too obviously to
Chinese pressures. Japan's reluctance to conclude the
PFT was due to Chinese insistence that it include Article Seven of the 1972 joint communiqué -- the "anti-
hegemony" clause. Because of opposition from the pro-
Taiwan group in his own party, and a fear of becoming

entangled in Sino-Soviet rivalries, Prime Minister Miki Takeo decided not to push the treaty negotiations, and in May 1975 discussions were suspended.

Attempts to rekindle negotiations were discouraged by distractions on both sides: the Lockheed scandals in Japan and the deaths of Mao and Zhou in China. By mid-1977 stabilization in China and a new government in Japan under Fukuda opened the way for the resumption of the stalled talks. Despite pressure from leading members of his party, Fukuda remained wary of the same reasons which had inhibited his predecessor -- the pro-Taiwan faction in the LDP and the Chinese pressure for an anti-hegemony clause. The Keidanren (Federation of Economic Organizations) pressured Fukuda to proceed with treaty negotiations as early as possible.

The Japanese ambassador to the PRC informed his government that China wanted to reopen negotiations on the treaty. Fukuda moved cautiously, but had appointed Sunao Sonoda, an enthusiast for the treaty, to the post of Foreign Minister. China's stand on the hegemony clause appeared to soften, and Deng Xiaoping stated that it was not directed against any third power.

The treaty was technically a bilateral affair. But the Sino-Soviet treaty of 1950 contained an anti-Japanese clause, and had to be abrogated in order to avoid the contradiction of China proclaiming opposition to Japan in one treaty, and friendship with Japan in the other. Despite these and other problems, Sonoda's personal interest in the treaty was a major factor in guiding the negotiations to a successful conclusion.

The 1950 Sino-Soviet treaty was technically in force. If Sonoda had insisted on abrogation of the treaty before conclusion of the Japan-China treaty, the consequences might have been: (1) China could have protested Japan's intervention in domestic affairs, and break off negotiations until after the treaty expired; or (2) Sonoda could have used the demand to abrogate the 1950 treaty as bargaining leverage with China to modify or eliminate the troublesome hegemony clause. However, both sides preferred to minimize the 1950 treaty as no longer having any force, and therefore a negligible factor in the negotiations.

The Japanese Foreign Ministry, moreover, had announced that before negotiations began, it would not insist on abrogation of the 1950 treaty.[14] This was because the Chinese side had indicated that the "Sino-Soviet Treaty has the name but no substance," and that China had no intention to continue it. (The objectionable Article One stated that both countries "will jointly take all possible measures against aggression by Japan and any country connected with Japan.") The treaty was effective for thirty years, and would be extended for five years if neither party notified the other one year before expiration. This meant that the treaty would expire in April 1980 (the thirtieth anniversary) if by April 1979 China or the USSR announced their intention to abrogate.

Some quarters called for immediate abrogation before the PFT was concluded: According to Nihon Keizei "it is inconsistent to conclude a Sino-Japanese treaty ... while letting the Sino-Soviet treaty, which takes a hostile view toward Japan, continue to exist."[15] The Foreign Ministry preferred not to raise obstacles to the treaty: "The Sino-Soviet Treaty is a treaty between China and the Soviet Union, which are third countries for Japan, and it (Japan) is in no position to say anything in the form of intervention in internal affairs."[16] It probably was fruitless to insist on abrogation of the Sino-Soviet treaty, which had become a scrap of paper within a decade of its signing by Zhou Enlai and Vyshinski in Moscow.

Since the late 1950s, the Sino-Soviet dispute had far overshadowed the goodwill embodied in the treaty. Neither side wanted to initiate the necessary discussions which would inevitably become an occasion for further contention in already tense relations between the two powers. The Chinese government preferred to announce its intention to abrogate the treaty with as little fanfare as possible.[17] During negotiations with Japan, representatives of the Chinese government repeated that the Sino-Soviet treaty was no longer in force, and would not be renewed. Non-official Japanese arguments that formal abrogation precede the conclusion of the Japan-China treaty were treated as pretexts to stall negotiations.

The LDP's "Asian Problem Research Association" had drafted a study of the effects of the proposed PFT with China, and asserted that co-existence of the Sino-Soviet and Japan-China treaties would lead to Japan-Soviet confrontations.[18] Japan was specified as the potential enemy in Article One of the 1950 treaty, and China's anti-hegemony statements had left no doubt that the USSR was the implied enemy in the hegemony clause to be included in the Japan-China treaty of peace and friendship. Therefore, the logic of these two clauses meant that China would be in an ambiguous -- if not contradictory -- position vis-a-vis Japan and the USSR. These latter states, however, would be placed in mutual hostility, regardless of their intentions. The LDP study further maintained that if the hegemony clause took effect, it would violate Article Three of the 1950 treaty:

> Each Contracting Party undertakes not to conclude any alliance directed against the other Contracting Party and not to take part in any coalition or in any actions or measures directed against the other Contracting Party.

Sonoda visited Moscow in early 1978 and informed the Soviets of forthcoming negotiations on the peace and friendship treaty. China had not mentioned any changes in the 1950 treaty directly to Moscow, and the Soviet leaders said that any responsibility for altering the 1950 treaty would be with the Chinese.[19] When the Japan-China treaty was concluded in August, Sonoda indicated that the Chinese "will take necessary measures for the abrogation of the Sino-Soviet Treaty of Alliance in April (1979)."[20]

As promised, the Standing Committee of the Chinese National People's Congress abrogated the Sino-Soviet Treaty on 3 April 1979. The next day, Moscow issued a statement warning that all responsibilities concerning the suspension of the validity of the Sino-Soviet treaty rest with the Chinese side: "The Soviet Union will probably draw a proper conclusion from the Chinese side's action."[21] Before the treaty became null and void on 10 April 1980, the two sides intended to open negotiations on the treaty relationship. However, the Soviet invasion of Afghanistan a few months earlier prompted the Chinese to cancel futher talks. Vice-ministerial talks took place in Moscow during 1979, and were scheduled to continue in Beijing. Since the end of 1979, however, Sino-Soviet relations cooled even further, and renewal of the 1950 treaty seemed unlikely in the post-Afghanistan atmosphere.

THE ANTI-HEGEMONY CLAUSE

Chinese hostility towards Japan expressed in the 1950 treaty turned out to be a minor impediment to concluding the PFT. The hegemony clause, however, remained a sticking point which dragged out negotiations, and it undoubtedly adversely affected Japan-Soviet relations.

The PRC negotiators insisted that it be incorporated in the main text of the proposed treaty. Chinese polemics against the USSR as the major hegemonistic power in the world left no doubt as to the target of anti-hegemony sentiments. Beijing was unwilling to make any concessions on the issue.

Most Japanese were aware of Soviet opposition to Japan adopting the principle of hegemony.[22] Because the principle implied symbolic identification of the USSR as an expansionist power, Japanese acceptance of the hegemony clause could be construed as alignment with China against the Soviet Union. To dilute this effect, the Japanese negotiators argued that, first, Japan had no intention of joining an anti-Soviet alliance with the PRC, and second, there had to be an additional clause in the treaty stipulating that relations with any third nation would not be affected by the treaty.[23]

The Japanese interpretation of hegemony did not agree with the Chinese interpretation. The Japanese government considered it an unnecessary stimulation of Soviet anxieties. To the Chinese, however, the hegemony clause symbolized that they did not stand alone against the USSR, and that an international united front was taking shape. Some members of the ruling LDP asserted that acceptance of the hegemony clause would involve Japan in the Sino-Soviet dispute, and would raise problems with the US-Japan security treaty structure.[24] Nevertheless, the government negotiators accepted the controversial clause as long as the treaty included a disclaimer that it was not aimed at any third nation.

Deng Xiaoping sought to quiet Japanese reservations about the hegemony clause. In talks with Komeito Secretary-General Yano Junya, he said the concept was invented by the Americans, and accepted by Prime Minister Tanaka in 1972.[25] Deputy Premier Geng Biao said that the clause will relieve those who fear a revival of Japanese militarism or Chinese expansionism, since the two countries would also be bound under the clause.[26] Vice Premier Deng stated that the USSR had no reason to object to the clause. Only when Prime Minister Miki raised the issue of the clause as a problem did the Soviets begin to oppose it and to threaten Japan if the clause was included in the proposed treaty. Deng was ignoring that China had used the notion of hegemony as a synonym for Soviet expansion, and had imparted a specific national identity to the term in recent years. Deng's statements to Yano urged Japan to be firm with the USSR, and not to retreat from the position taken in 1972. Nothing, he said, could be accomplished by being diffident to the Soviet Union.[27]

China wanted Japan in an anti-Soviet front. The 1972 Communiqué had been issued within a firm US-sponsored defense structure. But by March 1978, American intentions in Asia were less clear to Japan. To antagonize the USSR under those circumstances could leave the country more vulnerable to pressures to rearm, or to move closer to the PRC, or to make compromises with the USSR. After the visit of Dr. Brzezinski, Carter's advisor on national security, to China in May 1978, and the rapid rapprochement between the US and China, it became clear that the US was tilting toward China.

In late April, PRC Vice Minister of Foreign Affairs Yu Zhan mentioned four reasons why the inclusion of the anti-hegemony clause would be in the best interests of China and Japan:[28]

(1) It will clarify that China will not undertake acts of hegemony, even after modernization.

(2) Japan will have better relations with other Asian nations by clarifying its position of not seeking hegemony.

(3) It will contribute to the reversion of the northern territories.

(4) China and the US advocated opposition to hegemony in the Shanghai Communiqué of 1972, so the clause will not be in conflict with Japan-US relations.

Furthermore, Yu Zhan stated that Soviet opposition to inclusion of the clause in the treaty "is proof that it is seeking hegemony."

The first point was not very meaningful. In February 1979 the PRC launched an attack into Vietnam to "punish the small-scale hegemonists." From the Vietnamese perspective, the PRC had engaged in an act of "hegemonism": a notion too vague to have precise meaning in a treaty or international law. Moreover, a treaty stipulation can last only as long as the contracting parties agree to abide by it, as the 1950 Sino-Soviet alliance testified.

As to Yu Zhan's second point, the domestic barriers to a rearmed Japan were far more effective than any treaty clause renouncing hegemony. The peace constitution had been a formidable barrier to rearmament for over three decades. Opposition parties at home helped to preserve the pacifist structure of the Japanese state. Moreover, the phenomenal prosperity induced in part by low military spending in Japan provided a further incentive to avoid prewar-type militarism.

The Chinese vice-minister's third point was dead wrong. The point assumed that Japan's bargaining strength with the Soviets would be enhanced by partnership with China, and the northern territories could be pried loose. In fact, the opposite occurred, and reversion of the northern islands to Japan has never been more unlikely than after the spring of 1978.

Finally, his fourth point ignored the very different international settings. In 1972, the US security umbrella was more credible, even to the point of US willingness to enter a war entailing large sacrifices. By 1978, the Vietnam war had weakened the American will, possibly to the point that other commitments were not as reliable as the past. Where Nixon had proclaimed opposition to hegemony, Carter raised his voice against violations of human rights. The supporting security structure of Japan was no longer as certain as a few years earlier, and an anti-hegemonistic posture could complicate Japan's relations with the USSR at a time when US guarantees were coming into question.

The conservative daily Sankei suggested that China's stiff insistence on the hegemony clause was itself a sort of hegemonism, in that China sought to compel Japan to accept Chinese national interests.[29] China's national strategy was "basically the formation of an anti-Soviet international united front" centered on the "three worlds" approach.

To dispel doubts about the proposed treaty which were raised in public, the Foreign Ministry clarified

its policy in a pamphlet published during the summer of
1978. Director General Nakae of the Asian Affairs Bureau
stated that the PFT had to be concluded in a way which
does not have the USSR in mind as a specific third nation.[30] The pamphlet indicated that the government accepted the Chinese rationale of the hegemony clause:
"The clarification of their basic way of thinking that
(China and Japan) will not seek hegemony and that they
are opposed to it, will bring no harm at all." The face-
saving formula, that the clause really was directed
against the co-signers of the treaty, became the Foreign
Ministry's official rationale for accepting anti-hegemony. Thus, Japan would tolerate the notion in the
treaty because it was harmless, as they explained. Beyond this, there was no conceivable purpose for Japan
accepting the clause.

To place this rationale in its best terms, the
hegemony clause reiterated the sentiments of the Japan
peace constitution -- that Japan would never again engage in belligerent activities except in self-defense.
Perhaps some people in Southeast Asia saw the growth of
Japan's Self-Defense Forces as a cause for concern. In
the years prior to Sino-Japanese normalization, there
had been Chinese concern about Japanese militarization.
From this perspective, Japan's renunciation of hegemony
was welcomed by those countries which suffered Japanese
invasion and occupation until 1945.

Similarly, Chinese denunciation of hegemonism, if
restricted to its own future actions, was also welcomed.
Certain Asian countries feared that a modern and powerful China might follow the path of previous late modern-
izers, such as Japan and Germany, and seek expansion at
the expense of smaller or weaker neighbors. PRC renunciation of hegemonism did not foreswear the use of force
against Tibet or Taiwan, since these were regarded by
China as integral territory and therefore strictly internal matters if military force were used.

This interpretation of China and Japan restricting
their own external application of force was not the Soviet interpretation, which saw anti-hegemony unity as a
thinly-disguised spiritual alliance against itself. When
the final draft of the treaty was signed, the hegemony
clause was included. The Japanese Foreign Ministry defined it as conforming to universal and established
ideals.[31] After long negotiation, the "third nation
clause" was included as an independent article, and
broke the long stalemate over the treaty.

Sonoda's statement on the treaty provided the Japanese interpretation.[32] He indicated that Article Two did
not refer to any particular country: "Both Japan and
China will not seek hegemony, and they will oppose at
tempts of any nation or group of nations to establish
hegemony." Article Four prescribed that the treaty did
not exert any effect on relationships with third

nations. However, the fact that Article Three, on economic and cultural exchanges, was interposed between the highly controversial clause and a clause which Japan demanded to neutralize Article Two, indicated hard bargaining and compromise. China had conceded inclusion of the "third nation clause," but only by separating it from the anti-hegemony clause. By inserting Article Three between the two (the principle of anti-hegemony, and the denial of its reference to any specific third countries), the Chinese accomplished separation, and watered down the effect of Article Four.

Sonoda expressed optimism after signing the treaty, stating that it gave a sense of relief to other Asian nations that China and Japan would not invade each other, and would become good friends. He warned that Japan must not become involved in the Sino-Soviet confrontation, and that the Japan-China treaty must not become an anti-Soviet alliance.[33]

.THE "NON-PROBLEM" OF THE SENKAKU (DIAOYUDAI) ISLANDS

The Japanese negotiators, as we have seen, were reluctant anti-hegemonists, and hoped that their concept of non-specific anti-hegemony would be understood by the USSR.[34] The differing expectations of anti-hegemony was the second anomaly in the treaty, one which indicated that both sides were unable to conclude a conceptually satisfactory treaty relationship.

This reluctant willingness to live with bilateral ambiguity at the expense of legal precision was also evident in a third area of potential disagreement -- ownership of the Senkaku Islands. These islands, named the Diaoyudai in Chinese, were claimed by Japan, the PRC, and Taiwan, as the Republic of China. The anti-treaty group within the LDP preferred that the Senkaku issues should be resolved before concluding the treaty.[35]

Their reservations and doubts were reinforced in April 1978 when a flotilla of Chinese fishing boats entered the waters around the islands and appeared to challenge Japanese claims of sovereignty. According to the Japanese Maritime Safety Agency, 19 Chinese fishing boats carried out fishing operations within the 12 mile limit of Uotori Island on April 14. Agency officials warned the boats to leave the waters, but the orders were disregarded. Two days earlier, the Agency's radar detected about 100 Chinese boats in the area.[36]

The Chinese government claimed the islands in a Foreign Ministry statement of 30 December 1971, but had not mentioned them at the time of the Okinawa reversion agreement in 1972.[37] The Japanese prime minister and foreign minister were perplexed by this development, coming at a time when treaty negotiations were about to resume in earnest. Information that the ships came from

various parts of China, and that there were also included intelligence ships indicated that the presence of
the flotilla was not an accident.[38]

The Japanese requested that the Chinese boats be
withdrawn, and the Chinese side reiterated that the area
in question was Chinese territory. Nevertheless, neither
side wanted to push the issue to the point of endangering treaty negotiations. One Diet member of the Fukuda
faction argued that negotiations should be shelved until
the question of Senkaku ownership was settled.[39] At the
time of the 1972 normalization, there was a "gentlemen's
agreement" not to debate or discuss the question of ownership. Each side wanted to remind the other of its
claims through action. The Chinese fishing fleet which
materialized in the Yellow Sea in April was one such
reminder.

As an island nation, Japan was naturally concerned
about ownership of various islands -- however small --on
its perimeter. For years, the American administration
of Okinawa had been a point of friction between the two
countries. With reversion of Okinawa to Japan in 1972,
Tokyo turned attention to other irredenta. Takeshima
was occupied by the ROK, and claimed by Japan and the
PRC. Its waters were important fishing grounds, and
were potential petroleum reserves. The USSR occupied the
northern islands after the second world war, and Japan
demanded their retrocession. In these island disputes,
friction among the claimants was inevitable.

There was a further complicating factor in the
Senkaku dispute. The decision to shelve this territorial
problem during normalization in 1972 was a necessary
postponement. If the issue was again shelved in 1978,
the Soviets could demand similar postponement of the
northern territory issue when peace treaty negotiations
between Tokyo and Moscow occurred.[40] That is, the USSR
would interpret shelving of the Senkaku question as a
further sign of Japan's pro-China tilt if the same flexibility was not accorded equally to it. It was not considered an important point, however, and the government
was not interested in pursuing its equidistant diplomacy
to this extent.

Sonoda made fairly generous gestures to the Chinese, preferring to get on with the treaty negotiations.
The April "violation" was treated as an unforeseen accident, and was not raised in negotiations. Japan separated the treaty and the territorial issue, despite demands from LDP hawks that the government increase the
number of patrols around the islands and make firmer
statements about Japanese ownership.[41]

There was speculation that the Chinese flotilla had
been engineered by local opposition within China to in-
terrupt the treaty negotiations. Fujian province, opposite the islands, was the site of various resistance
movements to the central government, and the incident

was seen as an attempt at resistance by remnants of the Cultural Revolutionary group.[42]
Despite differences within the party, Sonoda and the SDA Director-General Kanemaru Shin wanted to push ahead with the negotiations, and keep the Senkaku question separate.[43] On April 21, the Chinese Foreign Ministry responded and explained the incident as "an unforeseen accident."[44] It was not an apology, and there was no admission of Japanese sovereignty over the islands. As a result, some LDP members strongly opposed resumption of negotiations.[45]
Sparring on the territorial question continued, but at a reduced level. Both sides asserted their claims to the Senkakus, but did not let these claims intrude into the treaty talks. In late April, Vice Foreign Minister Yu Zhan stated his government's position that the islands were China's inherent territory, adding that "both sides have agreed to handle the territorial problem by separating it from the negotiations for the proposed treaty."[46]
In order that the Japanese claims to the islands would be strengthened, the Executive Board of the LDP passed a resolution on 17 March, urging the government to construct a relief port so as to clarify Japan's effective control.[47] When Sonoda later met with the Executive Board, he claimed that even if a port and light house had been built, the April incident could still have occurred.[48] In another meeting, the foreign minister asserted that Japan's sovereignty over the Senkakus was already established by the fact that the government had loaned them to US armed forces as a firing range.[49]
A source of Sino-Japanese contention was the nature of oceanic boundary lines. Japan's view was that the international boundary was the "intermediate line," while China claimed territory on the basis of the natural extension line.[50] Such differences had also contributed to friction over the proposed Japan-ROK continental shelf agreement, which China had protested on several occasions. The most recent protest, on 10 May, was interpreted by the Gaimusho as linked to Premier Hua Guofeng's visit to North Korea. Others in Japan interpreted it as a counter-protest to Japanese reactions to Chinese intrusions in the Senkaku area. With the Chinese remarks coming during Diet deliberations on the continental shelf-related bills, some Diet members accused China of interfering in domestic affairs.[51]
When negotiations on the treaty entered their final stage, the territorial issue had been defused. Sonoda said that the Chinese had assured him that disputes or incidents similar to those in April would not recur.[52] According to Deng Xiaoping, it was best to leave the Senkaku question to future generations to resolve.

THE US AND THE 1978 TREATY

Japan was negotiating a treaty in which the PRC and USSR had vital interests. Moscow watched closely to see if Japan would tilt towards its adversary, while the PRC needed Japan's economic and diplomatic support. Not only was Japan important because of economic superpower status, but also because it was closely linked to the US by the security treaty. Japan was the vital bridge between the PRC and the US, and the increasing possibility of a closer relationship among the three worried the USSR.

The US-Japan treaty insured coordination of foreign policy through annual summit talks and various bilateral committees. It also provided a nuclear umbrella for Japan, allowed Japan to maintain a low level of defense spending because of the stationing of US forces. To proponents of the treaty, the security relationship lessened the chances that Japan would remilitarize. The postwar constitution prohibited Japan from possessing armed forces capable of waging aggressive war, so the US military presence filled the gap between the constitutionally possible and the strategically necessary.

This arrangement eliminated the necessity of military agreements with other countries. But in order to maintain the relationship with the US, Japan had to coordinate with -- or at least favorably consider -- US policy objectives when diplomatic initiatives occurred. But as the US appeared to move towards optional presence in East Asia during 1977, Japan reexamined the need for more autonomous diplomacy, especially if there was a possibility of destabilization on the Korean peninsula.

Another development affecting Japan was the 1978 tendency towards US rapprochement with the PRC -- a trend which was manifested much faster than the Japanese had anticipated. Thus, Japan faced two tendencies from the US: disengagement from Asia and rapprochement with the PRC. The tendencies were mutually reinforcing, because US-PRC friendship allowed troop withdrawals from a region ostensibly safer from declining Chinese threats. The strategic logic of the US was compelling, but it downplayed the Japanese factor. The US assumed that nothing had happened to affect Japan's diplomatic and security position.

Japan's subordinate role to the US was possible in earlier years, when American economic and military dominance was evident. During the 1970s, Japan had been overtaking the US in economic performance and proved to be a formidable competitor. At the same time, the USSR was catching up to the US in military strength. Although the best of friends, the US and Japan were also engaged in rivalry for the China market, and so US rapprochement with China was suspected as a way of penetrating and capturing that market. The rapprochement was also a

means of counteracting the Soviet buildup by supporting
the PRC.

US rapprochement could be seen as a substitute for
the previous widespread deployment of US forces in Asia,
and as a tacit admission that US military strength was
no longer sufficient to contain the USSR. Under these
circumstances, Japan could not remain a passive bystan-
der. For Japan not to push ahead with the PFT would
allow the US to seize the diplomatic advantage and capture a major share of the China market at Japan's expense. Also, if Japan had capitulated in the face of
Soviet objections to the PFT, then Tokyo would be seen
as having given up diplomatic autonomy. This was particularly dangerous if the US defense umbrella was weakening in relation to the Soviet threat, and could mean the
"finlandization" of Japanese foreign policy.

It was suggested in late 1977 that Japan ought to
wait until the US and the PRC normalized relations before signing the PFT.[53] Sonoda answered that President
Carter, in earlier summit talks, said that a stalemate
over US relations with Taiwan was preventing any progress in normalization. Sonoda also said that the President had expressed no opposition to the PFT, so Japan
need not worry that it would cause friction over this
point.

On the question of anti-hegemony, the US seemed to
support the principle, so inclusion of the clause in the
treaty would not be a departure from US priorities.[54]
But it was one thing for the US as a superpower to es-
pouse "anti-hegemony," and another for Japan to include
the vague concept in a bilateral treaty and risk Soviet
antagonism.

Naturally, Japan hoped to avoid antagonizing the
PRC, USSR, or the US. But if Japan postponed negotiations too long in order to consult with the US, as some
were urging, there was the risk of China losing respect
for Japan as a sovereign nation. Beijing had already
given hints of a lack of faith in Fukuda's "sincerity"
in desiring the treaty.[55] A Foreign Ministry source
also indicated that if negotiations with the PRC were
postponed until after the Fukuda-Carter talks, the USSR
would have additional material with which to denounce
the PFT. That is, by bringing the US into early stages
of negotiations, the peace treaty might be attacked as
the prelude to a tripartite alliance against the USSR.

The public attitude of the US administration ranged
from insouciance to mild approval. US Ambassador to
Japan Mansfield stated:

> A Japan-China treaty is purely a Japanese and a
> Chinese matter, and it is not a matter on which I
> should comment...The Japanese and Amerian peoples
> share a basic interest in promoting peace, stabi-
> lity and development in East Asia, and in this

context, the achievement and improvement of
friendly relations between Japan and China should
be considered as a positive and major accomplishment.[56]

In part because of the Senkaku incident, negotiations were postponed until after the US-Japan summit
talks. Prime Minister Fukuda returned from Washington
with a more positive attitude towards the PFT, but he
declined to relate this new attitude to Carter's statement of support for its conclusion.[57] Diet politics may
have been a factor: Members of the opposition parties
were starting to support the US-Japan security treaty,
in contrast to longstanding disapproval. But if Japan's
relations with China were not stabilized, the opposition
might become restless again, and stimulate legislative
instability as in 1960.
        Another factor was that Fukuda probably learned of
Carter's intention to speed up normalization with China.
This meant that the treaty was in harmony with US diplomatic trends on the one hand, and on the other hand,
Japan might lose valuable momentum in penetrating the
China market if the treaty was not concluded quickly.
As the American intention to normalize became clear, the
Japan-China treaty was welcomed by both the US and PRC
as smoothing the way. Parallel improvement of Sino-
Japanese and Sino-American relations implied mutual
priorities were in harmony.[58] If this was the case,
then Soviet anxieties about the parallel US and Japanese
movement towards China appeared well-founded.
        There was evidence that the US government was not
watching Sino-Japanese developments as attentively as
the Gaimusho assumed. Asahi Shimbun analyzed the US as
an "unconcerned spectator,"[59] and noted that Washington
had issued a statement welcoming the treaty two days
before its actual signature -- a diplomatic faux pas.
The American view, according to Asahi, was that the PFT
was little more than a supplement to the 1972 Zhou-
Tanaka Joint Communiqué, and of no major importance.
There was no US anxiety over Soviet retaliation against
Japan. For the Carter administration, the treaty's
major significance was that it confirmed China's international pragmatism. It also meant that the US had to
move quickly if it expected to march the advantages won
by Japan in the China market.
        The summer of 1978 was critical in the turn of
events in East Asia. The US pullout of ground forces
from South Korea was appearing less practical. Japan's
treaty with China would help to strengthen existing
trade, and to stimulate further economic exchange between the two countries, giving Japan a competitive edge
over the US. The post-Mao leadership in China affirmed
its moderation and anti-Soviet stance, and Washington
saw the PRC as a potential counterweight to the USSR,

which was active in Angola and other areas. These considerations encouraged the administration to move ahead
with normalization, even at the expense of cutting ties
with Taiwan.

In retrospect, the PFT was a catalyst to significant shifts in the Far East. It may have helped to
accelerate Sino-US rapprochement. It undoubtedly helped
to alienate the USSR from Japan, a factor which has made
rearming more palatable to many Japanese. It may have
stimulated the USSR to pursue treaties of alliance with
Vietnam and Afghanistan with more vigor, since a China-
Japan-US coalition would be a formidable barrier in Asia
to further Soviet influence. Thus, 1978 may be remembered as the year when the Sino-Soviet dispute expanded
to include non-communist industrial powers as unwitting
participants.

Footnotes

1. See Gerald L. Curtis, "Japanese Security Policies and the United States," Foreign Affairs (Spring
1981), pp. 852-874.
2. Rodger Swearingen described the role of the
Soviet in SCAP in The Soviet Union and Postwar Japan
(Stanford, Ca.: Hoover Institution Press, 1978), Ch. 2.
3. The vulnerability of Japanese air defenses was
demonstrated on 6 September 1976 when Lieutenant Belenko
defected, and piloted his advanced MIG-25 to Hakodate,
Hokkaido.
4. Swearingen, ibid.
5. The linkage beween friendly economic and political relations was strongly emphasized in a conversation
between a senior Soviet diplomat and the author in
Tokyo, 1981.
6. Text in Lee Chae-Jin, pp. 210-212.
7. "Both Contracting Parties undertake jointly to
adopt all necessary measures at their disposal for the
purpose of preventing the resumption of aggression and
violation of peace on the part of Japan or any other
state that may collaborate with Japan directly or indirectly in acts of aggression. In the event of one of the
Contracting Parties being attacked by Japan or any state
allied with her and thus being involved in a state of
war, the other Contracting Party shall immediately ren-
der military and other assistance by all means at their
disposal." "Article One" Treaty of Friendship, Alliance
and Mutual Assistance Between the People's Republic of
China and the Union of Soviet Socialist Republics. 14
February 1950.
8. George Sansom, A History of Japan to 1334
(Stanford: Stanford University Press, 1950), Ch. 4.
9. For a fascinating account of the Russo-Japanese
War, see Denis and Peggy Warner, The Tide at Sunrise

42

(New York: Charterhouse, 1974).
10. According to one partisan, "Our (Japanese) forces now fighting in China are not there merely to kill - but to bring birth to a new Asia, in which Japan and China each maintaining her full independence, will be merged into one system to create and foster a new life - a new solidarity of the Asiatic races." Tatsuo Kawai, The Goal of Japanese Expansion (Tokyo, 1938), p. 75.
11. China Quarterly, No. 41 (January-March 1970), p. 176.
12. New York Times, 23 January 1972, p. 1.
13. Christian Science Monitor, 29 May 1973.
14. Foreign Minister I. Hatoyama told a Diet Committee in late 1977 that Japan would seek annulment of the anti-Japan clause in the Sino-Soviet Treaty. Japan Times Weekly (hereinafter JTW), 19 November 1977, p. 1. By the end of November, however, Fukuda reshuffled his cabinet and installed Sonoda as foreign minister. Sonoda reversed his predecessor's stand, and considered the 1950 Sino-Soviet Treaty inoperative, NK, 26 December 1977, p. 2.
15. NK, 26 December 1977, p. 2.
16. Ibid.
17. See Daily Report: China, 17 April 1979, pp. C1-C4. (Hereinafter DR:China.)
18. TS, 25 March 1978, p. 2.
19. MS, 10 August 1978, p. 2.
20. YS, 13 August 1978, p. 1.
21. TS, 6 April 1979, p. 2. On China's reaction to Pravda's attack against China's decision not to renew the 1950 treaty. See People's Daily, 17 April 1979, "Why Does Moscow Fly Into a Rage?"
22. Soviet Ambassador Polyansky was quoted by the Japanese Broadcasting Company (NHK) as follows: "Should the Sino-Japanese treaty be concluded with an antihegemony clause, the Soviet Union will look upon it as having the same character as the Japan-Germany Anti-Comintern Pact." JTW, 1 April 1978, p. 5.
23. TS, 15 March 1978, p. 2.
24. TS, 25 March 1978, p. 2.
25. NK, 16 March 1978, p. 4.
26. YS, 16 April 1978, p. 1.
27. NK, 16 March 1978, p. 4.
28. MS, 27 April 1978, p. 1.
29. SK, 7 July 1978, p. 6.
30. TS, 15 July 1978, p. 1.
31. MS, 18 August 1978, p. 1.
32. YS, 13 August 1978, pp. 1,3.
33. Ibid., p. 3.
34. Ibid., pp. 1,3.
35. TS, 25 March 1978, p. 2.
36. AS, 14 April 1987, p. 2.
37. Ibid.

38.   The "woodpecker" theory offered by Representative Masaaki Nakayama was that the Chinese provoked the
incident to draw Fukuda out of his cautious attitude toward the PFT.   In ancient Chinese military theory, the
woodpecker hammers on the trunk to force worms out of
their hole, and then "gobbles them up." JTW, 6 May 1978,
p. 5.

39.   AS, 15 April 1978, p. 3.
40.   AS, 16 April 1978, p. 2.
41.   NK, 18 April 1978, p. 2.
42.   Ibid.
43.   SK, 18 April 1978, p. 1.
44.   MS, 22 April 1978, p. 2.
45.   TS, 22 April 1978, p. 1.
46.   MS, 27 April 1978, p. 1.
47.   MS, 14 April 1978, p. 1.
48.   NK, 13 May 1978, p. 2.
49.   AS, 31 March 1978, p. 2.
50.   AS, 11 May 1978, p. 2.
51.   NK, 13 May 1978, p. 2.
52.   YS, 13 August 1978, p. 1.
53.   AS, 28 December 1977, p. 2.
54.   YS, 16 April 1978, p. 1.
55.   SK, 7 July 1978, p. 6.
56.   MS, 27 April 1978, p. 1.
57.   AS, 8 May 1978, p. 1.
58.   MS, 18 August 1978, p. 1.
59.   AS, 13 August 1978, p. 7.

4
Japan's China Tilt

The timing of the PFT was linked to three factors. First, the PRC was emerging from the upheavals of the Cultural Revolution. After the Fifth National People's Congress in March 1978, the leadership appeared stabilized. The direction of modernization, within an emerging legal structure and with foreign participation, seemed to be unsettled. The treaty would give Japan a special relationship with China at a time when the system was becoming more accessible to foreign participation. This relationship would also overcome China's suspicion towards Japan.

Second, Japan's autonomous diplomacy had been under the shadow of US foreign policy, and the treaty was an opportunity to carry out an independent initiative. The proposed treaty did not run contrary to American policies and Japan did carry on consultations with the US. As an initiative, the treaty was not a radical departure from past patterns. But if the US was reducing its presence in the region, Japan had to assume a more visible role in diplomacy. The Japan–China treaty was a first step in structuring the East Asian environment into a system based on cooperation between the two powers.

Third, Tokyo was seeking a way of exerting leverage over the USSR. Moscow refused to discuss the territorial issue, while Japan wanted to reopen the question of the northern territories. Sonoda realized the danger of playing off China against the USSR, and repeatedly stated that negotiations with China had nothing to do with third countries. This did not entirely convince the USSR, which saw the previously neutral Japanese drifting into economic and political intimacy with the major Asian adversary, the PRC.

During the treaty negotiations, Japan was aware of the danger of involvement in the Sino–Soviet dispute via the hegemony clause. It was China's intention to bring Japan as a major economic power into its anti–Soviet international united front. Visions of trade, investment and regional stability were consolation to Tokyo.

Moreover, the announcement that US and PRC diplomatic normalization would begin on 1 January 1979 convinced the Foreign Ministry that the PFT had been concluded none too early. If not for the treaty, the US might have received important advantages in China at Japan's expense.

But if there were reasons for promoting the PFT, later events indicated that the same document may have been the trigger to an intensified Sino-Soviet rift. In November 1978, the USSR and Vietnam signed a Treaty of Friendship and Cooperation. The simultaneous preparations for Sino-US normalization took the appearance of joint anti-Soviet rapprochement. Subsequently, in February 1979, China "counterattacked" (Beijing's term) Vietnam, and reserved the right to mount a second punitive attack if Hanoi persisted in "provocations." China was warning Moscow and its allies that it would not acquiesce in encirclement.

This turn of events created a dilemma for Japan, which was proving economic aid to Vietnam - a nation which China denounced as a regional hegemonist. Closer to home, the Soviets strengthened their forces on the island of Etorofu. This move, in the spring of 1978, was linked to the treaty negotiations between Japan and China, and openly expressed Soviet displeasure. It was becoming clear that one cost of Japan's improved relations with China was to be an unwelcome involvement in the Sino-Soviet cold war.

The PFT was seen by Japan as a move to stabilize the region and to exert diplomatic autonomy. By early 1979, however, the treaty appeared more as a link in the China-US-Japan triangle of cooperation. More important, and against Japan's wishes, the triangle was appearing as an anti-Soviet configuration.[1]

CRITIQUES OF THE TREATY

Japan negotiated the treaty in expectation of economic benefits and political stabilization on the continent. In the determination to conclude the treaty, the government may have minimized the possible negative effects. The press and the government's own studies warned that the treaty would antagonize the USSR, so the Foreign Ministry could not claim to be surprised by developments. Within the government there was tacit acknowledgement that the treaty was a calculated risk.

The benefits were attractive, but the dangers were crucial. The Japanese negotiators preferred the following outcome: The USSR would accept Japan's disclaimers that the treaty was not anti-Soviet. If the PRC insisted on proclaiming the treaty as a victory against hegemonism, let China take the consequences. Soviet umbrage would dissolve after it became clear that Japan was not to align with China in specific anti-hegemonism, or in any anti-Soviet activity.

If this did not occur, Japan was in a dangerous position. The arms buildup by the USSR against China could be directed against Japan as well. This situation would increase Japan's dependence on the US defense umbrella and possibly necessitate a major arms buildup in Japan. This direction of events, along with the US-PRC rapprochement, increased Soviet anxiety over the possibility of an anti-Soviet triangle. Japan as a sub-ordinate of the US, or as a rearmed equal, within this arrangement could only heighten Soviet anxieties over the combination of Chinese unpredictability and ideolo-gical unorthodoxy, Japanese technological sophistication and irredentism, and American military might. Moscow had to prevent coalescence of the new entente, in which Japan was the most reluctant ally, and most vulnerable to Soviet intimidation.

The Japanese government had examined the options when preparing to negotiate with China. In February 1978, as the Foreign Ministry was resuming negotiations, the Japan Defense Agency analyzed possible reactions to the treaty by interested countries - especially the USSR and Taiwan. The JDA analysis indicated there would probably be no change in the military situation in the short run. In a longer period, however, it was expected that the USSR would continue to strengthen its naval forces in the Far East.[2] Another effect of the treaty, according to the analysis, was that other industrial countries, including the US, would resent Japan's rapid inroads into the China market if additional major econo-mic exchanges resulted.[3]

The USSR responded to the proposed treaty by an-nouncing its own draft of a Soviet-Japan treaty of friendship and cooperation. This was perceived by the JDA as a countermove against increased cooperation among China, Japan, and the US. Japan could expect harassment from the USSR if the treaty with China went ahead, espe-cially because Japan lacked adequate military power to resist.

The JDA also anticipated the following after the PFT:[4] (1) The USSR would accelerate the commissioning of an aircraft carrier and the deployment of Backfire bombers in the Far East. (2) The USSR would further restrict Japanese fishing operations in northern waters. (3) Testing of missiles, and naval maneuvers, would increase in areas close to Japan, and possibly during the fishing season, as further signals of displeasure. (4) Taiwan would not remain indifferent to closer Japan-PRC relations, and might study improving relations with the USSR. The study thus concluded that the price of the treaty would be problems with the USSR and Taiwan.

The Defense Agency was more circumspect than the newspaper <u>Sankei</u>, a frequent critic of Tokyo's growing intimacy with Beijing. An article appearing soon after

48

the JDA report questioned whether the treaty was in
Japan's best interests.[5] In contrast to China, the Japanese government was portrayed as lacking any clear
strategy, and relying on "sincerity." Now that the USSR
had proposed a treaty based on the idea of Asian collective security, Japan's approval of either treaty would
amount to entry into the Sino-Soviet dispute.

For years, Japan pursued "equidistant diplomacy."
This was a term which referred to neutrality between the
PRC and USSR, while relying on the alliance with the US
as the primary axis. Now Japan was moving toward a pro-
China policy, while maintaining that there was no change
in policy toward the USSR. Sankei suggested that, instead of focusing on the technical language of the proposed treaty, the government should be examining its
effects on Japanese security.[6] If Moscow saw the treaty
as directed against itself, then new threats against
Japan were being created by the tilt toward China.

The situation in early 1978 was exacerbated by the
appearance of American disengagement from Asia, and continued Soviet military buildups. Under the Carter administration, which was reluctant to commit military forces, Japan could not be certain of American "unconditional, immediate, and automatic intervention" if Japan
faced an external threat to its security. It might be
better, to avoid adverse consequences of the treaty, to
strengthen the US-Japan security structure and the defense forces of Japan before proceeding with the PFT.

Finally, according to Sankei, the hegemony clause
would cause grave problems in the future. It meant one
thing to China, and Japan could not accept the Chinese
definition. Its vagueness meant that it could be interpreted according to the dictates of the moment, such as
when Vietnam became a "regional hegemonist" by the end
of 1978. It was meaningless to include in the treaty a
clause which itself was a cause of dispute between the
two partners.

Criticisms of the proposed treaty did not deter
Fukuda and Sonoda. The JDA analysis focused largely on
the security implications of the treaty. Other anti-
treaty arguments may have been dismissed as originating
from pro-Taiwan members in the LDP or from other
conservative groups. The treaty issue was not unrelated
to internal factional disputes in the party.

The Soviet response remained most problematic. A
few people realized the impact the treaty might have on
the PRC and on other third countries, but nobody could
foresee that US recognition of Beijing would follow so
closely. Sankei dismissed the possibility of an early
US-PRC normalization. According to other government
analyses of the effects on security, it was probable

that the USSR would expand its military strength if faced by a China-Japan-US combination in the Pacific region. At the most, the government expected some "unpleasant actions" by the Soviet Union, but not any major military move.[7]

The government stressed that the treaty had no military references, and expected the USSR would accept Japan's peaceful intentions. There has been increasing Soviet military activity in the western Pacific for a number of years, as well as naval and air activity near Japan. This was related to a challenge to US command in the region, rather than as a direct threat to Japan.

But if Japan wanted to remain aloof from the US-USSR-PRC rivalry, the 1978 treaty was not the best means. Former Secretary of Defense Schlesinger told Japanese leaders that the PRC "had become to sixteenth (unofficial) member of NATO," in light of the role China was playing in containing the USSR and tying down troops in Siberia. In the 1978 US Defense Report, China was depicted as a counterweight to the Soviets. Under these circumstances, Soviet anxiety about a tripartite coalition on the eastern flank was understandable.

Foreign Minister Sonoda continued to interpret the treaty as a benign instrument of peace, stability, and Japanese national interests. When he was asked by the Diet Foreign Affairs Committee whether the treaty could be interpreted as a move to contain the USSR through a US-Japan-PRC link-up, he replied that such an encirclement was inconceivable.[8] He indicated that Japan had done nothing improper, and owed no explanations to Moscow. If the Soviets should propose talks, then possibly a Japan-Soviet peace treaty could be concluded, but only if some settlement could be reached on the northern territories. But, the foreign minister said, if there are threats, Japan will resist them.

Despite Sonoda's reassurances, it was impossible to dispel the feeling that Japan was being brought into the emerging Sino-American strategy against the USSR. The Soviet press did not accept his explanations, and perceived something of an Oriental NATO emerging on the foundation of the Japan-China Treaty.[9] According to Sankei, Japan had entered the US-China-USSR power game as a result of the treaty.

American moves toward China and growing enthusiasm for the "China card" were giving increased credibility to the "Oriental NATO" thesis. Brzezinski, and Assistant Secretary of State Richard Holbrooke, left no doubt that the US supported a strong and stable China.[10] Japanese spokesmen also indicated that the Japan-China treaty was in accord with US strategy, although they did not mean it in the sense of creating an alliance against the USSR. But this pro-China tilt was not supported by Secretary of State Vance, and American policy was not irreversible.

But as the US moved abruptly toward China and against the USSR, Japan found itself exposed to pressures related to security problems. Even if the Japan-China treaty was as harmless as Sonoda wanted the USSR to think, other linkages and antagonisms in the East Asian region negated that claim. The major relations in East Asia by early 1979 were the following: the US-Japan security treaty, US-PRC rapprochement, a decline in US-Soviet détente, longstanding Sino-Soviet confrontation, and the Japan-China PFT. Given these relationships, it was probable that the USSR would see Japan as a potential additional threat.

A hardened Soviet stance on the issue of the northern territories was one cost of the 1978 treaty. When the USSR strengthened military forces on the island of Etorofu and Kunashiri in late spring of 1978, it was a move probably linked to the treaty negotiations. The islands were near the coast of Hokkaido, and the Soviet buildup could be interpreted as a direct threat to Japan's northern defenses.[11] US Defense Secretary Harold Brown confirmed this linkage to the Japan government, based on CIA information, more than a year after the treaty. There was no doubt that Soviet moves in the northern territories were countermoves against the Japan-China treaty.

The revelation was not welcomed by the Japanese government, which had claimed that the treaty would contribute to the peace and stability of Asia. Tokyo may have been somewhat fatalistic about some form of harassment or quantitative increase in military strength of the Siberian mainland, but strong, permanent bases on the northern islands which were demanded back by Japan was a high price to pay for peace and friendship with China. It demonstrated Japan's vulnerability, since nothing could be done to prevent the buildup, and it presented a severe warning against military collusion with the PRC.

The 1978 buildup brought the number of Soviet military personnel to 6,000, but equipment for 12,000 troops was reportedly in place on the northern islands by October 1979.[12] Japanese estimates indicated that these numbers were far more than considered necessary for defense of the islands. In addition, the original force of 1,500 border guards was increased to 5,000 men. Some Japanese saw the buildup as a potential threat to Hokkaido, while popular novelists wrote fictional scenarios about a future Soviet invasion of Japan from the north.

CHINA'S MOVE TOWARD PRAGMATISM

Events in China prior to the PFT provided opportunities for Japanese diplomacy. These opportunities may have been considered sufficiently attractive to risk Soviet displeasure.

Sino-Japanese relations had been restrained by international tensions and China's post-revolutionary antipathy towards a one-time conqueror. During Mao Zedong's reign, official and economic relations remained cool. During the period of US-PRC hostility, China blamed US imperialism for supporting reactionary forces in Japan:

> ...a democratic Japan must, first of all, also be an independent country. In order to control Japan forever and drag it along the old path of war and aggression, U.S. imperialism will never permit the Japanese people to step onto the road of peace and democracy. On the contrary, the United States has continually supported the most reactionary forces in Japan and carried on activities to revive militarism. Is it not true that the Japanese militarist forces have once more gained power in the last few years? [13]

The thaw began around the time of Nixon's visit to the PRC in early 1972, and the subsequent normalization of Japan-China relations. Until 1976, Japan was uncertain on how to deal with the Beijing government ruled by an aging figurehead, and rocked by factional disputes.

With Mao's death on 9 September 1976, and the subsequent overthrow of the Cultural Revolutionary Group, a coalition of leaders was formed, based on four party veterans: Hua Guofeng, Deng Xiaoping, Li Xiannian, and Ye Jianying. The major question was whether twice-purged Deng could cooperate with Mao's anointed successor, Hua Guofeng - Mao's State Minister of Security during Deng's last purge. If the new combination proved unstable, it would be difficult for Japan to move towards settlement of a treaty with China.

During the months after Mao's death, the structure of authority at the top levels became clear. In 1977, a Party plenum announced that the Fifth National People's Congress (NPC) would be convened soon. Provincial congresses were held, and the long dormant Chinese People's Political Consultative Conference (CPPCC) was resurrected as the institutional expression of the united front. The former guiding principle of class struggle was replaced by calls for unity, democracy, legality, and modernization.

When the Fifth NPC met in Beijing, Hua Guofeng mentioned China's desire to conclude the peace and friendship treaty with Japan. To observers, it appeared that China had abandoned the radicalism and hostility towards the US and Japan of the Cultural Revolution. A new "Hundred Flowers" period of blossoming in art, science and economy was written into the constitution. The appearance of "Democracy Wall" in Beijing indicated a willingness to experiment with some forms of political expression.

In the realm of modernization, China's leaders called for major efforts in the four fields of defense, agriculture, industry and science - the so-called "Four Modernizations." Foreign investment and technology would be welcomed, in contrast to the goal of self-reliance of the Maoist days. With an eye towards Japan, the US, Western Europe and the overseas Chinese community, Beijing intimated that it was willing to incur foreign debts in order to finance modernization. Limited domestic liberalization of the economy also occurred, in order to free productive forces from the bureaucratic and ideological straightjackets of years past.

Foreign governments and firms were attracted to participation in Chinese modernization for several reasons. First, access to a gigantic consumer market promised sizable profits. For many years revolutionary puritanism had prohibited conspicuous consumption in China. In 1978, these restraints were eased, and old-guard veterans complained of creeping Western decadence in their society. Nevertheless, non-communist consumer goods - from Coca Cola to Seiko watches - became part of the new availability.

Second, China has large reserves of untapped resources. New oil reserves have been discovered. For Japan, access will reduce dependence on Middle Eastern petroleum. Moreover, shipping lanes from distant oil fields are vulnerable to interdiction in war or hostile blockade of strategic straits. Interruption of oil flow could bring the Japanese economy to a standstill within a few months, if stockpiling is not promoted. Japan has been eager to participate in the exploration of Chinese oil and other resources.

A third attraction of Chinese pragmatism is access to Chinese labor. Japanese wage levels were already approaching the range of other industrial nations, and labor rates in advanced developing countries such as South Korea and Taiwan were also becoming expensive. China has a large reservoir of inexpensive labor, which has provided replenishment for Hong Kong industry as a side phenomenon. Numerous foreign companies hoped to establish operations in the PRC and take advantage of labor conditions there.

But if there were attractions, the obstacles were also formidable. Without stable political order in China, long-range plans were difficult if not impossible. Before the second world war, the foreign treaty ports and concessions in China had operated as havens of stability during the decades of civil wars and revolutions. By operating within the protections offered by extraterritoriality, these concessions were managed as quasi-colonies. Chinese government authority did not penetrate into these areas.

In large part because these enclaves operated

within Western or Japanese law, and were insulated from the vagaries of prewar Chinese politics, these concession areas prospered with inexpensive Chinese labor, modern industrial management and technology, and extensive consumer markets in China. These islands of industrialism were resented by successive Chinese governments and nationalists - despite the fact that politicians and intellectuals had often found sanctuary and freedom there, in flight from repression of domestic rulers. These concessions and the other remnants of the unequal treaties were abolished in 1943, although not all territory claimed by China was returned.

The PRC had no intention of reviving the foreign concession system, but some assurance had to be provided that foreign investments and loans would be protected. In the months after the Fifth NPC, a Legal Commission, under direction of Peng Zhen, drew up a number of new laws which came into force in 1980. In addition to new criminal and electoral laws, joint investment laws were passed and promulgated. These, combined with the introduction of insurance and other banking and currency reforms, have reassured foreign investors of commercial and legal protections.

Years of the Cultural Revolution and other upheavals had been enough to disillusion many Chinese with Maoist radicalism. The educational, scientific, artistic and economic life of the country was nearly in shambles. Those involved in revolutionary activities or who had received a "revolutionary education" became a "lost generation." To drive home the point that the period's upheavals would not be revisited on China, the leadership (increasingly dominated by Deng and his appointees) has blamed post-Mao ills on the notorious Gang of Four. Those who continue to act in the spirit of the extreme leftism exemplified by the Cultural Revolution are urged to change their thinking and behavior or face the consequences.

Repudiation of the Cultural Revolution, the trial of the Gang of Four, and dismissal of key figures in the party and government were signs of political and ideological purges to assure citizens and foreign friends that Maoist anarchism would not recur. The reform regime of Deng Xiaoping promised an end to "cults of personality" and lifetime tenure in office. Attacks on bureaucratic arrogance, official corruption, and ideological error have underlined the seriousness of the task. Other changes included the retirement of Hua Guofeng from the state premiership, and discrediting of the Dazhai model for agriculture.

The multiple reforms have not masked the unprecedented problems facing China in the 1980s. A stagnant economy and an exploding population are major problems and the central government has now taken the lead in reducing population growth rate.

Stability and security remain major priorities in
China today. Externally, the country requires a peaceful environment which will allow modernization without
diversion of scarce resources to military preparations.
Since the mid-nineteenth century, China has been distracted by domestic and foreign conflict. From the opium
wars to the present, China's vulnerability vis-à-vis
other major powers has resulted in a perennial sense of
insecurity. For generations, the experiences and anxiety
of foreign intervention and civil war have moulded the
political consciousness of China's political leaders.
After 1949, the threat from the US, and fear of US-sup-
ported Japan and Taiwan revived apprehension over external intervention. In 1960, the polemics between China
and the USSR evolved into a new threat of intervention
against China.

After PRC entry into the UN in 1971 and subsequent
improvement of relations with the US, the USSR remains
the major threat to China. This hostility is expressed
in ideological polemics, but the central danger comes
from mutual distrust and military buildups on their common border. Since the Vietnam war ended, the Sino-Soviet
dispute has intensified and extended as both sides no
longer confine their search for support to communist
parties and states. The Soviet search for clients has
led to Cuba, Vietnam, Afghanistan, and Angola as well as
in other areas. This expansion of Soviet influence is
what China calls hegemonism.

China has retaliated by strengthening ties with
NATO and Yugoslavia, and by continuing to support revolutionary movements abroad. In East Asia, a main counterattack to Soviet hegemony was the treaty with Japan,
and normalization of relations with the US. While Japan
denied involvement in China's search for allies against
the USSR, the US less reluctantly entered into what was
evolving as a de facto alliance to contain Soviet expansion. In effect, China had brought two major industrial
nations of the Pacific region into its confrontation.
Originating as a sectarian dispute, the Sino-Soviet rift
produced military confrontation, and now has widened into a larger arena of international politics. While there
have been a number of causes in the broadening dispute,
major triggers in the Pacific region have been the Chinese strategy of the international united front, the
Japan-China treaty of 1978, the US-China normalization
in 1979, Vietnam's pro-Soviet tilt, and Soviet invasion
of Afghanistan.

Japan's reluctant partnership in China's realpolitik has come about in part because the government preferred to minimize the negative arguments against the
treaty, and to believe that Article Four neutralized the
hegemony clause. The government also minimized the Soviet reaction to the treaty. In public, the foreign
ministry focused on anticipated benefits and glossed

over potential problems.
We might sum up the working hypothesis of the Foreign Ministry as follows:

The PFT is a major opportunity to improve and enhance mutual diplomatic relations. It will provide
Japan with a privileged position in economic relations during the period of modernization. The new
relations will also strengthen stability in the
region as consultations on mutual problems are
facilitated. The treaty is not directed against the
USSR or any other power, it is not a prelude to a
Sino-Japanese alliance, and it should not be interpreted as such.

Despite such optimistic projections, subsequent
events confirmed only part of the hypothesis. In retrospect, we can see that Japan may have underestimated
China's determination to project the treaty as an anti-
Soviet symbol.
The Japanese Foreign Ministry was encouraged by the
Fifth NPC and saw it as a signal of China's intention to
modernize and seek stability. Compared to the secrecy
and stridency of the previous congress, the Fifth NPC
indicated moderation, and even a step towards more legislative power in the government. These developments
reinforced the positive expectations of Tokyo. Prior to
the Congress, the Foreign Ministry indicated that the
government could watch the NPC to see if the post-Mao
Chinese structure was in firm command. If so, this
would be important in the decision to go ahead with
negotiations. The Congress had already been delayed
because of reported rivalry between Hua and Deng, but
proceedings indicated that a stable balance had been
attained. Deng's visit to Burma and Nepal was also seen
as a positive sign that Beijing was renewing diplomatic
activity on a unified basis.
With the continuation of Hua as Party Chairman and
State Premier, stability at the top seemed assured. A
truce was struck in which beneficiaries of the Cultural
Revolution were not purged if they supported the new
order. This apparently included Hua Guofeng. Also, Mao
Zedong was not brought into the criticisms of the rampant radicalism which he had inspired and encouraged.
Officials and veterans who had been purged in the Cultural Revolution or earlier, were rehabilitated, some
posthumously. Slowly but deliberately, Deng was consolidating his position to get on with rebuilding the
nation and to expunge the influences of Mao's last revolution.
For Sonoda, the fact the preliminary talks on the
treaty had been held during the NPC session was an indication that China was eager for serious negotiations.
After the NPC, the Japanese foreign minister waxed

enthusiastic:

> ...China has finished the consolidation of its
> footing, centering on Chairman Hua Guofeng. It has
> now formulated a realistic plan for modernization,
> and is taking first steps in that direction. [14]

Sonoda saw China "heading for a new age," with the line-
up as moderate, with right persons selected for the
right posts. [15]

On the Sino-Soviet question, Sonoda interpreted
Chinese statements as more realistic and flexible. He
suggested that Japan would be willing to assist in Sino-
Soviet reconciliation, but added that his suggestion to
Moscow in January 1978 had not been answered. He thought
that conclusion of the Japan-China treaty might allow
Japan to promote friendly relations with the USSR. Y.
Inayama Yoshihiro, the board chairman of Nippon Steel
Corporation, agreed that the treaty would facilitate
talks with the Soviet government - an overoptimistic
expectation as it turned out.

Sonoda was heartened by the changes since Mao's
days of ascendancy, preferring to interpret Hua-Deng
relations in the most cooperative light:

> There was kind of severity in the days when Chair-
> man Mao was the leader and when Premier Zhou was in
> charge of administration. With the team of Premier
> Hua and Deputy Premier Deng, it appears they are
> both helping each other, while faithfully upholding
> the teaching of Chairman Mao. In any case, the two
> must help each other and must walk in unity and
> solidarity. Regarding the Japan-China peace and
> friendship treaty, there is nothing arbitrary in
> Premier Hua's Political Report. The attitude toward
> 'hegemony" remains unchanged, but he does not espe-
> cially refer to it. [16]

His optimistic expectations were shared by the
Nihon Keizai, which editorially welcomed the stable and
forward-looking structure that emerged at the Fifth
NPC. [17] China's decreased anxiety over national security
was noted, especially with the easing of its relations
with the US since 1972, and the ending of the Vietnam
war. Deng's role was seen to be that of a major support
for the revived participation of intellectuals in national life. His chairmanship of the CPPCC promised to
give greater scope to that institution as representing a
much broader spectrum of political values and choices
than was possible during the Cultural Revolution. The
plans announced at the Congress provided Japan an opportunity to expand the scale of intercourse. Moreover,
with new emphasis on legality in China, the editorial
urged Japan to implement the Long Term Trade Agreement

which had already been concluded. Treaty negotiations
should be accelerated so as not to miss an important
opportunity to take advantage of the favorable possibilities.

Minoru Shibata, writing in Sankei, took a more
guarded view of the Fifth Congress. He examined the new
constitution, compared it with the 1975 document which
it superseded, and noted that the basic principle of
foreign policy was opposition to Soviet expansion.[18]
His analysis of the expansion of the governmental NPC
power, at the expense of the party, indicated a trimming
of Hua's power as party chairman. Shibata indicated
that the party chairman's authority in military affairs
had also been reduced in the new constitution. A potential source of conflict where Japan had to be cautious
was the Preamble statement: "We will liberate Taiwan,
without fail, and achieve the great task of unifying our
fatherland."

As it happened, the year of the Fifth NPC witnessed
a brief equilibrium of the Hua and Deng forces. In early
1980, the so-called "whatever" faction was purged, and
Hua became increasingly isolated. At the third session
of the Fifth NPC, he stepped down as premier in favor of
Deng's protégé, Zhao Ziyang.

Deng's determined comeback to power, accompanied by
major redirections in state policy, was undoubtedly
abetted by major support for abrogation of Mao-inspired
excesses of the previous years. He has emerged as perhaps one of the most astute statesmen in modern China,
along with Zhou Enlai. His consolidation of political
power was accomplished with speed and efficiency. But
this was not as clear at the Fifth NPC as Sonoda said,
and his optimism might have been premature and displaced
if Hua had rallied more support. However, Deng's maneuvers avoided the instability which Japan dreaded.

CHINA'S INTERNATIONAL UNITED FRONT AND JAPAN

Japan and other nations welcomed China's stabilization and drive towards modernization, since it would
present opportunities for economic and political bridge-
building. China's new entry into the non-communist world
of diplomacy after Mao's demise was evidence to many
that a new era of peaceful cooperation was beginning. At
a time when the US seemed intent on winding down its
Asian commitments, China's moderate foreign policy held
out promise of fulfilling Roosevelt's plan for China to
provide regional stability.

This enthusiasm for a greater China connection may
have led Japanese leaders to minimize the anti-Soviet
thrust of China's policy. Possibly, once China became a
member of the United Nations, the International Monetary
Fund, the World Bank and other international organizations, China's anti-Soviet anxieties (which saw

expansionist aims in practically everything Moscow said
or did) would be reduced. In any event, Japan felt com-
pelled to go along with China's pressure for the hegemony clause, hoping that explanations and protestations
of neutrality in the Sino-Soviet dispute would be adequate against Soviet countermeasures.

Japan was aware that failure to conclude the treaty
would have adversely affected bilateral trade with China. In September 1977, Tan Zhenlin, vice chairman of
the Standing Committee of the NPC, met a delegation of
editors from Kyodo News Service. If Japan failed to act
promptly on the treaty, he said, China would strengthen
trade relations with Western European countries.[19]

Tying the treaty to improved trade relations provided a major inducement for Japan. But the diplomats minimized Japan's other interests in their rush to go ahead.
The Sino-Soviet dispute had not abated after Mao's
death, and Beijing was determined to expand international support for China's position: The major non-communist
nations, including Japan, the US, and Western Europe,
had to realize that the USSR was a danger to world peace
and a threat to the sovereignty of all nations.

In an August 1977 article entitled "A More Dangerous Superpower," the People's Daily portrayed the USSR
as seeking world domination:

> The lopsided development of the Soviet economy and
> the inflation of its military strength have greatly
> stimulated its appetite for world domination and
> re-division of the world...Like the United States,
> the Soviet Union today is following an imperialist
> policy of accession, expansion, and contention for
> the domination of the world. The only difference
> is that the Soviet Union is on the offensive while
> the United States is on the defensive in their con-
> tention for world hegemony. U.S. imperialism, which
> is aggressive in nature, certainly wants to domin-
> ate the world, but at present, though it sometimes
> assumes the offensive, what it can do is mainly to
> try to maintain the status quo and protect its ves-
> ted interest because it has overextended itself and
> its strength is not equal to its ambition. The So-
> viet revisionists, burning with ambition, are push-
> ing a counter-revolutionary global strategy for
> world hegemony. Their objective is to control and
> dominate Europe, extend their spheres of influence
> in Asia, Africa, Latin America and other areas,
> take over the dominant position occupied by the
> United States and establish their rule over every
> corner of the globe. Not long ago, Brezhnev declar-
> ed: "We now have to reckon in one way or another,
> with the state of affairs in virtually every spot
> on the globe." This is a confession of Moscow's
> wild ambition![20]

The USSR has played the anticipated role, and has helped to validate China's thesis. Whether Japan accepted the thesis or not, it certainly did not want to enter an anti-Soviet front with the PRC. The antipathy between the USSR and China was nearly two decades old by the time of the Japan-China treaty. It had earlier affected Japan on several occasions. For example, the Japanese film "Dersu Uzala," produced by Kurosawa with Soviet cooperation, was denounced as an "out-and-out anti-China film" because it "depicted the Chinese people as ugly and savage." Moreover, it allegedly "beautified the old tsars' expansionism against China."[21] According to the leftist Da Gong Bao in Hong Kong, "Soviet revisionism solicited some individual Japanese movie workers to participate in directing and producing this film. This was designed to drag others into trouble in a vain attempt to damage the friendly relations between the Japanese and Chinese people."[22]

From cinema to armed intervention, the USSR is depicted as an aggressive threat to world peace. Chinese Foreign Vice Minister Yu Zhan warned that the USSR will commit aggression whenever there is an unguarded moment. China's policy was to support various countries against the Soviet Union.[23] Indeed, if there was any sector of PRC state policy that has escaped the sweeping changes which followed 1976, it was China's antipathy towards the USSR. In October 1975, the theoretical journal Red Flag published an article entitled "The Economic Root Cause of the Soviet Revisionists' Quest for World Hegemony."

In line with the class struggle standpoint which predominated at that time, a resurgence of capitalism was blamed as the cause of Soviet expansionist behavior:

The economic base of the Soviet Union today is state monopoly capitalism brought about by the Soviet revisionists' all-round restoration of capitalism. The bureaucrat-monopoly capitalist class holds sway in the ownership of the means of production, in the relationship between man and man and in distribution. The characteristics inherent in this economic structure make the Soviet revisionist social-imperialists more brutal in their aggression and expansion abroad and in their striving for world hegemony.

Compared with that of the capitalist-imperialist countries, the state monopoly capitalism of the Soviet Union is more monopolistic, more concentrated and more tightly controlled. All its economic lifelines including the war industry are directly controlled by the Soviet revisionist renegade clique which takes firm hold of the state machine...

To grab maximum profits, the Soviet revisionist
bureaucrat-monopoly capitalist class steps up its
aggression and expansion abroad, annexes new territories, plunders cheap raw materials and unloads
its commodities abroad, exports capital and shifts
its crises onto others.[24]

Less than two years later, after the collapse of
the Cultural Revolutionaries, the same journal again
denounced Soviet "social-imperialism." The interpretation of Soviet expansionism as derived from economic
factors was embellished, and the USSR had set out on the
path of past historical imperialism based on monopoly
capital:

In its acquisition of maximum profit, Soviet state
monopoly capital is both sucking the life-blood of
its own people and madly pursuing a policy of aggression and expansion and committing the most
ruthless colonialist plunder abroad. Soviet social-
imperialism has become one of the biggest international exploiters.[25]

According to PRC interpretations, Soviet imperialism was far more dangerous than previous capitalist
imperialism because it has massive military power to
back up its ambitions, it has made strategic moves enabling it to outflank Western Europe, and it is on the
strategic offensive against the US. "It is reaching out
with voracious appetite to swallow the whole planet."[26]
   Under these circumstances, China insisted that the
Japanese stand up and be counted. In 1975, Vice Premier
Ji Dengkui told an academic delegation that China was
determined to include a hegemony clause in the China-
Japan treaty.[27] The absence of such a clause, he said,
would imply that the contracting parties would seek
hegemony. He added that the USSR is opposed to the
clause because it is seeking hegemony. This position
remained consistent through the negotiations in the
ensuing years.
   During negotiations, the Chinese wanted replies to
specific problems, such as whether expulsion of Chinese
residents from Vietnam could be considered as "local
hegemonism."[28] The Chinese government wanted Fukuda to
commit himself to an anti-hegemony posture, and to stand
up to the USSR in Asia - which is precisely what Tokyo
wanted to avoid. Beijing wanted not only peace and
friendship with Japan, but anti-Soviet agreement as
well. The Chinese were asking Japan to make radical
changes in foreign policy.
   Sino-Vietnamese relations continued to decline
while negotiations were in progress. During the Vietnam
war, both China and the USSR had supplied significant
amounts of aid to Hanoi. Subsequently, Vietnam leaned

towards the USSR, in part to avoid dependence on the Chinese. In July 1978, China suspended aid to Vietnam - prompting comparison of this act to Soviet suspension of aid to China in 1960.[29]

This worsening of Sino-Vietnamese relations caused concern to Japan for at least three reasons: First, it could not avoid affecting Japan-China treaty negotiations. China was claiming that Vietnam was an "Asian Cuba" and a regional hegemonist. This was bound to expand the Chinese usage and definition of hegemonism. Hegemonism was a concept which referred to expansionist tendencies of a state. To the PRC, the US was also engaged in the struggle for hegemony, which had come to mean political, military, and strategy domination of other countries. In the Chinese concept, it is the political equivalent of monopoly capitalist imperialism, but far more deadly. Not all territorial expansion was hegemonistic. When India annexed Sikkim in 1975, for example, the arsenal of synonyms included "aggression," "expansionism," "chauvinism," "imperialism," "colonialism" - but not hegemonism.[30] In an article in a Thai paper quoted by Xinhua, India was called "a running dog of Soviet social-imperialism." Thus Soviet hegemonism worked through regional agents, and formed a worldwide conspiracy. Acceptance of this world view was impossible for the Japanese Foreign Ministry.

A second complication of the Sino-Vietnam dispute was that Japan had made economic aid commitments to Vietnam.[31] Would China then consider this as assistance to local hegemonism? This would be a legal contradiction, if Japan opposed hegemony in the treaty with China and simultaneously assisted "local hegemony" through development aid.

Finally, the ASEAN countries were already fearful that the Sino-Soviet conflict would extend into their region. Before the treaty was concluded with China, Japan sought to reassure ASEAN that their interests would not be adversely affected. The redirection of aid and investment from Southeast Asia to China was an area where Japan had to be cautious.

China continued to pressure Japan for clarification of its stand. Kuno Chuju, an LDP diet member (Tanaka faction), visited China shortly before final negotiations on the treaty, and reported that Beijing desired to reach accord with Japan on basic international problems, including the Sino-Vietnam dispute, the border problem with the USSR, African problems, and the Japanese northern territory dispute.[32] Although Kuno's information was unofficial, it indicated that Beijing not only wanted Tokyo to accept the posture of anti-hegemony, but also hoped for closer alignment in their mutual foreign policy. Kuno indicated that the dispute with Vietnam was a major factor in China's current anxieties about foreign affairs.

China had supported the Japanese position on the
northern territories for a number of years, and hoped
for reciprocal support from Tokyo. But while Japan
continued to bring up the territorial issue as a local
question, China saw it as a symptom of general Soviet
hegemonism:

> The Soviet revisionists have made gigantic efforts
> to promote hegemonism and carry out aggression and
> expansion in Asia in a most unbridled way...The
> Soviet revisionists have also forcefully occupied
> the territory of other nations and regarded it as
> their own. The four northern islands of Japan are a
> good example. While stubbornly refusing to return
> these four Japanese islands, the Soviet revision-
> ists have also established naval and air bases
> there, frequently intruded upon the territorial
> airspace and waters of Japan, and conducted ruth-
> less activities against the Japanese fishermen.[33]

Japan, however, did not request or need this ideological support from China, and found it embarrassing in
the content of treaty negotiations. For the Chinese,
Soviet occupation of the northern territories was proof
that Japan had a national interest in resisting hegemonism.

When the PFT was signed, Sonoda insisted that the
main thrust of the hegemony clause was that it imposed
self-restrictions on China and Japan.[34] Opposition to
hegemony was a principle which demonstrated that Japan
would not revive militarism, and as such was already
implicit in the sentiments of Article Nine of the 1947
Constitution. Therefore, the foreign minister averred,
the inclusion of the hegemony clause in the treaty did
not break any new ground.

Deng Xiaoping was unwilling to let Sonoda's innocuous interpretation of hegemony stand as definitive. In
the Great Hall of the People, he urged Japan to strengthen self-defense power.[35] He referred to Vietnam's
actions as a case of local hegemonism, supported by the
arch-hegemonist, the USSR. Now that Vietnam had become
a member of COMECON, East European nations were also
supporting Vietnam with assistance. Sonoda responded
that he understood China's way of thinking, but hoped
that it would not do anything to "set off a fire in one
corner of Asia." Deng was noncommittal on this point.

After August 1978, the Chinese continued to stress
the common interest of Sino-Japanese opposition to Soviet hegemony. Deng said that the USSR opposed the
treaty because it was disadvantageous to their expansionist policy.[36] Deng Xiaoping, in an interview a few
weeks after the treaty, again encouraged Japan to increase its defense power. Sonoda stressed the anti-
militarist intention of the treaty, but Beijing was

giving an opposite meaning - that the closer relationship allowed the PRC to speak more frankly and directly
on Japan's security affairs.
The vice premier did not envisage military cooperation with Japan. Ignoring the evidence and Soviet anxieties, he denied that increased military preparations by
China, Japan, Western Europe, or the US would stimulate
the USSR to further arms races. The Chinese perception
was that the growth of Soviet armaments - especially in
conventional weapons - was independent of whatever self-
defense preparations were undertaken by other countries.
Soviet social imperialism was projected as an inherent
characteristic of the "fascistic dictatorship of the
Brezhnev clique," and had to be resisted.
Strategic considerations assumed priority in Chinese thinking, and helped to alienate leftist support in
Japan. Although the socialists and communists favored
the peace treaty as a progressive step, they benefited
little from its conclusion. Deng wanted Japan to increase self-defense, but this was resisted by the opposition parties in Japan. He also indicated that China
was not seeking to separate Japan from the US - a relationship which Japanese leftists found distasteful.
Japan-US relations should come first for Japan, he said,
and Japan-China relations second.[37] When this hierarchy
of priorities was combined with approval of the US-Japan
Mutual Cooperation and Security Treaty, Japanese leftists felt betrayed by Mao's successors.
With regard to Vietnam, Deng did not directly criticize Japan's aid, but said that China would no longer
cooperate with Vietnam since that would be tantamount to
cooperation with the USSR. In this post-treaty summing
up, Deng reminded Japan of its unredeemed northern territories, and mentioned that the USSR was extending its
influence into South Korea. Thus Japan's security interests were endangered by Soviet hegemony in the region.
The month following the conclusion of the treaty
saw a flurry of worldwide diplomatic activity. The PRC
sought to broaden international support in its growing
confrontation with the USSR and Vietnam, which China
considered a Soviet surrogate. Deng's mention of Soviet
influence in the Republic of Korea may have referred to
the visit of Seoul's Health and Social Affairs Minister,
Sin Hyon Hwak, to Alma Ata - the first ROK cabinet minister in office to visit the USSR.[38]
In less than a week after the Japan-China treaty
was signed, Hua Guofeng and Foreign Minister Huang Hua
visited Rumania, Yugoslavia and Iran. These vists were
marked by economic and technical agreements. These three
states, on the perimeter of the Soviet Union, noted PRC
concern about their independence.[39] With Hua's visit so
soon after the treaty with Japan, it indicated China's
general strategy of strengthening ties around the Soviet
rim. In Deng's press conference of 6 September, he

stated that the 1950 Sino-Soviet treaty was to be abrogated. These developments, and the growing Sino-Vietnam tension were ample evidence of worsening Sino-Soviet relations, and a cause for Japanese anxiety over the implications of its new treaty relationship.

In October 1978, Deng Xiaoping visited Japan for the purpose of exchanging the treaty instruments of ratification. It also gave more Japanese the opportunity to size up the man, described by one journalist as "a realist who has risen above being a mere socialist."[40] His public statements in Tokyo called for opposition to hegemony, and wanted Japan to join against the USSR. He conveyed the impression that he was more interested in Japanese cooperation against hegemony, than in Japan's aid to China's modernization. Because there was no problem with the latter, he felt it necessary to push the former. His emphasis on anti-hegemony at his Tokyo press conference embarrassed the Foreign Ministry, which insisted that opposition to hegemony had not been brought up in this way at the treaty negotiations during the summer. On October 23 Deng stated that "opposition to hegemony prescribed in the treaty will deal a severe blow to a hegemony nation." The prime minister could hardly welcome such an interpretation of the treaty, and emphasized that the treaty was not directed against any third nation.

The further deterioration of PRC-Vietnam relations in the wake of the Japan-China treaty may not be directly linked. Nevertheless, on 3 November, less than three months after the treaty, the USSR and Vietnam, signed a treaty of friendship and cooperation. Yu Zhan, one of the nine vice foreign ministers in the PRC government, maintained that the Japan-China treaty would not impede relations between China and countries of Southeast Asia. Deng's visit to the region was designed to further strengthen good relations, and to allay fears of Chinese expansionism. The real threat to the region's peace and stability, he noted, was Vietnamese expansion, as proven by the invasion of Kampuchea. Yu Zhan stated that the USSR's hegemonism was standing behind Vietnam's regional hegemonism. This was the real meaning of the Soviet-Vietnam Friendship and Cooperation Treaty.[41]

When the new Ohira government came to power, China indicated that relations were on the right track. Retention of Foreign Minister Sonoda in the cabinet assured continued good relations.[42] However, the PRC hoped that Ohira would stand up to Soviet hegemonism, which was threatening Asia.

By the beginning of 1979, attention had shifted from Asia's northeast to the southeast as a potential area of conflict. Deng indicated that there was little or no chance that North Korea would attack the South.[43] His government was seeking a peaceful solution to the Taiwan question. Now, Vietnam was becoming the major

flash point again, he said, because of its military
alliance with the USSR. Soviet naval power was becoming
stronger in the Pacific region as well.
The Chinese had watched the USSR build up its naval
power for a number of years, as it grew from a coastal
defense force into a formidable ocean-going fleet. In a
review of S.G. Gorshkov's The Maritime Power of the
State, Xinhua saw "a wonderful self-portrayal of Soviet
maritime hegemony":

> The author as one of the war-maniacs in the Kremlin
> wantonly advertises arms expansion and war prepara-
> tions and energetically advocates the strengthening
> of the Soviet naval power as a means of obtaining
> supremacy over the seas and throughout the world.
> Driven by the rapacity and unrestrainable hegemonic
> desire of a late-comer to the imperialist marine
> feast, the author arrogantly declares, "We are now
> in a new stage of the struggle for dividing and
> exploiting the seas and oceans in service of the
> economic and military purposes." He clamours, "Can
> the Soviet Union agree to the permanent rule of the
> Western maritime powers over the seas? Of course
> not!" He says, "It is necessary to build a navy as
> powerful as it is appropriate to the interests of a
> world power," adding "without a powerful navy Rus-
> sia could not have been able to join the ranks of
> powers."[44]

Discounting the rhetorical overkill typical of Cultural Revolutionary prose, the Chinese take the Soviet
maritime threat most seriously. The ultimate goals of
Soviet naval power were seen as: (1) to defeat the US in
a world war; (2) to unleash "local wars" against small
countries; and (3) to carry out "gunboat diplomacy." In
this strategy, Japan and Vietnam were vital to control
of sea lanes in East Asia. The straits through Japan's
waters were choke points which could affect Soviet naval
operations in the Sea of Japan and Sea of Okhotsk. If
the USSR acquired naval bases in Vietnam, these would
provide ports to threaten US naval power and its allies
in Southeast Asia.
In the West, Deng Xiaoping considered the strengthening of the US and West European alliance more important than any SALT treaty.[45] Alliances against the USSR,
not treaties with the "chief hegemonist," were the only
effective means of blocking Soviet expansionism. This
imperative was also a criticism of Japanese opinion that
a peace treaty with the USSR was needed to restore good
relations. Brezhnev had proposed a treaty of friendship
and cooperation to visiting Labor Minister Ishida on 15
June 1977, but Fukuda called it unaccepable if it did
not consider the question of the northern territories.[46]
The Japan-China treaty had not led to the peace and

stability of Asia as Japanese proponents had hoped. In fact, it probably exacerbated Sino-Soviet tensions in at least four ways: First, the inclusion of the hegemony clause indicated to Moscow that, from China's viewpoint, the treaty was not a neutral instrument. Second, because of the close relations between Japan and the US, the treaty smoothed the way for Sino-American normalization, which probably would lead to a harder anti-Soviet stand by both. Third, the treaty and subsequent Japanese loans to China may have strengthened the PRC's confidence to attack Vietnam in February 1979. Fourth, Japan's insistence on abrogation of the Sino-Soviet treaty of 1950 raised an issue which China preferred to let die quietly. It was done as quietly as possible, but the USSR claimed that the onus for breaking the alliance was on the Chinese.

The PRC continued to string together a worldwide united front against Soviet hegemony. After normalizing relations with the US, Deng visited the country in February, stopping in Tokyo on February 7. Ohira pressed for a peaceful settlement of the border issue with Vietnam. Deng replied that China was handling the problem cautiously, but also hinted at the action his country would take within a few days: "It is necessary to inflict necessary punishment to some extent on the actions of Vietnam."[47] Deng also welcomed Japan's aid and diplomacy towards ASEAN, and requested economic aid for China's anti-Vietnam client, the auto-genocidal Pol Pot regime in Kampuchea.

In talks held simultaneously between the respective foreign ministers, Sonoda asserted that Japan would not support any attempt to settle the Vietnam problem by force. Huang Hua called Vietnam the "Cuba of Asia" in reference to its relations to the USSR, and indicated that it was necessary to respond strongly to Vietnam's "provocations."

Deng also met with ex-Prime Minister Fukuda, and repeated the strong line that Soviet hegemony was undermining Asian stability. He saw Soviet pressure on Iran, and considered India already under Moscow influence. Confronted with these developments, China could not sit back and do nothing, he said. Also, important shipping routes were endangered by Soviet hegemonism, and Japan must stand up for its vital interests.

The reference to Vietnam becoming a "Cuba in the East" was not hyperbole. For several years, the USSR had used Cuban troops in Africa as surrogates to assist pro-Moscow forces. Since the Bay of Pigs debacle, the US denounced the pro-Soviet regime for engaging in subversion and covert military actions in the Caribbean region and elsewhere. China would not tolerate an Asian Cuba on its southern borders. Vietnamese invasion of pro-Chinese Kampuchea proved the "Cuban" tendencies of Hanoi. Only decisive action in the form of military

attack was considered sufficiently effective to halt
Soviet-backed expansion by the Vietnamese.
     The statements of the Chinese vice premier and for-
eign minister in Tokyo stirred Japanese anxieties. Frequent border skirmishes between Chinese and Vietnamese
forces and the reported buildup of the Chinese military
in the region indicated that a dangerous situation was
developing.[48]   Nihon Keizai placed blame on China for
the sudden growth in tension in Asia and the Pacific.
China defended its subsequent invasion of Vietnamese
territory as a legitimate counterattack against previous
Vietnamese intrusions of Chinese territory.[49]
     China had embarked on a new brinkmanship, risking
that the USSR would not intervene. If China had not responded forcefully to Vietnamese provocations, Deng later
asserted, the Chinese people would have been regarded as
weak. China was demonstrating that it would not shrink
back from the use of force when challenged by a regional
hegemonist - a client of a major hegemonist. Military
force and the credible threat of its use were the most
effective means of resisting hegemony.
     During the remainder of 1979, Beijing continued to
consolidate the domestic political structure, renovate
the economy, and cultivate the American connection. The
Soviet invasion of Afghanistan in December reinforced
China's perception of the USSR as expansionist. The US
was finding the claim more credible now. The Afghan
intrusion was a further move in the Sino-Soviet dispute
as well, and it was Moscow's turn to demonstrate that it
would not hesitate to use military force to support or
establish a regime consonant with Soviet interests. As
a result, the once-neutral Afghan state became a Soviet
satellite, and China's close ally in the subcontinent,
Pakistan, became a frontline state.
     Several interpretations may be suggested for the
Soviet action in Afghanistan. One is that the USSR
responded to a strategic encirclement attempt by the
PRC, which included the US, NATO, and potentially, Japan. The USSR had demonstrated its will and capacity to
break any attempt to create a perimeter network of anti-
Soviet states. In this perspective, the Soviet install-
ment of the Karmal regime marked an intensification of
Sino-Soviet conflict.
     Another interpretation is based on the Chinese
hegemonism thesis - that Soviet expansion is the result
of some national aberration which the present regime has
inherited. It could be termed the imperialist proclivi-
ties of the tsarist forebearers, the combination of
state monopoly capitalism and late developing nationalism. But whatever the roots of this tendency towards
expansionism, the Chinese maintain that this hegemony
can be contained only by resisting with force and making
it clear that it will be opposed everywhere.

A third explanation is that the Sino-Soviet dispute has enhanced traditional patterns of Russian expansionism. Historical Russian expansion incorporated buffer territories so as to provide greater national security. This was apparent in Ivan the Terrible's or Peter the Great's reigns, when Mongol and Tartar retreats were followed by Russian conquest, or after world war two, when Eastern Europe became a system of Soviet-dominated buffers against possible Western attacks in Soviet Europe.

With the Western borders stabilized, the USSR has turned its attention to its eastern regions, where it sees an increasing Chinese threat. The Soviet-oriented Mongolian People's Republic provides one buffer, and the pro-Soviet Kabul regime may have a similar buffer role. Weak, unstable states between the modern Soviet empire and its rivals are considered dangerous to that empire's security, and must be replaced with pro-Soviet regimes. If such regimes are not possible, these buffers must preferably be weak countries susceptible to Soviet pressures.

In this interpretation, the historical insecurity of the Russian state has led to the tendency of absorbing neighboring territory in the name of enhancing security. Since the 1960s, Soviet expansive tendencies have confronted the Chinese state in Asia. The end of US military involvement in Indochina reduced "American imperialism" in Beijing's active demonology, leaving mainly Soviet hegemonism and its regional agents as the major threats to China. In its search for allies, the PRC has sought to arouse the US, Japan, and Western Europe to the Soviet danger. Perhaps to the extent that China has been successful, the USSR has responded to a perceived threat with greater belligerence - thus helping to validate the Chinese accusations of hegemonism.

A fourth interpretation is that Soviet intervention was sui generis - an isolated event which was the result of a Soviet-backed regime on the brink of collapse. Rather than risk this collapse, and the consequent expulsion of Soviet advisors, Moscow intervened and installed a new client, defended by its military might. [50]

In response to the Afghan crisis, Deng Xiaoping has advocated the formation of an anti-Soviet alliance. [51] He portrayed the Western response to the affair as stopgap and piecemeal. Although a superpower, the US did not have the ability to stop Soviet hegemony alone. He saw the USSR as increasing power in East Asia and the Pacific, evidenced by its naval expansion and links with Vietnam. Next, he expected a Soviet move against Iran or Pakistan, the Indian Ocean having been the target of advances since tsarist days.

Deng admitted that China was poor, weak, and backward, but his nation had consistently viewed things from

a long-run standpoint. This contrasted with non-communist, both Western and Japanese, politicians who viewed
only the short-run. Implicit in Deng's statements was
the critique that democratic politics is not always
appropriate to the conduct of long-range foreign policy.
The Chinese harbored few illusions about Carter's motivations in agreeing to normalization - they understood
presidential politics sufficiently to realize that the
approaching 1980 election was one factor. And it was no
secret that Fukuda's decision to support the Japan-China
treaty was closely linked to his rivalry with Ohira for
the LDP presidency.

     In the international system, the continued resis-
tance of "Democratic Kampuchea" against Vietnamese occupation was one bright spot seen by Deng. The vice premier said that victory for the resistance was possible
even if 80 per cent of the country fell to Vietnam.[52]
Vietnam was subsisting on Soviet aid - about $2.5 mil-
lion per day. If resistance could be maintained, both
Vietnam and its Soviet sponsors would be weakened -just
as the US had been. Deng preferred to ignore that the
"heroic Kampucheans" had murdered hundreds of thousands
of their countrymen, and made the Pol Pot government one
of the most morally repugnant in the world.

     If the USSR succeeded in outflanking China and
neutralizing all external resistance, the fallback position was clear to Deng: it would mean "living in caves
and eating millet," as in the days of Yanan. Before
that happened, however, China would follow a three-pron-
ged strategy to avoid defeat. The first was to build up
the People's Liberation Army through greater professionalization and modernization. Admission of Mao's mistakes
has also cast doubt on his doctrines of people's war,
which receives less emphasis in the present regime. It
will be many years before China possesses a modern military force capable of defeating Soviet forces in the
field. The Soviet operation in Afghanistan was ample demonstration of Soviet blitzkrieg efficiency. Ironically,
the performance of the Afghan resistance movement continued to demonstrate the viability of guerrilla warfare
in preventing a technologically superior military force
from consolidating control over rural areas. From the
Kampuchean and Afghan examples, the Chinese military
leadership may draw the conclusion that it is premature
to opt for total modernization, which is very expensive
and also not always the best means of defense. There
are also conflicts between military and civilian budget
priorities. In the spring of 1981, the Chinese Defense
Minister Geng Biao said that in terms of budget priorities, defense was the fourth of the four modernizations.[53]

     The second prong of Chinese strategy is to keep up
pressure against Soviet invaders and their proxies by
direct action as well as assisting allies, as in the

case of Kampuchea. However, material aid does not insure
postwar alignment, as Vietnam demonstrated. Even full-
scale participation of Chinese troops on the side of the
North Koreans did not guarantee "undying friendship"
from Pyongyang. Kim Il Song has navigated cautiously
between China and the USSR.

In recent years, the Deng strategy has stressed a
third approach: to encourage resistance to Soviet ambitions on the part of uncommitted nations and regional
groupings. In Europe, Beijing has become an unofficial
member of NATO and is a supporter of anti-Soviet sentiments there. In Southeast Asia, where China had earlier
denounced ASEAN as an imperialist plot, the Chinese
leader paid visits and worked for friendship there.

In this last part of PRC strategy, the most significant gains were the Japan-China treaty and the restoration of Sino-US relations in an environment of growing
anti-Soviet pressures. In both cases PRC diplomats displayed knowledge and realism concerning the weaknesses
and emotions of the countries involved. With Japan, the
search for peace and stability was stressed as the guiding principle. Even the hegemony clause was announced
as self-restrictive by both parties so as to avoid embarrassing Tokyo before the treaty was concluded. China
also played on the so-called "China fever" current in
Japan, as the pandas in Ueno Zoo became a symbol of this
sinophilia.

"Panda diplomacy" was merely one weapon in the Chinese diplomatic arsenal. To China, Japan remains a bourgeois capitalist nation. The prospect of trade, investment, and access to resources became a powerful inducement for Japan to cement closer relations. Against these
economic, emotional, and cultural ties, the USSR was no
match. In addition, there remains a residue of war guilt
for atrocities and invasion against China, which the PRC
has not discouraged.

It appears that despite Tokyo's formal commitment
to equidistant diplomacy, it is unlikely that Soviet and
Japanese ties can ever be as strong as the bonds between
Japan and China. The reforms and economic direction map-
ped out by Deng Xiaoping conform to a vision with which
middle-class Japan can agree. It is based on rational
planning and contains the mixture of state leadership
and foreign investment in a spirit analogous to Meiji
modernization strategy. Except among intellectuals, the
Cultural Revolution had few admirers in Japan. The four
modernizations represent a spirit of orderly change and
reform more akin to the nation-building programs of Sun
Yat-sen than to Marx and Lenin and Mao. More important
to the Japanese, China's current modernization welcomes
their participation - or at least their capital and
technology.

An astute estimation of the US was also involved in
the steps towards normalization. When China's new regime

indicated that the economy would not shut out international capital, Washington saw new opportunities to
move, or else US business would be squeezed out by Japan
and Western Europe. The Nixon visit in 1972 to Beijing
had already broken the ice, and after 1975, no Vietnam
war remained to place US and China interests in sharp
contradiction. Moreover, Soviet expansion of influence
in Africa had made Carter retreat from his original
optimism over détente. The "China card" was becoming
attractive for business and strategic reasons.

As in Japan, pro-Chinese sentiments were far stronger than pro-Russian sympathies with the US. Several
generations of missionaries, businessmen, and journalists maintained emotional ties with China. The China
they remembered before 1949 had only a weak government
and was victimized by ousiders and native predators.
The new China had stood up, and nationalistic excesses
could be forgiven. The Korean instance of Sino-American
war, according to PRC sympathizers, was the result of
MacArthur's errors and Soviet machinations. Even the
Cultural Revolution could be understood as an orchestra-
ted movement to rid society of undesirable feudal features. A romanticized version of the PRC emerged, and
the US was urged to learn from some of these social
experiments. After Mao's death and the denunciation of
the Cultural Revolution, PRC sympathizers were mollified
by the prospects of normalization, which helped to overcome any reservations about the Chinese turnaround.

In contrast, the affinity of any sizable sector of
US public opinion for the USSR has never been very high,
perhaps with the exception of the period of US-Soviet
cooperation during the second world war. Soviet repression of East European independence, persecution of Jews
and dissidents, spies and espionage revelations, and
Stalin's pact with Hitler have poisoned American perception of Soviet intentions for decades. Chinese leaders
recognized that below the official movement toward détente there remained considerable mistrust of the USSR.
China's anti-Soviet pronouncements in the 1970s thus
coincided with American sentiments, and eased the path
to rapprochement, which culminated in normalization.

However, when the Republican presidential candidate
said, during the 1980 campaign, that his administration
would reconsider US relations with Taiwan, Beijing expressed concern that the delicate structure of Sino-
American relations might become strained if the Taiwan
issue were revived. Reagan was expressing concerns of
his party that Carter may have accommodated the PRC too
generously, without quid pro quo guarantees about the
security of Taiwan.

Objectively, the strategic elegance of China's
post-Mao diplomacy is to be admired. From a position of
weakness and vulnerability Beijing contributed to the
halting of the US withdrawal tendencies from Asia, and

indirectly exacerbated Japan-Soviet suspicions. Those
who believe that the US-Soviet impasse of the 1980s is a
continuation of the postwar Cold War may fail to note
its new nature - the extension of the Sino-Soviet conflict onto a worldwide scale now involving West Europe,
the US and, to a lesser extent, Japan.

Footnotes

1. For a review of selected books on Soviet policy
in the region, see Kimura Hiroshi, "Soviet Strategy in
Northeast Asia," Problems of Communism, 30:5 (1981), pp.
71-76.
2. On Soviet naval expansion, see Elmo R. Zumwalt,
"Gorshkov and his Navy," Orbis 24:3 (1980), pp. 491-510.
3. NK, 28 February 1978, p. 2
4. Ibid.
5. SK, 6 March 1978, p. 4.
6. Ibid.
7. MS, 11 August 1978, p. 2.
8. MS, 18 August 1978, p. 1.
9. SK, 4 September 1978, p. 4.
10. Ibid.
11. SK, 23 October 1979, p. 1.
12. Ibid.
13. "Peace, Independence and Democracy, the Only
Bright Road for the Japanese People," Renmin Ribao
Editorial, 20 November 1958, in Oppose the Revival of
Japanese Militarism (A Selection of Important Documents
and Commentaries), edited by the Chinese People's
Institute of Foreign Affairs, Peking: Foreign Languages
Press, 1960, p. 4.
14. AS, 9 March 1978, p. 6.
15. Ibid.
16. Ibid.
17. NK, 8 March 1978, p. 2.
18. SK, 8 March 1978, p. 1.
19. DR:China, 26 September 1977, p. A4.
20. DR:China, 22 August 1977, p. A4.
21. DR:China, 10 April 1975, p. A1.
22. Ibid., p. A7.
23. MS, 27 April 1978, p. 1.
24. DR:China, 7 October 1975, p. A7.
25. DR:China, 8 July 1977, p. A5.
26. Ibid., p. A3.
27. DR:China, 23 April 1975, p. A18.
28. TS, 5 July 1978, p. 2.
29. MS, 7 September 1978, p. 2.
30. DR:China, 23 April 1975, p. A18.
31. YS, 4 July 1978, p. 1.
32. SK, 7 July 1978, p. 2.
33. DR:China, 20 October 1975, p. A8.
34. YS, 11 August 1978, p. 2.

35. Ibid.
36. MS, 7 September 1978, p. 2.
37. Ibid.
38. NK, 12 September 1978, p. 2.
39. Ibid.
40. TS, 26 October 1978, p. 3.
41. TS, 20 November 1978, pp. 1-2.
42. NK, 12 August 1978, p. 4.
43. YS, 15 January 1979, p. 2.
44. DR:China, 2 June 1976, p. A7.
45. YS, 15 January 1979, p. 2.
46. JTW, 25 June 1977, p. 1.   DR:China, 20 June 1977, p. A11.
47. YS, 7 February 1979, p. 1.
48. NK, 9 February 1979, p. 2.
49. MS, 27 February 1979, p. 4.
50. The author is grateful to Professor Allen Whiting for suggesting this interpretation.
51. YS, 30 March 1980, p. 1.
52. Ibid.
53. DR:China, 15 April 1981, p. D1.

5
China and Japan: Diplomatic, Economic and Military Relations

American withdrawal from Vietnam in 1975 was translated into a general policy of disengagement from potential Asian conflicts. President Carter's policy of advocating human rights, and the desire to avoid situations which could lead to American military involvement, indicated a new direction in foreign policy.[1] To allies in East Asia, the new direction meant that American support in emergencies was less certain than in the past.

Japan was facing a new international reality in the late 1970s. A new regime was taking shape in post-Mao China, and the US was withdrawing ground forces from continental Asia. On the one hand, a more rational and pragmatic leadership in China would substantially reduce the threat to Asian stability from Beijing. On the other hand, some quarters feared that US withdrawal from Korea could have a destabilizing effect.[2] One or the other of the Korean regimes might seek to unify the peninsula by force, and the decreased presence of US forces made American participation less certain than in the past.

These and other factors were producing a new configuration of international forces in the region. By the end of the Carter administration, the East Asian situation was as follows:

(1) The PRC and the USSR were in severe confrontation, due to a number of quarrelsome issues. Most recent were the Soviet invasion of Afghanistan, and the expansion of the Soviet ally at the expense of Laos and Kampuchea.

(2) The US had tilted towards the PRC since normalization, and was tending to confrontation with the USSR. Carter had cemented the China relation at the expense of Taiwan. Simultaneously, the PRC was seeking to induce Taiwan to reunite with the mainland, and end the half-century of civil war.

(3) Japan had cemented diplomatic and economic relations with the PRC, at the cost of cooler relations with the USSR. The security treaty with the US continued in force, but Japan-US friction on various trade matters

continued.

(4) In Southeast Asia, Vietnam became the bête
noire of peace and stability. ASEAN, Japan, the US and
PRC opposed Vietnamese domination of Indochina, and
continued their cooperation in a wide range of issues.

Thus, the balance of power in East Asia emerged
with a loose coalition of nations opposing the USSR and
its ally, Vietnam. In no small part, Deng Xiaoping had
fashioned an anti-hegemony united front out of the diverse nations of the north Pacific region. Unlike NATO,
the de facto united front in East Asia was geographi-
cally scattered, as well as linguistically, historically
and culturally fragmented, and at different phases of
industrialization. It would therefore be impossible to
achieve the coordination present in NATO, particularly
in military matters. But within these existing limitations, Beijing had managed to tilt much of the region
towards an anti-Soviet and anti-Vietnam orientation.

In accomplishing this, China's diplomacy has emphasized themes and inducements which broke down Japanese
and US reservations. For Japan, the China market offered
attractions such as opportunity for investment and access to energy resources. When Japanese business or
government negotiators displayed hesitation, the Chinese
would hold out the prospect of European or American rivals who offered alternative financing. Also, by expressing peaceful intentions and commercial pragmatism, the
Chinese assured Japan that the PFT would facilitate stability in the region. This promised a combination of
economic opportunity and increased tranquility which was
difficult for Japan to refuse--making the PFT's hegemony
clause easier to accept as a cost of doing business.

Inducements to the US differed slightly. American
business interests felt they were being shut out of the
China market by the rapid advances made by Japan and
Western Europe. Previous objections to the abandonment
of Taiwan were overcome by the PRC shift to the line
calling for peaceful unification. Also, the anti-Soviet
posture of the PRC appeared useful to US strategists who
sought ways to checkmate Soviet expansion without invok-
ing direct US-USSR confrontation. The anti-hegemony
notion of China was much less objectionable to the US
than to Japan.

Simultaneously, China had been courting support in
Southeast Asia. Although China continued support for
native communist parties, it also cemented closer relations with existing governments. Criticism of ASEAN was
transformed into moral support for an organization which
provided stability and resistance to Vietnamese expansion.

When Japan was negotiating the treaty with China,
it did not want to be part of an anti-Soviet alliance.
Officially, Japan followed its omnidirectional diplomacy
with regard to China and the USSR. In practice the line

has been applied selectively.

A major task of Japanese diplomacy since the treaty has been to avoid an excessive pro-China tilt which could antagonize the USSR into overt hostility. High level visits of Deng Xiaoping and Zhang Caiqian* in 1978, and again by Deng in February 1979 provided evidence for Moscow's claims that a growing Sino-Japanese relation was being consolidated. China appeared to play a moderating influence over North Korea and held bilateral discussions with Japan on the Korean situation. This reinforced Japanese expectations on the stabilizing effects of the relationship with China. However, the Chinese attack against Vietnam in February 1979, following Deng's visit to the US and Japan by a few days, aroused second thoughts about China's peaceful intentions.

Nevertheless, the primary connection between China and Japan has been economic. With the signing of the Long Term Trade Agreement in February 1978, great possibilities appeared for Japanese commerce and industry. The agreement also smoothed the way for the PFT. China has put aside the former policy of self-reliance and invited foreign investment on a large scale. Financing was first on a private basis, and later, government loans were negotiated. For Japan, access to China's vast untapped energy resources was a central factor in economic cooperation. The visits to China by Prime Minister Ohira Masayoshi in late 1979, and to Japan by Premier Hua Guofeng the following May, produced new agreements of cooperation.

Although the economic links were desirable for their own sake, China's bargaining strategy included other industrial nations besides Japan. Moreover, Japan's competitive edge was eroded by an increasingly expensive yen, and by the entry of the US into the China market. In economic intercourse, Japan had fewer chips than the PRC.

China needed foreign investment and technology to aid in the program of modernization. Beijing also hoped that a military relationship could by forged with Japan. Ideally, a combination of Chinese ground forces, Japanese air and naval forces, and US strategic capability would be a formidable counterweight against the USSR. Fukuda wanted no part of any such combination. The peace constitution, domestic opposition, and fear of reprisals by the USSR were sufficient reasons to resist military cooperation with Beijing. In addition, Sino-US normalization provided an alternative source of military cooperation, taking some pressure off Tokyo.

The perennial promise of the China market was materializing to Japan, and cooperative relations blossomed.

---

*Deputy Chief-of-General Staff, People's Liberation Army (PLA), General Headquarters.

78

The Chinese National People's Congress passed a number of new laws to accommodate joint ventures, and the government has undertaken other reforms in banking, insurance, and finance to facilitate importation of foreign investment and technology. Leaders and businessmen in the industrial nations hoped that the Chinese recognized the superiority of non-Soviet and non-Maoist methods of organizing capital and labor. To a limited extent, this element was present in the post-Mao reforms, but not to the degree of dismantling central control and socialist planning. However, excessively ambitious plans and changing priorities have resulted in confusion and dislocation.

Whether or not economic modernization succeeds to the degree proposed will affect the future survival of the Beijing leadership. But in the realm of foreign affairs, the promise of modernization, and the invitation to non-communist industrial nations to participate in that modernization, has already accomplished one purpose - to end China's isolation from the US and Japan, and to give the "bourgeois capitalist" countries an economic stake in the new Chinese order. This new face of China - oriented towards legality and economic growth - makes the country more acceptable as an ally to the US and countries of the "second world."

SINO-JAPANESE SUMMIT DIPLOMACY, 1979-80

The history of Sino-Japanese relations in the twentieth century has been marked by inequality, conflict, and mistrust. Japanese diplomatic support for Taiwan and the link with the US after the war strongly determined Tokyo's policy orientation, while mutual suspicion during the Cultural Revolution inhibited close relations. For its part, China accused Japan of embarking on a program of remilitarization in 1971, and PRC spokesmen made statements which were considered as interference in Japan's internal affairs.[3]

After the Nixon visit, which occurred without consulting Prime Minister Sato, there was a groundswell of sentiment for Japan-China normalization: Prime Minister Tanaka even claimed that his cabinet might collapse if normalization did not take place.[4] According to Lee Chae-Jin, the rapid emergence of a pro-Beijing mood in Japan in the early 1970s "reflected the nearly universal acceptance of China's great power status and the demonstrable erosion of the US containment policy towards China."[5]

After normalization, a hiatus in further improvement of relations occurred. With the 1978 PFT came a new flood of mutual visits, agreements, exchanges - and problems. PLA General Zhang Caiqian stopped over in Tokyo in September 1978, preceding Deng's treaty-signing visit in October. Zhang's visit proved an embarrassment

to Tokyo, and gave a momentary military hue to the new
relationship. Deng's October and February visits also
stressed China's anti-Soviet stand, to the consternation
of Japanese hosts. These moves by Deng and General Zhang
indicated China's determination to build a coalition
with the US and Japan against the USSR and Vietnam.
    Even before the treaty had been signed, there were
clear indications of China's goals. Vietnam was expelling Chinese residents, the China-Vietnam border dispute
was intensifying, China suspended economic aid to Vietnam, and Hanoi had joined COMECON – the economic organization of the Soviet bloc nations. Vietnam's Foreign
Minister Phan Hien visited Japan and told Fukuda and
Sonoda that his country would uphold autonomy, independence and non-alignment. He also indicated a readiness
to hold normalization talks with the US. Sonoda instructed Japan's ambassador to the US to assist in mediation
between Vietnam and the US. [6]
    Mediation did not have good prospects in the con-
text of growing US distrust of the USSR. Moreover,
critics saw a certain inconsistency in Japanese policy –
trying to act as an intermediary between the US and
Vietnam, while engaged in negotiating a Peace and
Friendship Treaty with China. [7] While these moves were
theoretically derived from omnidirectional diplomacy,
the Tokyo Shimbun criticized them as leading to unprin-
cipled behavior. The Chinese saw the Russians behind
Vietnam's actions, and did not sympathize with Sonoda's
attempts at peacemaking. Japanese officials remained
optimistic that China would understand the continued aid
to Vietnam, despite what China called "small-scale hegemony." [8]
    Japan's omnidirectional diplomacy could only oper-
ate under conditions where the US itself followed equidistance between the USSR and PRC. As the US began to
take sides in the Sino-Soviet dispute, there would be
little opportunity for Japan to exercise the autonomy it
desired. Linked to the US by trade and the Security
Treaty, Japan could not deviate too far from American
initiatives. At best, Tokyo's foreign policy could be
slightly ahead of Washington. But without adequate
military power, Japan's economic and moral influence was
limited.
    The Sino-Soviet confrontation could not fail to
affect Japan. Sonoda told Huang Hua that he hoped China
would not attempt to settle the Vietnam dispute by
force. Huang replied that the Soviet Union uses Cuba
all over the world, and now Vietnam is serving Soviet
hegemony. A firm answer to provocations had to be
given. [9]
    The 1979 war and its preceding events led to the
disillusionment of many Japanese intellectuals who had
supported China's road to socialism and the Vietnamese
revolution against foreign countries. China's dismant-

ling of the Cultural Revolution, Vietnam's invasion into
Kampuchea, and the Chinese attack on Vietnam were profound shocks to those who had opposed US involvement in
Vietnam.[10] Socialism, it appeared, was unable to solve
national confrontations and border problems. Moreover,
Vietnamese communists were expelling many thousands of
citizens, and creating refugees as a matter of national
policy.
     Japanese leftists faced a major crisis of confi-
dence. The Chinese and Vietnamese models of socialism
became tarnished in 1978. Not only did Deng Xiaoping
fail to meet with leaders of the Japan Socialist Party
(JSP) on his trip to Tokyo, but he even approved the US-
Japan Security Treaty as necessary in opposing Soviet
hegemony. With the outbreak of the Sino-Vietnamese conflict, Asian socialism could claim little relevance to
international politics.
     Japan expressed official concern about the Vietnam
action through its embassy in Beijing. Huang Hua reiterated China's position that it was a counter-offen-
sive for self-defense.[11] A proposal had been presented
in the UN Security Council, calling for withdrawal from
Kampuchea. The PRC foreign minister maintained that
these were two separate issues,[12] implying that his
country's action was purely for self-defense, and not
intended as punishment of Vietnam for ousting China's
ally, the Khmer Rouge, from much of eastern Kampuchea.
Still, China would consider the ASEAN proposal to link
Chinese and Vietnamese troop withdrawals.
     During the first year of the PFT, Japan became a
concerned witness to the intensification of the Sino-
Soviet conflict. Ohira postponed his awaited trip to
China, partly in consideration of relations between
Japan and the USSR. In the wake of Deng's strong statements in Tokyo on his two visits, the prime minister did
not want to antagonize Moscow by rushing to visit Beijing. Ohira hoped to restore some balance in diplomacy
towards the two continental rivals, and so the government announced that he would visit both countries.[13]
     His visit to Beijing had been planned for September
1979, but was cancelled because of general elections.
Also, negotiations for a visit to the USSR were not
successful. The realization of omnidirectionality was
increasingly difficult. Ohira's visit to China would be
in the name of peace and friendship. But in the proposed
visit to the USSR, the northern territories would be an
unavoidable subject when the peace treaty was discussed.
     Finally, Ohira decided to visit China in December
1979, without scheduling the Moscow trip as planned.
Foreign Minister Okita said that the purpose of the
visit was to pave the way for "mature relations."[14] This
term referred to more routine visits by heads of state,
rather than the visits of opportunity and stopovers
which had occurred since the treaty was signed in 1978.

Okita emphasized that Sino-Japan relations would not exert effects on third nations, and specifically mentioned the USSR.

An immediate purpose of the Ohira visit was to make final arrangements on certain loans and joint projects, but it also had significance in the wider context of the Asian international system. For one thing, Ohira's visit would be the first Japanese move within the formal framework of Japan-China treaty relations. It set in motion more summit talks between the two countries in the future. China was rapidly improving relations with the US, West Europe and ASEAN, wrote the Nihon Keizai, and Ohira's visit was a timely step.[15] Presumably, to postpone the trip further would not help Japan's relations with China.

Increasingly, summit talks were used to exchange views on important issues and to reduce differences where possible. Ohira did not intend to discuss the Senkaku Islands. Only Korea and economic exchanges were on the agenda. In the future, ministerial meetings would be held on an annual basis.

Akahata, the organ of the Japanese Communist Party (JCP) criticized Ohira's visit as a move to promote a Japan-US-PRC alliance. Such an alliance would lead to a revival of Japanese militarism and contribute to the US world strategy of encircling the USSR, it was claimed. The JCP was also critical of the government promise of huge aid to China, while freezing assistance to Vietnam.[16]

Ohira wished to avoid suspicion of Sino-Japanese collaboration against the USSR, or of Japan moving toward monopoly of the China market. To underline this, Ohira announced three principles in cooperation with China: (1) no military aid; (2) parallel cooperation with Europe and the US; and (3) a balance with ASEAN, so as not to reduce aid to the region.

The talks between Ohira and Hua Guofeng confirmed Japanese government loans of $1.5 billion to assist in building six major projects, most of which were concerned with port facilities and energy development. Japanese language training in China and acceptance of Chinese students in Japan were also agreed. On this, his third visit to China, Ohira, who had been foreign minister at the time of Japan-China normalization, noted that there was a five-fold increase in trade and personnel exchanges in the past five years.[18]

The prime minister mentioned that economic cooperation would be discussed annually, depending on progress and respective projects as well as relations to Japanese aid plans. Differences continued in international policies, and Ohira urged China and Vietnam to avoid resorting to force in settling their disagreements. Japan had already promised aid to Vietnam, and felt obligated to fulfill the commitment. In general, Ohira spoke of peaceful economic cooperation and the reduction of international tensions, unaware that later in the month, Asian problems were to increase with the Afghanistan affair.

The press communiqué on the visit referred to Japan-China economic cooperation and Asian peace and stability.[19] No mention was made of hegemony or any specific third country. Ohira also talked with Deng, the advocate of a hard-line against the USSR, but anti-Soviet sentiments were subdued on this occasion. This was partly in deference to Japanese sensitivities over relations with Moscow, which remained important especially in economic intercourse. In addition, the American-Chinese connection was moving in a direction advantageous to China by the end of 1979. With US opposition to the USSR, it was no longer urgent to push Japan into an anti-Soviet position.

The Ohira-Hua discussions also decided to hold high-level consultations annually, and the Chinese premier, who would step down in September 1980, accepted the Japanese invitation to visit Tokyo in May. During his Chinese visit, Ohira gave a speech to the Chinese People's Political Consultative Conference (CPPCC).[20] The CPPCC was the institutional expression of the idea of a united front, consisting of representatives from various "democratic parties and mass organizations." It was therefore appropriate, from the Chinese perspective, to have the head of government of Japan - a country which China ardently hoped would join the international united front against the USSR - speak before its members. His speech touched on international cooperation, although Deng, as CPPCC chairman, preferred a strong statement against the USSR.[21]

The Chinese avoided any embarrassment to their guests. Ohira's three principles allayed Western fears of Japanese market domination, and were designed to quiet Soviet anxieties over a Sino-Japanese military alliance. It had also been necessary for Japan to allay ASEAN concerns over a possible shift of financial resources from their region to China.

Foreign Minister Okita stressed the benefits of the visit and minimized any possible threat to the USSR. He intended to inform Moscow of the general terms of the talks through diplomatic channels, so as to head off any suspicions.[22] While he vigorously denied that Japan-China relations were directed against the USSR, there was no disguising the optimism held by Japan over the new relationship. For these two neighbors, however, it has been a case of "same bed, different dreams."

One area where China and Japan agreed - and could say so publicly - was on the need for peace and unification on the Korean peninsula. The topic had been discussed when Deng met with Ohira in Tokyo in February 1979.[23] At that time, Japan suggested China-South Korea

economic exchanges - a difficult proposition, considering China's close ties with Pyongyang, and Seoul's links
with Taiwan. On the subject of US withdrawal of ground
forces from South Korea, Deng indicated that it would
not have a destabilizing effect on the region. Deng and
ex-Prime Minister Fukuda also discussed the Korean situation. Deng concurred that Japan should communicate with
the south, and China would encourage the north in their
mutual dialogues. [24]
     The Korea question also came up in the Ohira-Hua
talks in Beijing, but was not mentioned in the communiqué. [25] Hua and Ohira agreed to create a stable international environment within which unification of the
peninsula could take place. Hua said that North Korea
would not attack the south, and that Pyongyang probably
would not seek reunification by force. China also echoed
North Korea's demand for "democratization" of the south.
     When Hua Guofeng visited Tokyo in May 1980, the
Korean issue was discussed again. Little progress had
been made in reunification. Moreover, with the political
turmoil in the south after the death of Park Chung Hee,
Japan was worried that the north might use the opportunity to move south. As the ROK army also became involved
in the political struggle, the defenses along the Demilitarized Zone were weakened. Hua denied that the army of
North Korea would take advantage of domestic distractions in Seoul. [26] He expressed concern that the ROK
military might create a conflict with the north.
     The direct discussion of Korean affairs by China
and Japan, and their exchange of accurate information
was useful to both nations. In addition, it provided
sources of information to Pyongyang and Seoul about each
other's potentialities and intentions. The north and
south have faced each other for three decades in intense
suspicion, so it is possible that the China-Japan connection can help to reduce tensions. The two states hold
different views and priorities on the Korean peninsula,
but both agree that an exchange of information would
help to maintain peace. In this environment, barring
intervention by other major powers, reunification might
make progress.
     While Hua Guofeng was visiting Japan to sign the
Japan-China Science and Technology Cooperation Agreement, Geng Biao was in the US holding talks on various
areas of cooperation, including military affairs. [27] In
Tokyo, Hua expressed general views on the Soviet threat,
but did not press Japan as Deng had done earlier. A
double election was coming up in Japan the following
month, and the Chinese were careful not to do or say
anything which could be construed as interference. Only
a few weeks earlier PLA General Wu Xiuquan had suggested
to Nakasone Yasuhiro that Japan could easily double its
defense expenditure. This statement was criticized by
the Gaimusho as improper, even if it was the general's

"private opinion."[28]

Hua met with ex-Prime Minister Tanaka, who was honored as the head of government that normalized Japan-China relations. Now freed from the restraints of high office, Tanaka stated candidly that it was necessary for Japan, the US and China to maintain equilateral triangular relations among them. Hua added that it was necessary "to have an eye all the time on the Soviet Union's attitude."[29] Meetings between Hua and Ohira were more subdued, and Hua appeared to be a more relaxed person than Deng. The prime minister was relieved over Hua's mild statements on sensitive topics. Ohira had written to Hua prior to his visit to Tokyo, requesting him to urge North Korea to exercise self-restraint towards South Korea.

Another request was that Premier Hua not involve himself in Japan's defense question. Hua already saw his position in Beijing eroding, and he had no intention of setting off a controversy which could supply his critics with ammunition to use against him. He met with Soka Gakkai and Komeito leaders Ikeda and Takeiri. The party had a special relation with China, and had sent numerous official delegations. In addition, the forthcoming election appeared that the result might be a coalition government including Komeito, and so it was no harm to cement good relations with potential members of that government.

With regard to the USSR, Ohira's view came close to China's interpretation of the Afghanistan affair.[30] At the time of Soviet intervention, Ohira did not characterize the action as expansive, as did the Chinese and Americans.[31] He subsequently realigned his thinking with various Western allies. In any event, the convergence of growing Western suspicions of the USSR, closer Sino-Japanese cooperation, and possible Sino-US military cooperation were visible signs of the very coalescence of Japan, China, and the US which Ohira strenuously denied. Japan's pro-China tilt was evident, and the government was reluctant to raise problems such as Chinese testing of nuclear weapons in the atmosphere, ICBM tests in the Pacific, and Japan-ROK oil development on the continental shelf which China protested against.[32]

The death of Ohira during the 1980 election campaign ended his political career, but his funeral became the occasion of talks between Hua and Carter over the Soviet threat in Afghanistan and Southeast Asia. The symbolism of the Tokyo talks was not unnoticed. The Soviet Union regarded the Carter-Hua talks as a strengthening of the China-US alliance, despite Carter's denials. Press Secretary Jody Powell pointed out that Japan shared a common interest with the US and China in the threat of the USSR in Afghanistan and Indochina. According to the Tokyo Shimbun, Powell hinted that there actually was a common understanding among Japan, the US, and China concerning the threat of the Soviet Union. [33]

After Ohira's funeral, Cabinet Secretary Miyazawa Kiichi warned against Japan becoming part of the US-China combination against the USSR. With increasing Soviet military superiority over the US, it was more and more dangerous to antagonize Moscow. However, Japan has become too closely linked to the US through trade and security to remain aloof from American policy. [34] Through trade and investment, Japan had also become linked with the PRC, although no military relations have been established. In this structure of relations of cooperation with two world rivals of the USSR, it has become difficult for Japan to convince other states of its omnidirectional diplomacy.

JAPAN-CHINA ECONOMIC RELATIONS: THE LONG TERM TRADE AGREEMENT (LTTA)

It is axiomatic that today Japan must trade or perish. It has few natural resources, and has become adept at processing, manufacturing, and selling a wide range of products which compete extremely well on the world market. Japanese efficiency in competition has led to demands for protection in major industrial countries. In addition, industrial development in other countries of East Asia has reduced Japan's competitive edge. Japanese industry must constantly innovate and seek new markets to prosper.

At the same time, the country must search for and secure resources of raw materials. Dependence on Mideast oil creates problems because of the instability of the region and long shipping lines. This vulnerability of resource supply and export markets influences not only Japan's economic health, but foreign policy as well. The protective relationship of the US has thus affected much of Japan's external policy.

These considerations have been valid in the development of Sino-Japanese relations as well. The PFT preceded US-China normalization by only four and a half months, and so was in line with US policy. It is also possible that the PFT facilitated normalization by demonstrating the Chinese intentions to US leaders.

But economic considerations, perhaps more than anything, led to the cementing of Sino-Japanese relations. Trade had increased after normalization in 1972, but the Chinese economy had slowed in the waning years of Mao's leadership. The emphasis on self-reliance also meant that China did not welcome foreign investment or loans while the spirit of the Cultural Revolution remained unpurged until 1976.

The new direction appeared with the rehabilitation of Deng Xiaoping in 1977. Party and government embarked on a program of modernization, and non-communist industrial countries were invited to participate. A major

boost for Japan came in February 1978, when business and
MITI (Ministry of International Trade and Industry) representatives travelled to Beijing to conclude the LTTA.
The agreement was signed by Inayama Yoshihiro, President
of the Keidanren. In form, it was a private agreement,
although government advisors had participated. Inayama's
Chinese counterpart, Liu Xiwen, signed for the other
side.   Liu was Chief of China's China-Japan Long Term
Trade Consultative Committee and Vice-Minister of Foreign Trade.
       The LTTA was to be in force for eight years, from
1978 to 1985. This period corresponded to the last three
years of the fifth Five Year Plan (FYP) and through the
full sixth FYP.[35] The value of the agreement was about
US $20 billion. Japan was to export technology, plants,
construction materials, and machinery worth $10 bil-
lion.[36] In return, China was to export crude oil, and
coal for coking and general use to Japan in gradually
increasing quantities during the first five years. Subsequent quantities would be decided by mutual consultation.   As to payment, Article Three of the agreement
stipulated that Japanese exports would be under a deferred payment formula. The remaining nine articles addressed certain technical matters of transaction.
       Inayama expected the LTTA to have an important
impact on the PFT negotiations.[37]   He also said that it
would relieve some Western resentment which had been
accumulating over Japan's export drives.   By 1978, the
international environment did not allow any more major
export offensives by Japan, so the Agreement with China
added to Japan's industrial security.   The diversifica-
tion of energy sources was also welcomed.
       Conclusion of the agreement proved to be easier
than its implementation. The high wax and sulphur content of Chinese crude caused problems for Japanese refineries which were set up for "sweet" oil from the Mideast and Indonesia. Nor was it certain that Japan could
absorb all the coal which was promised. Additional problems still had to be settled regarding interest rates
and deferred payments.
       Nevertheless, Sonoda and Inayama spoke enthusias-
tically about the economic prospects of the agreement.[38]
Sonoda saw the LTTA as a measure of diplomatic relief to
Southeast Asia, where countries could "now associate
with China with smiling faces," referring to the PRC
shift from revolution to modernization as the major
policy line.   Inayama was also optimistic and expected
few problems in China meeting the deferred payments.
       On the same day the agreement was signed in Bei-
jing, Li Xiannian, the vice chairman of the party and
deputy minister, urged Ambassador Sato of Japan to make
efforts for an early conclusion of the PFT.[39] The two
matters were kept separate by the Japanese government,
but to the Chinese, trade, peace and friendship were on

the same continuum: To paraphrase Clausewitz, trade is
the continuation of diplomacy by other means. Japan
faced difficulties in the tightening international market, so the prospects for flourishing bilateral relations were bright. The Chinese were making it clear
that the PFT would reinforce the special connection
between the two countries, a connection which was vital
to help the Japanese economy to survive and prosper.
    Business leaders were among the most ardent suppor-
ters of the treaty. Inayama pointed to the LTTA as preparing the way for the August PFT. Nihon Keizai interpreted the treaty as supporting the economic relations
which were rapidly becoming stronger.[40] Keidanren Chairman Doko described the treaty as showing the two nations' "resolve to build up mutual friendship and prosperity...far into the future." The president of the
Japan Chamber of Commerce, Nagano Shigeo, saw the PFT as
providing "supplementary relations where China provides
Japan with energy resources...and where Japan will offer
technology."[41]
    The February LTTA established economic and trade
cooperation which would assist in maintaining Japan's
industrial prosperity. Business circles welcomed the
PFT because it secured further political ties for that
cooperation. During treaty negotiations, China softened
its position on accepting loans to finance imports.
    The minister of MITI, Komoto Toshio, was the first
cabinet minister to visit China after conclusion of the
PFT. A major purpose of his trip was to discuss the expansion of the LTTA. According to Inayama, the agreement
was not merely for eight years, but was "endless."[42]
His optimism stemmed from the fact that Japan's target
of $10 billion worth of exports had been achieved in
less than six months.[43]
    The agreement was private, Komoto said, but the
government gave support in financing, consultations, and
other matters. The direct entry of the government into
LTTA cooperation was necessitated by the size of the
intercourse. In talks with Beijing two months after the
PFT, the two governments decided to extend the agreement
to 1990, and to expand its scope to more than $80 bil-
lion - an increase of more than four times.[44] Negotiations to renew the LTTA began in March 1979.
    The LTTA underscored the complementarity of the two
countries' economies. Japan had successfully initiated
modernization in the late nineteenth century. Prior to
1945, Japan attempted to emulate European nations in
building its own economic empire. Simultaneous with
Japanese industrial and political expansion, China had
been on the downward side of the imperial dynastic cyc-
le. Political fragmentation created a political vacuum
which Japanese industrialists and militarists sought to
fill with their own new order.
    The Cultural Revolution in China denounced foreign

participation in economic affairs, and sought to create
a new revolutionary state. In retrospect, it was an
impractical vision, and inhibited stable economic progress. The economic program of the four modernizations
was unveiled to make up for the lost years, and to dup-
licate what Japan had accomplished nearly a century earlier. Japan was a logical choice as a bridge to modernity for China. It has become one of the most powerful
economies in the world, and poses no military threat.
Japan welcomed the opportunities in China. The Japanese
exports successes were generating pressure for countermeasures in the industrial countries, while successful
industrialization in other East Asian countries was
creating competition for some Japanese products.
    Japan wished to sell, and China wanted to buy,
advanced technology. China had, and Japan needed, raw
resources, including crude oil and coal. Earlier, Chinese fears of Japanese remilitarization and the continued antipathy between China and the US had prevented
large-scale economic rapprochement between China and
Japan. After these factors had been removed or reduced,
Japan could participate fully in the economic life of
its near neighbor, with whom it had centuries of cultural and economic relations.
    The LTTA would help solve the three main bottle-
necks which Li Xiannian had said were inhibiting modernization: a shortage of construction funds, insufficient
production facilities, and a shortage of managers, ad-
ministrators and technicians.[45] At the Fifth NPC, an
ambitious economic plan was unveiled: In the period
through 1985, mechanization of agriculture was to be
increased to 85%. Manufacturing would increase by an
annual rate of 10%. The government planned 120 large-
scale construction projects, including metal plants,
coal mines, oil and gas fields, electric power stations,
railway lines and port facilities.[46]
    China had imported $3 billion worth of industrial
plants in the first years of the 1970s, and faced severe
staffing problems. The increasing emphasis on legality,
the declining role of Maoist ideology, and the appoin-
ting of technocrats and pragmatists to government minis-
tries indicated a new political environment in which
Japan could participate.
    When signing the PFT, Hua Guofeng stated:

    The National People's Congress decided on a 10-year
    economic plan, and efforts are being made. We are
    pursuing the building of our country by our own
    strength independently. However, we are definitely
    not exclusionist. We wish to learn advanced science
    and technology greatly. We also wish to increase
    persons to be dispatched abroad for study. We wish
    to spread advanced learning, too. We also wish to
    learn from Japan.[47]

Hua projected China's growth rate at 15% during 1978. These and other optimistic economic projections had attracted Japan and the US into a closer relationship with China. In 1979, economic priorities, especially in heavy industry, underwent revision. There appeared several problems due to overcommitment as well as budgetary deficits from the Vietnam war.

An editorial in People's Daily (24 February 1979) called for reduction of investments in iron and steel, and for increased emphasis on light industry and agriculture. This rearrangement of priorities was due to financial stringencies, according to Yomiuri.[48] This vitally affected Japanese business interests, because it caused suspension of negotations on oil development and plant construction.[49] The suspension of new contracts affected the giant Shanghai Baoshan Steel Works, and about 420 billion yen in investments. Numerous contracts for plants had been concluded, but not approved by the Chinese government because of problems in financing loans to pay for them.

In August 1979, Beijing consoled Japanese capitalists by claiming that China was not invalidating the economic plans, but merely revising them. A major policy change was also taking place in foreign loans. Deputy Premier Gu Mu officially requested government-to-government loans from Japan, in a departure from the previous policies of self-reliance.[50] In the past, the arrangements were that goods and projects would be paid in the form of deferred payments consisting of coal and oil exports. Gu Mu visited Japan in September, and requested $5.5 billion in loans.[51] In the wake of the retrenchment, China still needed and hoped for massive Japanese assistance. A combination of careless planning and coordination of the projects, and a dubious ability of China to repay all loans on schedule had made Japan more cautious. However, Japanese leaders and business circles were reassured that the risk was manageable when planning improved, the number of projects was reduced, and a US loan of $2 billion through the Export-Import Bank was promised. Japan went ahead with more cooperation in major projects when Ohira was visiting Beijing in December. The immensity of China's requirements was underscored when Li Xiannian said that about $600 billion was needed to achieve the four modernizations.

The original program of the four modernizations bore characteristics of previous crash programs to mobilize all resources and leap into the twentieth century, except that this time, non-communist external assistance was invited. Two decades before, Mao Zedong's Great Leap Forward had plunged the country into years of political struggle, as the communists attempted to build new economic and social institutions. With the four modernizations, victims of previous campaigns were rehabilitated, sometimes posthumously, as in the case of Liu Shaoqi.

Modifications in the modernization program allowed greater initiative to provincial and municipal levels than earlier. In October 1979, a trade mission arrived in Japan to explore joint venture possibilities formulated at local levels.[53] The mission was sent by the National Planning Committee, but projects would be carried out at local levels. Economic priorities were shifted from chemical and heavy industry to light industry. Fifty-one projects were formulated at the subnational levels and proposed as joint ventures to Japanese enterprises. Further cuts were announced in heavy industry during 1980. The concern over funding of agriculture and light industry remained, especially as consumer production expanded.

In politics, the Deng leadership was dismantling the Maoist cult of personality and denied there had been benefits from the Cultural Revolution. The new regime had to maintain the loyalty of its billion citizens, a large number of whom were made cynical by the Maoist years and the subsequent revelations of palace politics. To overcome this, one approach was to improve livelihood and provide firm evidence that a return to radicalism was neither likely nor desirable.

The Dengists could not afford an economic policy which, emulating Stalin and Brezhnev, concentrated on heavy industry and military weaponry at the expense of the consumer economy.[54] To accomplish an improved livelihood, and demonstrate to the Chinese people that socialism meant more than state interference and huge steel mills, Deng appeared to compromise socialism if necessary - or at least the forms which were prevalent in the USSR and Maoist China.

China announced that the second stage of the Baoshan steel complex would be postponed, affecting $1.3 billion in contracts with Japan, and possibly another $900 million in related contracts.[55] Gu Mu said that plans would be revised in a way so as to not cause losses to foreign contractors. China's modernization, which had appeared as a major opportunity for Japanese traders and industrialists, was losing its earlier promise.

THE INTERNATIONAL SETTING OF SINO-JAPANESE ECONOMIC COOPERATION

Japan's eagerness to conclude trade agreements and various projects with China was only partly based on recognition of profits to be earned. With rapid improvement of US-China relations, Japan had to move fast or lose out in competition which also included Western Europe. While the US lacked ancient cultural ties and the proximity enjoyed by Japan, American willingness to support some aspects if China's anti-hegemony was a favorable factor.

Initial advantages enjoyed by Japan in 1978 were
less important in the next years as American and European competition moved in. Also, Japan could not move
too far ahead of its industrial allies because of certain agreements under COCOM and OECD. Also, the increasingly expansive yen made Japanese goods and loans less
attractive to the PRC. Proclamations of Japan-China
friendship notwithstanding, China used international
competition among the industrialized states to its own
advantage. Under these circumstances, Japan's economic
advantage could be eroded by the US and Western Europe
as they penetrated the China market.

Another aspect of Sino-Japanese economic cooperation involved the ASEAN group. Japan had promised major
financial aid to the region, and had developed investment and trade there.[56] With the development of Japan-
China ties, ASEAN countries wanted assurances that it
would not be pushed to second place in Japan's aid
priorities. Also, they feared that an economically
strengthened China might someday penetrate and dominate
Southeast Asian markets.

Japan could not move too far from the Western industrial countries due to the limitations of various
agreements. One restriction came from the Coordinating
Committee for Exports to Communist Areas (COCOM), which
had to approve exports to China. The purpose of COCOM
was to maintain strategic superiority over communist
countries and prevent advanced technology which had
military application from being exported to communist
states. In late 1979, Hitachi and the PRC government
agreed on the sale of large-scale computers for meteoro-
logical use. But because these infringed on COCOM restrictions, the US agreed to approve the sale only if
three conditions were met: reduction of memory capacity, establishment of a safeguard system to prevent
conversion to military use, and an inspection after
installation. China agreed to the conditions, and the
sale went ahead.[57]

The US has a major voice in COCOM. As relations
with China improved, some restrictions in exports were
relaxed.[58] The Chinese government also wanted relaxation
of COCOM restrictions. Such a move was a precondition
for expanded Japan-China economic exchanges, especially
in electronic computers.[59] In construction of the Baoshan steel complex, for example, the controlling computers exceeded limits set by COCOM. For this reason, MITI
Minister Komoto wanted elastic application of COCOM
rules, which was also the direction of US thinking.

By October 1978, the various members of COCOM were
working around their own rules in a way which threatened
to undermine the original purpose of coordination.[60]
Unnamed US sources claimed that Japanese businesses were
engaged in sales campaigns which bent COCOM restrictions. Britain and France were also stretching COCOM

rules with weapons exports, but these were defined as
purely defensive, and thus allowed under the stipula-
tions. COCOM members had not yet established a firm policy regarding technology exports to China, and the US
was accused of envy towards its allies because of their
success in entering the China market. MITI claimed that
Japan went through meticulous procedures in clearing
exports to China. Officials also expressed irritation
that COCOM cleared US exports to China fairly quickly,
while Japanese applications were protracted. The COCOM
restrictions were easing as the US moved towards normalization. [61]

US-Japan differences over COCOM were symptoms of
rivalry over economic relations with China. As long as
the US was bound to Taiwan by the Mutual Security Treaty, it had strategic reasons for opposing military technology sales to the PRC. As this rationale receded in
1978, MITI feared that COCOM might become an instrument
to slow down Japanese exports to the PRC.

Another case of friction between the US and Japan
occurred when the LTTA was under negotiation. The US did
not concur with the easier deferred payment formula
which China requested. [62] At US-Japan trade negotiations,
the US position was that the terms for granting export
credits to China should be repaid at a minimum interest
rate of 7.5% when the loan period is more than five
years. In this, the US referred to an OECD "gentleman's
agreement" concerning exports to low-income countries. [63]

Some of these various questions revolved on the se-
mantics of whether China was to be considered as a "developing country" or as a "socialist nation." Since at
least the early 1970s, China had proclaimed itself to be
a "developing nation of the third world." With regard
to urbanization and industrialization, it may have been
technically an accurate definition. The US, however,
considered China to be a communist nation, and therefore
subject to the same restrictions as Eastern Europe and
the USSR. The difference had practical consequences, in
that it affected loan terms. The US also feared that
competition among COCOM member nations would only be to
China's advantage, and undercut political solidarity.
The US wanted Japan to exercise moderation as a trading
partner with China. Some Japanese quarters felt that
Italy or France had easier conditions in extending loans
to China than did Japan. So Japan studied other means
of financing its sales. [64]

US and Japan competition for high technology sales
to China increased. [65] Rivalry for the China market did
not obscure the far greater importance of US and Japanese mutual trade. Even highly optimistic projections of
Sino-Japanese trade saw it attaining no more than 20% of
the US-Japan trade total during the period of 1978-
1990. [66]

The two industrial giants of the Pacific also

emerged as rivals in financing loans for deferred payments on exports. The US was entering a period of the
highest interest rates in history, while Japan and Europe managed to keep their rates considerably lower.[67] US
attempts to keep rates to China high met with protests
from allies. The US insisted on the 7.25% and 7.5%
rates in the OECD "gentleman's agreement." But Japan
rebutted that its deferred payment loans were different
than those covered in the OECD agreement. The president
of the Sanwa Bank revealed the mixture of emotion and
pragmatism which has characterized relations with China:
"Even in the sense of repaying China for its kindness in
abandoning its claim for reparations toward our country,
we ought to lower the interest rate to that extent.
Otherwise, there is the fear that the China market will
be eaten away by the US and European forces."[68]
    Japan's competitive edge was reduced by its indus-
trial rivals. Two major reasons cited for the necessity
to develop the China trade with all deliberate speed:
First, Japan's exports to industrial countries were
facing restrictions and resentment, and second, Western
countries were gaining on Japan in the China trade. Even
before the US normalized relations with China, American
firms moved quickly.[69] Government leaders in Tokyo and
Washington called for a more cooperative approach to the
China market, and established channels for regular discussion. To reassure Japan, Deng Xiaoping told Fukuda
that Sino-American economic relations would not affect
the connection with Japan - a nation which he said still
had priority.[70] Fukuda responded that Japan, the US and
Western Europe should work together with each other and
with China in achieving the four modernizations.
    Entry of West Europeans and Canadians into the
China market had begun years earlier. By 1979, a more
cooperative posture was called for among the industrial
nations, now that their diplomatic relations with China
were on a more equal basis. The European Economic Community (EEC) had also signed an LTTA with China, insur-
ing against any Japanese monopoly of the market.[71] The
Chinese took advantage of international competition.
Beijing looked for alternative sources of investment and
trade, and European banks responded by granting large
loans on favorable terms.[72] The higher value of the yen
was blamed for loss of business to West Germany, France
and Britain.
    Thus, the economic environment was a major induce-
ment for Japan signing the PFT with China. Japan may
have enjoyed certain cultural and geographical advantages, but these had been negated by decades of intervention in China up to 1945, and postwar suspicions due
to close alignment with the US. Parallel with the turnaround in Chinese attitudes toward Japan after 1972,
Beijing continued to pursue closer relations with the
EEC and the US. Japan gained some advantages from the

94

LTTA and the 1978 treaty, but these were not permanent as China sought to broaden economic ties with other industrial non-communist nations.
From a historical perspective, China did not want to allow any single country to have too much influence over its economy. In the prewar era, China had experienced considerable foreign participation in the economy, a situation which Mao termed "semi-colonialism." From the late Qing period until the 1930s, Japan and the Western industrial countries had penetrated China by methods used in the colonization of Africa an much of Asia. In the "scramble for concessions" in the late nineteenth century, China came to be divided into geographical spheres of influence. The US and Britain declared an open door policy to preserve foreign economic access and Chinese sovereignty which would have ended if China were carved into colonies.
A series of unequal treaties, treaty ports, and other devices gave the industrial nations considerable leverage over the Chinese urban economy.[73] Sizeable loans were granted to the central government, which were secured against state revenues. When the Guomindang came to power in 1928, it accepted the external obligations of previous governments. Much of the borrowed money had been dissipated in warlord politics, and in fighting to oppose the Guomindang revolution. However, the nationalist government in Nanjing counted on external investment to carry out its own modernization policies. To renounce previous government debts, as the Bolsheviks had done with tsarist obligations, would have resulted in international sanctions and a drying up of future credit.
The multiple participation of the foreign powers in China's economy before the war made the communist government wary of foreign loans and investments. Even the alliance with the USSR had not been an unmixed blessing, so Beijing came to insist on self-reliance, taking neither aid nor loans until the late 1970s. In 1978, various deferred payment schemes were introduced as thinly-disguised loans. By 1979, outright loans were granted to China by the US and Japan. Both devices became vital in financing China's modernization schemes.
After signing the LTTA, financial terms of implementation had to be worked out. The PRC reportedly had only $2-3 billion in foreign currency reserves.[74] Also, for the next few years, the prospects for Japan's exports to China were dim in comparison to import aspirations. Until Chinese oil reserves were brought into full production, and the shipping facilities for crude oil and coal were expanded, deferred payments for imports had to be arranged. In September 1978, the Japan Export-Import Bank agreed to a loan of $2 billion for the development of Chinese oil and coal. Japan would concentrate production to pay for the plants would not peak until

1983-1985. So financing was necessary in the interim.
A 6% loan was negotiated, bending the OECD agreement. Japan was anxious to take advantage of China's increased willingness to accept loans from private sources. The fiction of private loans was preserved in the following way: The Japanese government would deposit foreign exchange funds in city banks, and these would then extend financing to the Bank of China, using the dollar deposits as loan funds.[75] Japan had to move quickly, because West Germany and France were reportedly offering 3% loans to China. Inayama and others thought it necessary to humor China's sensibilities: If the Japanese government borrowed money from private funds and extended these funds to "private corporations in China, that will become the extending of loans from private circles in our country to private circles in China, and that therefore, this will be all right...it is not good to have the Chinese government mention debts."[76]

High yen rates were another factor in financing arrangements. The value of the yen had risen 8% in the first quarter of 1978 in terms of US dollars, and affected China's finance plans.[77] China resisted the strong yen as a loan currency, which made it more difficult for Japanese industries to compete against Western industries.[78] The Japanese Ministry of Finance opposed the Export-Import Bank making loans in dollars, which China preferred in developing the oil fields in the Gulf of Bohai.[79] Other devices, including preferential tariffs, were also introduced to facilitate Japan-China trade.[80] When China sought government loans through the OECD, ASEAN countries feared that China might absorb these soft loans - 3% at 30 years - which had been earmarked for them.[81] Japanese government officials assured ASEAN that loan expansion to China would not be at their expense.[82]

Japanese diplomacy was increasingly concernd with energy resources, especially since the oil shocks of 1973. The emergence of the OPEC oil cartel, Mideast instability, rising prices, and threats of war - all created severe anxieties in Japan over the stability of supply. Long shipping lines and the growing strength of the Soviet navy further underlined Japan's vulnerability to interdiction. The reliance on Mideast oil strongly affected Japanese policy in the region.

China had discovered large reserves of oil, and could use this resource for a number of purposes. Japan could not assume that its own needs would be met by the expansion of Chinese production. The modernization program targeted oil for chemicals first, and fuels second.[83] Also, China would use the oil and gas sales to earn much needed foreign exchange to finance imports of plants and technology. Petroleum reserves were also a powerful economic weapon. When Hua Guofeng visited North

Korea in 1978, he offered aid in various construction projects, and a price of oil that was only half the price charged by the USSR.[84] This was important to Pyongyang, which had suffered from large increases in price, a domestic shortage of energy, and problems repaying foreign debts. Oil imports decreased from 2.4 million tons in 1974-5, to 2.0 million tons in 1975-77.[85]

Japan's electric power and oil industries were reluctant to accept the heavy crude oil which had been contracted under the 1978 LTTA.[86] Oil demand was projected to reach 432 million tons by 1985, an increase of more than 140 million tons over 1978. The Chinese supply had to be expedited by improved transportation facilities, more efficient burning methods for power generation, and new refineries. According to MITI, 80% of Japan's oil came from the Mideast in 1978 and 20% from Asian sources (including Indonesia). He hoped that the proportion could be changed to two-thirds Mideastern oil and one-third Asian.

The disadvantage of relying on international oil companies became apparent in early 1979. Iran suspended oil exports in the wake of the Shah's overthrow, and the internationals reduced Japan's quotas. Japan requested China to increase its sales to make up for the shortfall, but China rejected the request for an additional half million tons.[88] Japan was paying a 1.4% premium on Chinese oil compared with Indonesian crude, but China had already decided on its production plans based on the quota agreed under the LTTA.

Aside from resource development, another sector of economic operation was worked out. The so-called "entrusted processing trade" was already a thriving arrangement between Japan and other non-communist states such as South Korea. Japan supplied factories with machines. Raw materials and parts were then fabricated into finished goods and exported back to Japan. China suggested a similar arrangement to Japan in 1978.[89] Japan was interested because of proximity and inexpensive labor. China would attach Japanese trademarks, use Japanese designs, pack the items in Japanese boxes, and signify "made in Japan."

As China expanded plans to include foreign firms in modernization activities, new laws and procedures were drawn up to facilitate economic cooperation. A Joint Venture Law was drawn up in mid-1979. It limited foreign investment in ventures to 49% of capital, and indicated that the presidents of such joint ventures must be Chinese.[90] However, when Vice Premier Yu Qiuli conferred with a Japanese mission in August 1979, he indicated that China would welcome 100% capital investment. He also said that even foreigners could assume the post of director of a plant.[91]

JAPAN-CHINA MILITARY RELATIONS

Although China's military forces had a number of
diverse missions during the Cultural Revolution, their
primary mission was national defense. This involved
defense of the Sino-Soviet border, the Sino-Indian border, as well as borders with Vietnam and North Korea.
Boundary disputes and fear of USSR attacks figured prom-
inently in China's security concerns. During the Cultural Revolution, the PLA had become highly politicized,
serving as a model for society as "holding Mao's red
banner." The PLA engaged in productive labor, emulating
the "Yanan spirit," and demonstrating the way to self-
reliance. During the Cultural Revolution, the PLA also
stepped in to maintain order at various times.

The PLA was generally organized for defensive operations. One exception was the mission to "liberate Taiwan." Since 1949, th PRC had sought to integrate this
last province into its state system - either by force or
by negotiation. As long as Taiwan was linked to the US
by defense treaty, the PRC was unlikely to attack. Gradually, US and PRC differences were narrowed to this one
obstacle to better relations - the status of Taiwan.

In the case of normalization between Japan and the
PRC, Taiwan was not as great an obstacle. Japan continued close economic relations with Taiwan, even while developing ties with Beijing. Japan had a security interest in Taiwan because the US-Japan Security Treaty included Taiwan within the scope of the Far East. Moreover
Taiwan was athwart the shipping lanes from Southeast
Asia and the Mideast to Japan.

Japan's military establishment was smaller than
other nations in a similar stage of industrialization.
The Self Defense Forces are limited by constitution and
public opinion from acquiring capability which would
enable them to engage in wars abroad. This was a stipulation introduced by the US occupation authorities to
prevent future remilitarization of Japan, and was continued by successive Japanese governments. Japan's economic and technological levels have left no doubt that the
nation could transform itself to a formidable war foot-
ing if its leaders and people so chose. The US nuclear
umbrella and the Security Treaty have allowed Japan to
concentrate energies on non-defense matters. Concern
over renewed conflict in Korea or a Chinese attack on
Taiwan were not major matters as long as the US maintained a credible presence in the Far East. Thus, there
has been little need for Japan to increase its military
establishment.

There was a brief flurry of concern over Taiwan in
1978 when rumors speculated than Jiang Jingguo might
seek to break out of growing international isolation by
links with the USSR.[92] In addition, China's new state
constitution of 15 March 1978 included in the preamble a

call for liberation: "Taiwan is China's sacred territory. We are determined to liberate Taiwan and accomplish the great cause of unifying our motherland." The previous constitution (17 January 1975) made no mention of Taiwan, and so the introduction of the territorial question was considered to be of new significance. Army Vice Chief of Staff, Wu Xiuquan, indicated that liberation could not be achieved without use of armed power. China continues to lack the naval and air power to subjugate Taiwan, so the threat remained more theoretical than actual.[93]

Modernization of defense was one of the four modernization programs announced in 1978. Military modernization meant greater emphasis on weapons and professionalization. Conventional warfare tactics were to be stressed over people's war. Nuclear weapons and missiles were to be developed. Wu Xiuquan admitted China was twenty years behind the US and the USR in armaments, but said the country hoped to catch up in ten years.[94]

Despite legal and political restrictions on Japan,s SDF, technology and training were high. As a close ally of the US, Japan had access to American military thinking and techniques. Because of the PFT, China hoped to establish closer Sino-Japanese military relations to facilitate its own military modernization. If such cooperation proved fruitful, Japan would probably come into closer alignment with China's anti-Soviet posture.

Precisely for that reason, Japan resisted military cooperation. The USSR was already highly suspicious of the Sino-Japanese connection, and would perceive military cooperation as one step short of alliance. Military cooperation could also rebound domestically, especially if the opposition parties interpreted it as a maneuver to circumvent the peace constitution. Germany, after world war one, had built up its military in several ways, one of them by sending officers abroad for training, despite allied proscriptions.

Chinese military modernization was conceived with the USSR as the potential enemy. A Chinese military authority said that the modern military technology would be introduced from advanced nations - including Japan - with their consent.[95] Modernization of the military could not take place without advancement of light and heavy industry, agriculture, and science and technology.

The Chinese considered Soviet buildups opposite the Xinjiang region a growing threat, especially since the region was sparsely populated and not favorable to the guerrilla warfare which China still relied on for defense. Modern Soviet tanks in the border areas could penetrate quickly and drive out Chinese forces. The Chinese predicted, despite the end of the US threat against the PRC, that world war three was inevitable. At best, it could be postponed for five or ten years.[96]

Western European countries were interested in selling advanced weapons to China. To overcome COCOM restrictions, an "escape clause" was cited - contraband
goods could be sold to communist countries according to
strategic considerations.[97] Weapons alone would not
create a modern military establishment - this was recognized by Chinese military leaders who felt that the
military system, principles of strategy, and military
attitudes had to be modernized simultaneously with the
introduction of new weapons. The best weapons had not
saved South Vietnam nor Iran's Shah. China did not see
Japan as a source of weapons, since the NATO countries
were capable and willing suppliers. It was hinted that
military advisors would be needed, and possibly Japanese
SDF officials could help in this respect. Japan's National Defense College and Defense Academy staff members
had expertise which the PLA hoped to draw upon. The
Chinese explored possible military exchanges through
various visitors. In the summer of 1978, several former
SDF officers visited China in an unofficial capacity,
invited through Japan-China Friendship Association channels.[98] Through these visits, indirect communication
was established between China and the JDA. In addition,
the PRC military attaché in Tokyo sought contacts with
SDF officers.

To avoid damage to relations with the USSR, the JDA
formulated its basic policy regarding interchange of
uniformed officers. The guiding principle remained
equidistance towards China and the USSR.[99] Proposed
visits of the SDF Joint Staff Council and Chiefs of
Staff to China were shelved, and the JDA decided against
inviting Chinese officers to Japan. There had been
numerous invitations of Japanese by China, and China was
also enthusiastic about sending officers to Japan. In
addition to stimulating problems with the Soviet Union,
this kind of exchange was regarded as one-sided: Japanese training facilities, for example, were far more
open than Chinese, and the Chinese were reluctant to
show much to Japanese visitors.

The JDA decided (23 November 1979) to dispatch a
mission of SDF medical officers to China. It was regarded by the JDA as necessary since China had repeatedly
requested some sort of military exchange. A medical
inspection visit was perhaps the least strategic and
also least likely to cause domestic opposition.[100] By
the end of the year, three high-ranking PLA visitors
already had gone to Japan since the PFT. The Japan
government considered that diplomatic courtesy called
for some reciprocity.

The international context contributed to China's
eagerness to modernize its military defenses. With the
dismantling of Maoist ideological strictures against
learning from the West and Japan, the PLA was pursuing
in military affairs what civilian counterparts were

attempting in economic affairs. It was a major surprise
to many Japanese that China had so quickly reversed
itself on evaluation of Japanese military affairs.
Since the first Sino-Japanese war in 1894, Japan
had a military presence on the mainland which lasted
until 1945. The possible combination of US and Japanese
forces against China continued to haunt Chinese security
planners. Historical legacies had made a reversal of
Chinese attitudes towards a Japanese military buildup
unlikely. So when a turnaround occurred, it caused
considerable surprise in Japan. The JSP in particular
was dismayed by China's reversal on the defense question. A JSP delegation in March 1978 found severe di-
vergence in their own and Chinese views. The Chinese
urged Japan to build up its defense power, and did not
think it necessary for one country, the US, to defend
another. The socialists claimed that stronger self-
defense would result in Japanese remilitarization.
Under the Security Treaty with the US, the socialists
argued, Japan became an American support base. The Chinese rejected the JSP positions and pointed to the
necessity of resisting the Soviet menace.[101]
While negotiating and concluding the PFT, China expressed faith that Japan's militarism was a thing of the
past.[102] Although the Chinese had proclaimed the opposite as late as 1972, their revised views were based on
the following considerations: First, after three decades, there seemed to be only residual militarism in
Japan. The SDF was restricted by public opinion, the
political parties, budgetary restrictions which emphasized high civilian industrial growth, and the peace
constitution. Second, the Defense Treaty with the US
was highly beneficial to Japan in that it freed Japan
from huge defense burdens. Third, with the conclusion
of the 1978 PFT, Japan had made special emphasis on
interpreting the hegemony clause as applying to itself
and China. This application was not only more prudent
than using it against the USSR, but it was also a simple
confirmation of widely-held principles in Japan. Fourth,
now that China's foreign policy had shifted to an anti-
Soviet role, pro-Western stance, it was useful to recognize Japan's role in this orientation. From the Chinese
perspective, the Japanese reaction against its own past
militarism had gone too far.
Since early 1978, the Chinese leadership has urged
Japan to develop self-defense capability to its full
potential.[103] On 8 September 1978, leaders of the PLA
separated defense power from remilitarization:

> The Sino-Soviet Treaty of Alliance was established
> in order to prevent the revival of Japan's militar-
> ism. However, the international situation has
> changed greatly since then, and we will declare its
> abrogation next year. We support Japan's having

defense power. To have defense power is a separate
problem from militarization. Viewed from the reality, Japan is at the stage of creating its own
self-defense power, and it is not at the stage of
heading toward militarism.

In November 1978, China-Japan Friendship Association Chairman Liao Chengzhi underlined basic differences
with the JSP regarding the defense issue.[105] China could
support the US-Japan Security Treaty now, he said, because the international situation had changed. It was
useful in light of Soviet expansion. He also said that
China supported Japan's possession of self-defense power
to defend national independence. Since 1952, Liao maintained, China had never supported unarmed neutrality.
    Further Chinese approval for Japan's defense build-
up was given in a Renmin Ribao (People's Daily) report
of 4 May 1979, concerning extensive discussions in Japan
on the defense question.[106] The report emphasized two
themes: The Japanese people overwhelmingly demanded
stronger defense; and the USSR was the target of stronger defenses. The article reviewed Soviet threats to
Japan and the expansion of Soviet influence in Vietnam.
It also mentioned the strengthening of the US-Japan
security system. The fact that the USSR was critical of
these developments "will only enable the Japanese people
to clearly see the ugly appearance of the Soviet hegemonists."
    Japan did not welcome this cheering from the side-
lines. Foreign Minister Okita insisted that China understood Japan could not join its opposition against "socialist imperialism."[107] However, Defense Vice Minister
Su Yu indicated that he thought it possible for Japan to
increase its defense budget to more than the 0.9% allotted.[108] To Iwashima Hisao of the Japan National Defense
College, Su Yu expressed China's desire for exchanges
with Japan, including a Maritime SDF training ship visit
to Chinese ports. Another PLA leader mentioned that Japan should further strengthen air power and anti-submarine capability.[109]
    Premier Hua Guofeng indicated China's support for a
stronger defense power to Nakasone, and emphasized air
power, especially to defend naval strength.[110] The hawkish Chinese views were expressed by General Wu Xiuquan:
"(The Japanese-US Security Treaty) carries positive significance for peace and stability in Asia. Some people
take the view that the US forces will withdraw from
Asia, but that will be disadvantageous for Asia."[111]
    Wu's statement touched sensitive nerves in Japan.
Okita criticized it at a Diet committee hearing:

    After the war, Japan has internationally pledged
    that it will not walk the path leading to becoming
    a military big power. It has also taken the basic

position that it will have defense power within the
necessary bounds, and that it will realize nuclear
deterrent on the strength of the Japan-US Security
treaty. To make a rash statement, without understanding the situation in Japan, the people's sentiments, and circumstances in Japan after the war,
is a kind of intervention in domestic affairs. [112]

To a question of whether or not China is a nation allied
with Japan, Okita replied that there were relations of
alliance between Japan and the US. China was a "friendly
nation."

* * * * * * *

In 1980, the rough dimensions of Japanese, Chinese,
and American diplomatic and economic cooperation had
been laid out. To a certain extent, the Japan-China PFT
played a role in achieving this cooperation. Once established, it provided a structure of trade and other exchange. Japan smoothed the way for US-China normalization, although not intentionally. After US Secretary of
Defense Brown visited China in early 1980, Vice Minister
of Foreign Affairs Han Nianlong explained to Japanese
Ambassador Yoshida the contents of their talks. [113]   It
was the first time contents of Sino-American talks were
officially transmitted to Japan - an indication that a
closer communication system was emerging among the three
nations. Because of the Soviet move into Afghanistan, a
communication and consultation system on security matters emerged.
China made a bid for closer defense cooperation
with Japan, and indicated support for stronger self-
defense arrangements, including the treaty linkage with
the US. Japan's demurral was not regarded as final, and
it is likely that China will bring the matter up again
in the future.
In sum, the PFT widened the base of Japanese diplomacy with China. It also facilitated consultations on
the Korean problem with China. The LTTA had already
broadened Japan-China trade, but it is not clear that
the 1978 treaty was a necessary reinforcement of the
February agreement.
On the first anniversary of the treaty, an official
of the Japan Foreign Ministry reviewed its impact: The
PFT had eliminated friction between China and Japan, and
established a foundation of stable relations. [114]   But
according to critics, the cost of the PFT has been high.
The USSR became anxious over Sino-Japanese partnership
and strengthened ties with Vietnam. Southeast Asian
countries feared for their own economic well-being when
a modernized and powerful China might begin economic
penetration into the region. Nevertheless, the Tokyo
view was that ASEAN regarded the PFT as a help to peace
and stability in the region.

China's national interests were served by the PFT. Despite reluctance, protests, and face-saving interpretations, Japan agreed to the hegemony clause. China's requests for anti-hegemony and military cooperation were rejected in the first round by Japan. But this disappointment was more than made up for by the progress toward the same goals in China's American relationship. Japan continued to proclaim principles with minimum defense and equidistant diplomacy. But with anti-Soviet China as a friend, and pro-China US as an ally, Japan's relations with the USSR could not avoid being adversely affected.

Footnotes

1. Senator D. Moynihan wrote of the period: "This was the view that had emerged in the course of the Vietnam war to the effect that the United States, by virtue of its enormous power, and in consequence of policies that were anything but virtuous, had become a principal source of instability and injustice in the world. We were, in short, a status quo power, and the status quo we were trying to preserve was abominable." "'Joining the Jackals': The U.S. at the UN 1977-1980," Commentary 71:2 (February 1981), p. 24.

2. JTW, 4 June 1977, p. 3.

3. Lee Chae-Jin, Japan Faces China (Baltimore: Johns Hopkins University Press, 1976), pp. 67ff.

4. Ibid., p. 119.

5. Ibid., p. 188.

6. TS, 7 July 1978, p. 4.

7. Ibid.

8. Ibid.

9. YS, 7 February 1979, p. 1.

10. AS, 19 February 1979, p. 22.

11. AS, 5 March 1979, p. 2.

12. Ibid.

13. SK, 29 August 1979, p. 1.

14. TS, 22 November 1979, p. 2.

15. NK, 21 November 1979, p. 2.

16. Akahata, 8 December 1979, p. 1.

17. TS, 8 December 1979, p. 4.

18. AS, 8 December 1979, p. 2.

19. AS, 5 December 1979, p. 2.

20. NK, 9 December 1979, p. 2.

21. See various comments on his speech in DR:China, 7 December 1979, pp. D6-D7.

22. TS, 8 December 1979, p. 2.

23. YS, 7 February 1979, p. 1.

24. NK, 7 February 1979, p. 2.

25. DR:China, 7 December 1979, pp. D2-D4.

26. AS, 30 May 1980, p. 3.

27. AS, 31 May 1980, p. 5.

28. AS, 16 May 1980, p. 2.
29. AS, 28 May 1980, p. 2.
30. YS, 31 May 1980, p. 4.
31. TS, 30 May 1980, p. 4.
32. SK, 30 May 1980, p. 10.
33. TS, 11 July 1980, p. 4.
34. See Yagisawa Mitsuo, "America's Four Umbrellas," Japan Quarterly 28:2 (1981), pp. 161-174.
35. AS, 16 February 1978, p. 1.
36. TS, 16 February 1978, p. 2.
37. AS, 16 February 1978, p. 1.
38. AS, 9 March 1978, p. 6.
39. NK, 18 February 1978, p. 2.
40. NK, 12 August 1978, p. 4.
41. Ibid.
42. NK, 9 September 1978, p. 3.
43. YS, 22 September 1978, p. 9.
44. AS, 12 October 1978, p. 1.
45. NK, 18 February 1978, p. 2.
46. NK, 8 March 1978, p. 2.
47. AS, 13 August 1978, p. 3.
48. YS, 28 February 1979, p. 1.
49. NK, 1 March 1979, p. 1.
50. NK, 18 September 1979, p. 3.
51. SK, 4 September 1979, p. 8.
52. NK, 5 September 1979, p. 4.
53. NK, 29 October 1979, p. 8.
54. Beijing Review, 13 July 1981, p. 3.
55. Christian Science Monitor, 8 December 1980, p. 1.
56. JTW, 30 July 1977, p. 1.
57. NK, 30 December 1977, p. 8.
58. Nikkan Kogyo, 14 July 1978, p. 1.
59. NK, 17 September 1978, p. 1.
60. AS, 27 October 1978, p. 1.
61. Nikkan Kogyo, 24 November 1978, p. 1.
62. MS, 13 February 1978, p. 1.
63. Nihon Kogyo, 31 March 1978, p. 1.
64. Ibid.
65. Nikkan Kogyo, 14 July 1978, p. 1.
66. YS, 22 September 1978, p. 9.
67. MS, 18 October 1978, p. 7.
68. Nikkan Kogyo, 4 October 1978, p. 1.
69. NK, 19 January 1979, p. 3.
70. NK, 7 February 1979, p. 2.
71. NK, 18 February 1978, p. 2.
72. MS, 24 October 1978, p. 9.
73. See Robert Bedeski, State Building in China (Berkeley: Institute of East Asian Studies, 1981), Chapter 5.
74. YS, 11 September 1978, p. 1.
75. AS, 10 September 1978, p. 1.
76. NK, 9 September 1978, p. 3.
77. MS, 1 April 1978, p. 7.

78. MS, 24 October 1978, p. 9.
79. AS, 13 August 1979, p. 1.
80. NK, 20 November 1979, p. 1.
81. NK, 30 August 1979, p. 3.
82. NK, 18 September 1979, p. 3.
83. NK, 30 August 1969, pp. 1-5.
84. MS, 22 June 1978, p. 1.
85. Ibid.
86. Nihon Kogyo, 6 October 1978, p. 1.
87. YS, 22 September 1978, p. 9.
88. MS, 8 February 1979, p. 7.
89. SK, 28 July 1978, p. 1.
90. NK, 12 June 1979, p. 1.
91. NK, 30 August 1979, pp. 1, 5.
92. AS, 29 April 1978, p. 7.
93. YS, 17 December 1978, p. 2.
94. AS, 29 April 1978, p. 7.
95. NK, 9 September 1978, p. 1.
96. Ibid.
97. AS, 20 October 1979, p. 7.
98. AS, 30 May 1978, p. 2.
99. NK, 25 April 1979, p. 2.
100. SK, 24 November 1979, p. 1.
101. SK, 25 March 1978, p. 5.
102. NK, 9 September 1978, p. 1.
103. Ibid.
104. AS, 9 September 1978, p. 7.
105. AS, 22 November 1978, p. 2.
106. DR:China, 17 May 1979, pp. D2-D3.
107. TS, 8 December 1979, p. 2.
108. SK, 14 March 1980, p. 1.
109. YS, 29 March 1980, p. 1.
110. AS, 16 May 1980, p. 2.
111. Ibid.
112. MS, 10 May 1980, p. 2.
113. SK, 26 January 1980, p. 1.
114. TS, 12 August 1979, p. 2.

6
Soviet Reactions
to the Treaty

When Japan signed the PFT with China, Soviet displeasure was anticipated. The two communist giants have
been at odds for nearly two decades, so Japanese declar-
ations of friendship with one state involved the risk of
antagonizing the other. Japan decided to take the risk
for several reasons: (1) The Foreign Ministry saw the
Long Term Trade Agreement as a tantalizing beginning of
a profitable economic relationship, which could be further cemented by the PFT. (2) To decline the PFT, when
the Chinese regarded it as a key instrument in their bilateral relations, might give Japan's industrial rivals
competitive advantages, especially those NATO countries
which were promising military weapons to the PRC. Japan
could not export weapons and was at a disadvantage in
this respect. (3) The PFT could demonstrate that Japan
would not be bullied by the USSR or any other country
with respect to its foreign relations. Autonomous diplomacy was more important than equidistance. (4) Domestic politics was also a factor. Fukuda reportedly calculated that conclusion of the treaty gave him an edge
in the contest for the LDP presidency. (5) As a political reinforcement of economic ties, the PFT could help
Japan out of the current economic slump.[1] (6) By forcefully asserting its sovereign rights as a nation, the
Japanese were demonstrating to the USSR that the latter's refusal to compromise on the northern territories
was having the effect of pushing Japan closer to China.
(7) Finally, the treaty signalled closer Sino-Japanese
cooperation, or at least consultation, on matters of
mutual importance, such as the stability of Korea and
Southeast Asia. Because the Carter administration initially favored a lower military role in East Asia, Japan
evisioned a greater political role for itself.
    The arguments were convincing in the abstract, but
the major flaw was inadequate consideration of Soviet
hostility to the PFT. The Russian ruled a Eurasian
empire which had expanded at the expense of past empires
and nations, including the Chinese and Japanese. A

108

diplomatic entente between the two, abetted by the US
and taking an anti-Soviet posture, was a development the
USSR did not take lightly.

CHINA THE ENCIRCLER?

Moscow's official opinion of China's diplomatic
strategy could be described as one-dimensional:

> Chinese foreign policy is well known. China has
> not put forward any proposals for international
> détente, disarmament or for the coordination of
> relations of reciprocal cooperation among countries
> and peoples. The ambition to undermine détente,
> (disrupt) disarmament, pit one country against
> another and sow the seeds of distrust among peoples
> is the motivation for the diplomatic activities of
> Peking's leadership.[2]

Therefore, Japan fell into the Chinese trap:

> One will naturally ask, "what are the advantages of
> concluding the Japan-China treaty envisaged by
> those Japanese who demand its conclusion?" It is no
> secret that the treaty with the antihegemony clause
> is directed against the Soviet Union, and the Chi-
> nese leaders clearly state this. This means that if
> Japan agrees to sign this treaty under China's
> conditions, Japan will be drawn into Peking's dip-
> lomacy whether it likes it or not.[3]

The Soviet reaction to the PFT was frigid as expected. According to Tass, the Chinese had "succeeded in
persuading Japan to include in the text of the treaty
the notorious article on opposition to 'hegemonism'."[4]
The Soviets noted that many Japanese in government and
in the media had urged caution, but the government had
capitulated to Beijing's pressures. The PFT was judged
dangerous by Moscow, and the inclusion of the article on
relations with third countries (Article 4) had done
nothing to neutralize Article 2 on hegemonism. The
treaty was interpreted as dangerous to the peace and
stability of Asia, since it encouraged "Han chauvinism"
and Japanese militarism:

> Indeed, the signing of a treaty between Japan and
> China took place against the background of an in-
> crease in Japan's armaments, amid statements of
> Japanese leaders that possession of nuclear weapons
> by Japan in the future allegedly did not contradict
> the spirit of the Constitution. Besides that, the
> top Japanese military leaders do not conceal the
> fact that they regard the Soviet Union as their
> main potential enemy. But in politics, just as in

nature, action produces counteraction. The formation of a Japanese-Chinese alliance which threatens
the destiny of relaxation of tensions and which is
fraught with international conflicts in the future
will inevitably produce counteraction by all the
people who hold dear peace and security in Asia.[5]

The Soviets clearly resented the PFT. It represented a failure of diplomacy towards Japan, and more important, it was the possible beginning of a triple entente against the USSR in the East Asian region. The
Soviet failure was underscored by several months of
threats and promises preceding the treaty. The threats
consisted of verbal attacks, while promises were made of
economic benefits from good relations. But the USSR
would not budge on the issue which probably could have
induced the Japanese to go slower in the tilt towards
China - compromise on the northern territories.

The Sino-Soviet dispute had lost little of its intensity since the death of Mao Zedong. Each side accused
the other of backing counterrevolutionary forces throughout the world, and of engagement in worldwide hegemonism. A most dangerous situation was emerging for the
USSR as China moved towards anti-Soviet understanding
with the US and Japan. Even if the two major capitalist
powers refrained from a military alliance or selling
advanced weapons to China, their ample economic resources would be a major form of assistance to Chinese modernization - which Moscow saw as ultimately augmenting
PRC military capability. (A Soviet diplomat in Tokyo
confirmed this view to the author, citing the example of
the Japanese nonmilitary investment in the South Korean
steel industry, which now manufactures heavy weapons.)

As China was cooperating with NATO and the EEC in
Western Europe, moving towards normalization with the
US, and enjoying warm relations with Japan, the USSR saw
its worst fears coming true - a pincer movement from the
east and west. In December 1977, PRC Foreign Trade
Minister Li Qiang visited Britain and France in connection with the program of four modernizations, which
Istvestiya proclaimed to be primarily in connection with
war preparations.[6] Some sectors of NATO welcomed the
strengthening of China's defenses, because this would
take some Soviet pressure off them. The Li Qiang delegation's interest in vertical takeoff military aircraft,
helicopters, and missiles was seen as ominous by the
Soviets.

The Chinese signed a five year trade agreement with
the Common Market, which gave China "most-favored-nation
status." Izvestiya interpreted this as a move which
would give the Nine greater hopes of business with China,
while China would find easier access to the advanced
weapons of NATO.[7] A few years earlier, the Chinese had
denounced NATO as an imperialist alliance. Now, by 1977,

it had moved to full sympathy with its anti-Soviet stance. The Chinese shift from hostility to sympathy for NATO, was a disturbing development to the USSR. The situation in Europe had been stabilized for a number of years in the postwar era. The USSR enjoyed the security provided by its East European buffers and massive troop deployment. With the new Beijing regime, however, a close cooperative relationship was emerging which would allow greater coordination with NATO.

Moscow saw capitalism's pursuit of profits as a major reason for the growing Chinese connection: "Hoping to derive good profits, the West European military-industrial complex has kindly opened its arsenals to Beijing."[8] The Western "munitions corporations" were competing for the Chinese military market, as preparations for modernization of the PLA gained momentum. In France, a Chinese delegation signed an agreement to purchase a large consignment of anti-tank missiles, and showed interest in various ship-to-ship, anti-aircraft, and other anti-tank missiles.[9]

Pravda considered the PRC's arms purchases to be part of plans to undermine détente, to harden Western attitudes towards the USSR, and to prepare for expansionism. Maoism did not die with Mao, and the new leadership continued to accelerate militarism. China has the world's largest army and spends 40% of the state budget on defense. Nuclear testing in the atmosphere and rejection of the test-ban treaty were evidence of China's heedless quest for war. Militarization "not only helps the Beijing elite to distract the ordinary Chinese from the burdens of life, but to foster a generation that could be used for implementing expansionist plans."[10]

In the Soviet perspective, no nation on China's borders is safe from Maoist expansionism. Historical maps were cited as proof of China's encroachments. Pretensions to additional territory included the Soviet Amur region, Sakhalin, part of Kazakhstan, part of India, Nepal, Bhutan, Burma, Thailand, Malaysia, Kampuchea, Laos and Vietnam, and many of the insular territories in the East China and South China seas.[11]

Soviet invectives stressed that the PRC was becoming a most dangerous enemy. China was ideologically dangerous because it claimed to be the inheritor of correct Marxism-Leninism. The split between the two parties had led to divisions in a number of communist parties around the world. Maoist claims to be the most advanced form of revolution had also stimulated differences between the two states as they vied for influence in the third world. But this difference became less strident as Beijing abandoned the Cultural Revolution, and adopted a more moderate line in international affairs.

With China's moderation and modernization also came a new source of danger for the USSR. China was no longer

attacking the West (including Japan), but joining the
West and attacking the USSR. Whether pragmatism or
revisionism, it represented the end of China's isolation
from the power centers of the world. New direct lines
of communication were opened between Beijing and other
Western governments in the 1970s. Not only governments,
but corporations, academic institutions, and various
"friendship" associations became recipients of Chinese
attention and hospitality. The Chinese did not have the
weapons to resist Soviet attack if it came, but they
were highly skilled in mobilizing foreign public opinion
to their side.

The Soviets suspected that the new face of China –
after the fanaticism of the Cultural Revolution – was a
part of the continued strategy against Soviet socialism.
To defeat the Soviet Union, take back territory it
claimed from past centuries, and do this without going
to war, the Chinese had a theory, the "three worlds,"
and a strategy, to encircle the USSR with hostile
states.

The three worlds theory was traced back to 1946,
when Mao Zedong told Anna Louise Strong that "between
the United States and the Soviet Union there lies a vast
zone which encompasses many capitalist, colonial and
semicolonial countries of Europe, Asia and Africa."[12]
In 1956, during the Suez crisis, he further elaborated
on "three forces": "first, the United States, the biggest imperialist country; second, the second-rate imperialist countries--Britain and France; and third, the
oppressed nations." In 1964, he distinguished a "first
intermediate zone," consisting of the countries of Asia,
Africa and Latin America, from the "second intermediate
zone" -the developed capitalist states except the US.

The notion of three worlds occurred in a 1974 conversation with a "third world leader": "In my opinion,
the United States and the USSR form the first world.
The intermediate forces, for example, Japan, Europe and
Canada, belong to the second world. And you and I belong
to the third world."[13] In April 1974, Deng Xiaoping delivered a report to the UN General Assembly which elaborated on the three worlds.[14]

The post-Mao regime enshrined the theory in party
doctrine when Chairman Hua Guofeng delivered his political report to the Eleventh National Congress of the Communist Party of China. Hua claimed that Mao applied the
method of class analysis to arrive at a "scientific conclusion regarding the present-day strategic situation in
the world." The theory, in Hua's formulation, provides
the basis for carrying on the international struggle:

> The two hegemonic powers, the Soviet Union and the
> United States, are the biggest international ex-
> ploiters and oppressors of today and the common
> enemies of the people of the world. The third

world countries suffer the worst oppression and
hence put up the strongest resistance; they are the
main force combating imperialism, colonialism and
hegemonism. The second world countries have a dual
character; on the one hand they oppress, exploit
and control the third world countries, and on the
other they are controlled, threatened and bullied
by both hegemonic powers in varying degrees. Chairman Mao's thesis differentiating the three worlds
gives a correct orientation to the present international struggle and clearly defines the main
revolutionary forces, the chief enemies, and the
middle forces that can be won over and united,
enabling the international proletariat to unite
with all forces that can be united to form the
broadest possible united front in class struggles
against the chief enemies of the world arena. [15]

Hua described China as a "developing socialist country
belonging to the third world," which supports other
developing countries.[16] China also supported countries
of the second world against the control, threat, and
bullying by the superpowers.

To the Soviets, the theory of three worlds and its
translation into foreign policy was simply more evidence
that China was "...joining with all the reactionary
imperialist forces in counterbalance to the Soviet Union
and the countries of the socialist community."[17] The
USSR finds the doctrine dangerous and wrong: dangerous
because it produces confrontation between the USSR and
other nations, and wrong because it lumps the two superpowers into one category, ignoring the "cardinal differences between socialism and imperialism."[18] Worse, the
doctrine claims that there is identity between "the policy of the world's first socialist and the course followed by the leading imperialist powers." In addition,
China considered the US to be the lesser of two evils:

The Soviet Union and the United States are the
source of a new world war, and Soviet social-imper-
ialism in particular presents the greater danger.
The current situation in their contention is that
Soviet social-imperialism is on the offensive and
U.S. imperialism is on the defensive.[19]

Under those circumstances, China was asking the US
to join the anti-Soviet alliance, supporting NATO and
purchasing weapons from its member nations, and cooperating with Japanese military circles.[20] In the Chinese
scheme of things, there was little if any distinction
between capitalism and socialism, according to the Soviet critics: "In the struggle for global hegemony
Peking is expressing a readiness to create blocs and
alliances with class enemies and a 'very broad united

front' including imperialism and reaction of every stripe."[21] The Albanians, once China's only communist ally against the USSR, now joined Soviet denunciation of Beijing: "(The theory of three worlds) is a theory of the dying away of the revolution, a theory of unconditional capitulation to the bourgeoisie..."[22]

The theory of three worlds is indeed a rejection of the relevance of socialism to international affairs. It stresses two major factors as central: the stage of economic-industrial development, and military-strategic capability. The second and third worlds differ in their degree of industrialization, and both differ from the first, the two superpowers, in their strategic leverage over the rest of the world. Although the emergence of the OPEC nations in the 1970s indicated the possibility of a fourth world - not industrialized but possessing considerable economic leverage - the doctrine of the three worlds has remained the public foreign policy of the PRC, and the basis of its united front strategy - to combine all nations against the USSR's expansionism.

Among the epithets aimed at the PRC, the USSR often includes "bourgeois nationalists" as a synonym for Maoism. The implication is that the real socialist revolution in China was betrayed, and that the present leaders are only sham communists. Beijing's use of the term "social imperialism" to describe Soviet external behavior, claimed Moscow, gave a clue to Maoist geneology. Chiang Kai-shek had used the term "red imperialism" to describe the USSR in 1929, and considered it more dangerous than "white imperialism."[23] Sun Yat-sen had divided the nations of the world into exploiter and exploited, adding that it was the moral duty of those nations which first achieved liberation to assist those still exploited.[24] In the context of Guomindang worldviews, Mao's "theory" of three worlds was not a radical innovation.

The three world doctrine establishes an international hierarchy of nations based on the morality of power - the least powerful are the most virtuous. Thus, in place of Marx's proletariat Mao sees a third world community of nations which will rise up and overthrow the evil superpowers. The second world is the intermediate zone of medium virtue because its members exploit and are exploited. Mao's strategy was to unite with the third world in an effort to check and defeat the first world, with the aid of the second if possible. In the history of the Chinese communist revolution, the strategy had been attempted twice before, in the united front with the Guomindang in 1924 and again in 1937.

Mao's successors in Beijing, however, were taking the theory and the strategy one step further - not only were they seeking to unite with the industrial capitalist states against their external enemy, but they were pursuing an intimate relation with one superpower - the

US. To the Soviets, such "opportunism" made a mockery
of the Chinese claim to belong to the socialist camp.
Deng had declared that a unified capitalist camp no longer existed[25] - a declaration reaffirmed by the People's
Daily on 1 November 1977.
     The doctrine of three worlds refuted the Soviet
claim to be the paramount socialist country. What mat-
tered was not the degree of conformity to Moscow's version of socialism, but the ranking in degree of exploitation according to Beijing. Socialism as the organizing
or legitimizing principle of a state guaranteed no political virtue, as the phenomenon of social imperialism
demonstrated. The three world theory further provided a
formula affording maximum flexibility for Beijing's
foreign policy. China no longer had to compete for support with the USSR among a limited number of socialist
nations, or within revolutionary movements. In the case
of the former, most of these sided with, or leaned towards, the USSR. With the latter, the USSR usually could
exert preeminence in providing advice and weaponry, and
thus outbid the Chinese. Moreover, support for a revolutionary movement did not guarantee that on coming to
power, the movement would reciprocate that support - as
Vietnam demonstrated to China.
     The tripartite division of the world allowed China
to choose trading partners and friends - not on the basis of ideology, but rather according to new criteria of
their anti-Soviet position. This, to the Soviets, was
"blatant reaction," as they announced with regard to
China's purchase of 250,000 bales of cotton from So-
moza's Nicaragua.[26]
     But more ominous was the way in which China was
structuring its relations with members of the three
worlds to the detriment of the USSR. The Chinese links
with EEC and NATO have already been mentionerd. In East
Asia, China was pursuing a policy of building an alliance consisting of itself, the US, and Japan, according
to Akahata, the organ of the Japan Communist Party. For
evidence, the paper noted that in a conversation with US
journalists, Deng Xiaoping "stressed the common anti-
Soviet interests of China, the United States, and Japan
and hinted at the need for joint actions by the three
countries against the USSR."[27] Deng agreed that China is
"an Eastern NATO," and emphasized the joint strategic
interests of China and the United States regarding Japan.
     The USSR also watched the Fifth NPC for indications
of the future course of PRC foreign policy. Unlike the
Japanese, they found little gratification. In three
specific areas, the Soviets detected a hard line - which
they hoped had vanished when Mao passed away: (1) The
theory of three worlds was reaffirmed, and although China opposed both social imperialism and capitalist imperialism, it was the former which was judged the more dan-

gerous. (2) Hua's Political Report called for improved
state relations between the PRC and USSR, but strongly
requested that Soviet armed forces be withdrawn from the
Mongolian People's Republic (MPR). (3) With regard to
the program of four modernizations, Moscow interpreted
this to be weighted heavily towards military modernization. In addition, Hua's call for the PFT with Japan,
and for increased contacts with the US signalled a trend
that ahd to be watched carefully.

Even before the Congress convened, Moscow indicated
that its expectations were not high:

> In order to mislead the world's people and the Chi-
> nese people, Peking's leadership resorts to the
> trick of holding a National People's Congress
> (NPC). The present Peking leadership is clearly
> aware that the congress will undoubtedly approve
> the documents dished up by the top leadership and
> thereby create a false impression that the Chinese
> people are backing them. In doing so, they are
> also trying to shift their responsibility for pur-
> suing an adventurist foreign policy, a policy which
> endangers China itself, to the Chinese people,
> making the people their accomplices. [28]

Hua's Report to the NPC reiterated the three world
doctrine, and called for the formation of "the broadest
united front against superpower hegemonism." His statement was almost verbatim from the preamble of the Constitution except that he added that it was "Chairman
Mao's theory of the three worlds." Although Hua generally spoke of "social imperialism and imperialism" in
tandem as attributes of superpower hegemonism, the greater onus was cast on the USSR. "A socialist country
should set an example in treating others as equals," he
said,[29] demanding a higher level of performance from a
state that espouses Marxism-Leninism. "A late-comer
among imperialist powers, the Soviet Union relies mainly
on its military power to carry out expansion; yet it
goes about flaunting banners of 'socialism' and 'support
for revolution' to dupe peoples and sell its wares. It
is the most dangerous source of a new world war."[30]
(author's emphasis) Hua said that expansion of the international united front against hegemonism was necessary to postpone the outbreak of a new world war. However, "some people in the West follow a policy of appeasement towards the Soviet Union with the fond hope of
saving themselves at the expense of others. This can
only whet the ambitions of the aggressors and hasten the
outbreak of war."[31]

Hua's statements left little doubt about the direction of foreign policy after the Congress. China would
oppose superpower hegemonism, form a broad international
united front, work against appeasement, and strengthen

China's own defenses against possible world war. These four ingredients indicated to the USSR that continuation of the Sino-Soviet conflict was unavoidable.

Nevertheless, both sides went through formalities in reducing tensions. On 24 February, at the beginning of the Fifth NPC, the Presidium of the USSR Supreme Soviet proposed to the NPC Standing Committee that the two countries come out with a joint statement on the principles of relations between the USSR and PRC.[32] According to Pravda, Beijing rejected the proposal and began "a new wave in the anti-Soviet campaign in China."

Responding to the Soviet attempt at mutual understanding, Hua listed China's requirements:

> If the Soviet leading clique really desires to improve the state relations between the two countries, it should prove its sincerity by deeds. First of all, in accordance with the understanding reached between the premiers of the two countries in 1969, it should sign an agreement on maintaining the status quo on the borders, averting armed clashes and disengaging the armed forces of both sides in the disputed border areas, and then enter into negotiations on resolving the boundary question. It should also withdraw its armed forces from the People's Republic of Mongolia and the Sino-Soviet borders, so that the situation there will revert to what it was in the early 1960's. How Sino-Soviet relations will develop is entirely up to the Soviet side.[33]

Hua was referring to a meeting of 11 September 1969 in Beijing at which an agreement was reached on restoring normal relationships, expanding bilateral trade, and settling the border issue so as to avoid armed conflict. Later, both sides took appropriate measures, including the exchange of ambassadors and the expansion of trade. On the border question, Moscow's position was the principle of recognizing existing borders: "The Soviet Union repeatedly stated that there is no, nor was there any, territorial problem between it and the People's Republic of China."[34]

Consultations were held in 1964 to specify the border line. Numerous areas within the Soviet territory were claimed by China on the topographic maps submitted. These were the areas which the Chinese have claimed are "disputed," and which the Soviets say are legally their sovereign territories. The Soviets refuse to withdraw their troops from what the Chinese consider "disputed areas," while the Chinese consider such a withdrawal necessary proof of sincerity, according to Hua's speech. Pravda referred to the Soviet submission of a status quo agreement to the Chinese on 11 February 1970, which would preserve the existing borders. But China would

link such an agreement to recognition of disputed area —
a condition Moscow rejects.[35]
   A minor border incident erupted in May 1979 when
about 30 Soviet soldiers opened fire on Chinese citizens
on the Ussuri River, after crossing into Chinese territory. Moscow expressed regret for the incident,[36] and
China formally protested the illegal river crossing and
wounding of local Chinese residents.
   Territorial claims have continued to exhibit a certain symmetry with regard to China, the USSR and Japan.
The USSR maintains that there are no territorial questions with regard to the Sino-Soviet border nor the northern territories. Moscow leaders feel that to relent or
compromise on the one would raise pressure for concessions on the other. After the PFT, the Soviet position
on the northern territories has hardened even more. The
USSR has pointed to the Senkaku issue as an example of
Chinese hegemonism towards Japan,[37] in the same way that
Chinese claims over "disputed territory" in the USSR
present hegemonistic behavior. For its part, Japan has
further aligned itself with China, at least in Moscow's
eyes, by not being forceful in the Senkakus, and insisting on retrocession of the northern territories.
   Hua Guofeng's insistence that Soviet troops withdraw from Mongolia was also rejected as unrealistic.
During the 1950s, at the height of Sino-Soviet friendship, there were few Soviet troops in the MPR.[38] The
present stationing of Soviet troops in Mongolia is

   at the request of the Mongolian Government because
   the freedom, independence, and socialist achievements of the Mongolian people are under direct
   threat from the predatory policy and malevolent
   actions of the Peking leaders.[39]

The MPR government rebuffed Hua's "presumptuous demand
to withdraw Soviet military units from Mongolia" in a
note of 12 April 1978.
   The USSR accuses the Chinese communists of continuing to seek annexation of Mongolia. In 1939, Mao told
Edgar Snow that the MPR would become a part of the Chinese republic, and in 1954, the Chinese allegedly sought
an agreement with a visiting Soviet delegation to Beijing that Mongolia be annexed to China.[40] Chinese incursions into the MPR have become more frequent, and increasing fortifications on the border are heightening
tensions, according to the Soviets, and led to the MPR
request for deployment of Soviet units in its territory.
   The third result of the Fifth NPC, from Soviet per-
spectives, was the Chinese determination to build up its
military capacity. Purchase of advanced weapons from
NATO countries was one indication. Accelerated modern
ization of the armed forces was the topic of at least
six Beijing conferences in 1977 and through May 1978.[41]

By the end of 1977, China's direct military expenditures accounted for 41.5% of the state budget, and one-half was used to produce missiles and other nuclear weapons.[42] Since Chinese armaments are estimated to be 10-15 years behind those of the USSR in quality,[43] the program of military modernization could hardly be considered provocative. Also, China's material poverty severely limits spending on defense. At the end of the 1970s, China's defense spending was $800 per man in uniform in contrast to other countries: $5560 in the US, $3680 for the USSR, and $3560 in Japan.[44]

M.I. Sladkovskiy, director of the USSR Academy of Sciences Institute of the Far East, saw the decisions of the Fifth NPC as placing "modernization of the economy in the service of militarism: the growth of the military industry, re-equipping the army and strengthening the PRC's nuclear missile armaments."[45] The Literaturnaya Gazeta quoted Deng Xiaoping on the desirability of modernization of science and technology because without it, it was impossible to create modern defense.[46] The journal also considered it significant that the first decree of the new NPC Standing Committee was to extend the term of service in the army.

Thus, the Fifth NPC kept the door closed to improved relations between China and the USSR. China was determined to strengthen military defenses, pursue closer relations with Japan, move towards rapprochement with the US - and stand up to the USSR. In this apparent determination, however, were two separate strategies. The first was based on the contingency of continued isolation. If the US and its allies continued their "appeasement" policies, and refused to join an anti-Soviet front, then China saw no possibility except to build up its military forces and fight alone if war broke out. Therefore, military modernization was pushed with as much speed as possible.

The other option (and the one which appeared less likely at the time of the Fifth NPC) was that NATO, the US, and Japan would actively resist the Soviet Union's expansionism. However, the Chinese were not certain the Japanese would risk antagonizing the USSR by signing the PFT. Certainly, normalization with the US on the basis of its derecognition of Taiwan seemed far in the future in March 1978. With the materialization of this second option by late 1978, the PRC saw that the risk of confrontation with the USSR was spread more widely among the capitalist nations, with the result that the "very broad international united front" came into being, and isolation was no longer the context of China's foreign and defense policy.

THE SOVIET UNION AND SINO-JAPANESE TREATY NEGOTIATIONS

A few years after the second world war, the USSR faced NATO in Western Europe. During the years after 1960, there was growing apprehension over the Chinese on the eastern flank, especially as territorial issues were raised. In 1978, the Soviets faced a new crisis as Japan and the US moved closer to China's orbit through diplomatic and economic steps. The USSR feared a modern, militarized and revanchist China as a potential threat, and deployed troops along the long border and in Mongolia as a cordon sanitaire. A new level of threat was seen in China's diplomatic realization of a broad international united front based on the theory of the three worlds, because of the increasing prospect of creating an "Oriental NATO" on the Asian flank. In order to avoid this possibility, Moscow tried to prevent Japan from linking up with China. To the Soviet leadership, the hegemony clause in the proposed treaty was the symbol of Tokyo's tendency.

Possibly the last opportunity for Japan to maintain its equidistant diplomacy was Sonoda's visit to Moscow in January 1978. The Japanese foreign minister held talks with Kosygin and Soviet Foreign Minister Gromyko to improve relations between the two nations. He explained Japan's intentions to enter negotiations with China on the Peace and Friendship Treaty.[47] Unexpectedly, the Soviet side presented a draft of a "good neighborliness, friendship and cooperation" treaty. The draft made no mention of any territorial problem - an omission which prompted the Japanese to dismiss the document. The Russians insisted "the Soviet Union's position is clear and definite: There is no so-called unresolved territorial issue in relations between the USSR and Japan. It has been resolved and is enshrined by the appropriate international agreements, which naturally must be observed."[48]

Sonoda claimed that his expanation to the Soviet leaders that resuming the talks with China was not directed against any third nation, would be sufficient. Having made the explanations, the foreign minister apparently thought Japan had secured its freedom of action with regard to China.[49] The Soviet side continued its criticism of any treaty with China which contained the hegemony clause. On his return from Moscow, Sonoda told Fukuda that the time was ripe for the conclusion of the treaty with China. According to Nihon Keizai, Sonoda "judged that conclusion of a Sino-Japanese treaty will not hinder Japan-Soviet relations, for he 'obtained Soviet understanding on our country's basic policy for peace diplomacy'."[50] On the basis of the ministerial talks, the Foreign Ministry concluded: (1) The USSR wanted improved relations with Japan; (2) the Soviet side still takes a "severe attitude" on the China-Japan

treaty and the territorial issue; and (3) by explaining
its position to Moscow, Tokyo has secured freedom of
action in dealing with China.[51] The Japanese delegation
also judged that Soviet retaliation over a China-Japan
treaty would not materialize.

The Soviet evaluation of Sonoda's visit was less
sanguine. No joint communiqé was produced, and as one
commentator wrote diffidently, "the sides confirmed the
existence of considerable reserves for the further development of cooperation."[52] Some spheres of relations
were already ripe for formulation on a firm basis, and
were included in the treaty proposed by Moscow, according to the article in Novoye Vremya. Such a treaty
would not rule out a Soviet-Japan peace treaty, and
talks could continue.

As to the projected PFT, Moscow considered it a
sinister step for Japan to take:

> The Soviet Union's position on the Japanese-Chinese
> treaty has been given frequently and is well known
> in Japan. The signing of this treaty with the in-
> clusion of a clause on opposing so-called hegemony
> would channel Japan into a foreign policy line hos-
> tile to the Soviet Union and to peace and the
> people's security—the line which the Chinese lead-
> ership pursues. This would seriously undermine
> trust in Japan's foreign policy and would by no
> means promote the strengthening of security in
> Asia. Whatever forms, even the most abstract, the
> clause on "hegemony" may assume, the essence and
> orientation of the Japanese-Chinese treaty will not
> change. Therefore, the Soviet Union's principled
> attitude towards it cannot change either. This was
> also quite definitely confirmed during the Japanese
> foreign minister's recent visit to Moscow.[53]

The Japanese foreign minister either misread the Soviet
attitude, or thought they were bluffing, or simply wanted the China treaty regardless of consequences.

When Japan's ambassador to Beijing was summoned in
Tokyo to consult on the treaty with China, the Soviet
reaction was predictably hostile. Citing China's "great
power ambitions" and "preparations for war as part of
its state policy," Novosti considered that the PFT would
"undoubtedly play the part of a kind of catalyst in
accelerating the militarization process which has begun
not only in China but in Japan too."[54] While Moscow
claimed that the Chinese were actively seeking a stronger Japanese military, and cooperation with it, the US
was considered to be against Sino-Japanese military
cooperation - at least in early 1978. The reason was
that the US was anxious over preserving its interests
and advantages and spheres of influence on the East
Asian region, "especially if the Japanese-Chinese mili-

tary alliance is spearheaded toward the south."[55]

By May 1978, a new view of US attitudes was propounded. In Fukuda's visit to Washington, Carter said he saw no problems with including the hegemony clause in the treaty. A _Pravda_ correspondent wrote: "(Carter's) position represents a deliberate attempt to push Japan onto the path of rapprochement with Peking on an anti-Soviet basis -- a rapprochement that obviously conforms with certain plans of the White House and the Pentagon."[56] It was at this time, following the Brzezinski visit to China, that the "oriental NATO" thesis appeared to gain additional momentum in Moscow.

Another theme in Soviet attacks, as treaty conclusion became more imminent, was that it was pushed by Japanese militarists. A radio commentary from Moscow saw suspicious implications in visits by military figures from Japan to China, although not mentioning that they were retired. Chinese leaders should not forget that they are "colluding with the Japanese militarist forces which time and again brought disaster to China in the past."[57] The people who are colluding with Beijing's anti-Soviet elements "have been continuously and stubbornly preparing new plans to establish the notorious 'greater East Asia co-prosperity sphere'."[58]

Both communist powers were using the Japanese territorial claims for their respective advantage. Vice Premier Ji Dengkui told LDP diet member Kuno that the only way for Japan to resolve the northern territory issue was to struggle against the USSR. A radio broadcast from Beijing soon afterwards said "The Japanese nation is a great nation and will not for long allow the Soviet Union to remain in its northern territories."[59]

The Soviets retaliated by pointing to the Chinese incursions around the Senkakus as evidence of Chinese encroachment on Japan's sovereign rights. Moscow closely watched Japanese opinion, hoping that the April incident would postpone or scuttle the treaty.[60] According to _Tass_, the islands were joined to Japan in 1895, and claimed by China only in 1968 when reports appeared that there might be large oil deposits in the area.[61] Chinese encroachment was not an isolated incident, but represented Beijing's general pattern of hegemonistic policy to expand at the expense of other nations, claimed Moscow. Although Sonoda wished to accept the Chinese explanation of the incident as accidental, the Soviets hoped to keep the incident alive. Moscow publicized a Shanghai wall poster which had been sent to Tokyo, describing a rally against Japanese claims over the Senkakus. Subsequently, the poster claimed, the Shanghai Fishery Department dispatched its fishing fleet to the Senkaku area and instructed the boats to mount a counterattack if Japanese attacked them - they were in "China's coastal waters." Thus, according to Moscow, "this poster clearly indicates the falsity of Peking's claim that the violation of Japanese territorial waters by the Chinese boats was accidental."[62]

The Soviets were leaving no argument unused in their barrage against the Japan-China treaty: The Japanese militarists wanted the treaty to form an alliance with China to subjugate Asia. The US wanted a three-way alliance to oppose the USSR. The Chinese needed weaponry and investment from the US and its NATO allies, and material support from Japan. China and Japan shared a common interest in that they claimed territory occupied by the USSR, so Japan's disclaimers that the hegemony clause was not anti-Soviet was discounted by the Soviets.

During the late spring and early summer of 1978, the Soviets probably overplayed their hand and resorted to crude pressures which may have pushed Japan closer to China. On 31 May, Kosygin told a group of Japanese newspaper publishers and editors that, essentially, support for the PFT with China meant support for war policies against the USSR.[63] Mission members told Kosygin that the treaty should not have an adverse affect on Japan-Soviet relations. He retorted that those relations could hardly be promoted by concluding a treaty with a country which advocated war with the Soviet Union, and wondered how Japan would react if the USSR concluded a treaty with a country advocating war with Japan.

The Soviets sought to appeal to pacifist and nationalist sectors of public opinion in Japan against the treaty. Beijing was portrayed as advocating preservation of the Japan-US security treaty, despite their longstanding opposition in the past. With Beijing supporting the security treaty and "advocating the augmentation of Japan's war potential...the Beijing leaders are apparently seeking to obtain equipment and industrial skills that can be used for military purposes."[64] Such cooperation would be a contravention of the Japanese constitution, and certainly would mobilize domestic opposition if it came about. Soviet sources insisted that the treaty was supported from "outside" (i.e., by the US), and that it would further reinforce the US-Japan security treaty, which allowed the stationing of US forces in Japan. Both were potent issues in Japan's democratic politics.

Moscow was grasping at straws in arguments against the PFT. For years, a broad range of public opinion in Japan supported improved relations with Beijing, and the treaty was generally welcomed when it was concluded. Tokyo avoided a fight over the Senkaku incident, and little note was given to Soviet goading from the sidelines. Their own occupation of the northern territories gave them little credibility on territorial issues. Few in Japan believed the altruistic motives the USSR claimed for itself in criticizing the PFT - that it would destroy détente in Asia, that it would lead to remilit-

arization of Japan, that it would make Japan into a
subservient puppet of China and the US, or that the
nations of Southeast Asia would be helpless targets of
Sino-Japanese exploitation.

In July, as the PFT settlement was becoming more
probable, the Soviets resorted to near-naked threat to
prevent Japan from signing the PFT:

> All developments in Japan-Soviet relations clearly
> indicate that an anti-Soviet policy will bring
> nothing good to Japan, but on the contrary, will
> lead it to the darkest page in its history. This
> fact should be constantly kept in mind, since the
> conclusion of the Japan-China peace and friendship
> treaty directly contradicts the interests of the
> USSR. The USSR does not intend to remain an indif-
> ferent bystander. Should anyone in Japan think
> that the anti-Soviet treaty with China would add to
> Japan's international prestige, he would be greatly
> disappointed. No nation can have its international
> prestige enhanced by means of an alliance with a
> country pursuing a reactionary policy that is hos-
> tile to the whole world and bound to fail.
>
> The proposed anti-Soviet treaty is reminiscent of
> the notorious treaty Tokyo concluded during World
> War II which is well known for its ugly purpose.
> The majority of the Japanese people are aware that
> what the handful of politicians working for the
> conclusion of the Japan-China treaty have in mind
> is not in the interests of Japan.
>
> Problems stemming from the treaty issue place a
> heavy responsibility on Japan because the projected
> treaty goes far beyond the framework of bilateral
> relations with China. This should be clearly remem-
> bered by those attempting to have Japan change its
> course and lead it toward a hopeless future and a
> political confrontation with the USSR, to cause
> setbacks in Japan-Soviet relations, and to create
> an atmosphere of tension in the Far East. [65]

In another commentary, Moscow warned Japan of serious consequences: "It must be clearly understood in
Tokyo that, in the event of a further intensification of
anti-Soviet trends in Japanese foreign policy, our country will be obliged to take corresponding retaliatory
measures to defend its interests." [66]

With such threats, Japan could not be complacent
that the USSR was only bluffing. Nor could Japan easily
step back from the negotiations because of Soviet displeasure.

The PFT - which settled no territorial issues,
created no formal alliances, and involved no economic

124

transactions - consisted largely of sentiments and words
which had different meanings not only to the two parties, but to a third party - whom the Japanese insisted
was not a third party. In other words, the treaty was a
collage of symbols, as well as an instrument of serious
diplomacy. The Chinese saw the PFT as a symbol of common
anti-Soviet sentiments between itself and Japan -a leap
forward in implementing the "broad international united
front." To the Japanese, it was the final step in normal
relations with China - and a reluctant concession in
order to gain economic benefits. The Soviets officially
interpreted the PFT according to the Chinese intentions,
although they have held back from treating Japan as a
full ally of the PRC.
       Japan had reluctantly acceded to the hegemony
clause only after the insertion of Article Four in the
PFT.   To the USSR, this reluctance mitigated Japan's
error in signing. Also, the Japan government "yielded"
to Beijing's demands during negotiations, according to
Izvestiya. [67]   Taking these into account, the Soviets
stepped back from the pre-PFT polemics and threats
against Japan. Nevertheless, the USSR lodged an official
protest against the PFT through its Tokyo embassy. The
verbal protest was made by acting Soviet Ambassador Bor-
is M. Zinovyev to the Administrative Vice Foreign Minister Arita Keisuke at the Japanese Foreign Ministry. [68]
The Soviet diplomat said that his country would take
necessary steps when Moscow thought that the Sino-Japan
PFT conflicted with Soviet interests.   He maintained
that it was still anti-Soviet in nature.
       Moscow, possibly appreciating Japan's efforts to
subdue the hegemony clause, shifted the blame to China
and the US.   Japan was by no means blameless, but "by
signing the treaty...has helplessly found itself in the
position of objectively promoting the implementation of
the Chinese leadership's foreign policy objectives, and
it is well known that these schemes are of a frankly
chauvinistic and expansionist nature." [69] The Chinese had
proven their hegemonism, so to speak, by forcing their
views of hegemony on the Japanese. Sonoda's and Fukuda's
words on their government's intention to exert efforts
to improve relations with the USSR, following the treaty
conclusion, may also have mollified Moscow. [70]
       The Japanese government officials were relieved at
this evidence that the Soviets would not take retaliatory steps directly against Japan. However, relations
could not return to their pre-PFT status. The Soviets
had already taken retaliation before the PFT was concluded - in the form of major reinforcement of the northern territories in the late spring of 1978.   This
action has made improvement of Soviet-Japanese relations
more difficult.   This reinforcement will be examined
after a glance at the treaty proposed by Moscow in early
1978.

THE SOVIET-JAPANESE DRAFT TREATY OF COOPERATION

When Sonoda visited Moscow for ministerial talks,
he was presented with a draft of a treaty of good-neigh-
borliness and cooperation, which would serve as a prelude for a peace treaty between the two countries. The
peace treaty issue has been deadlocked between them over
the northern territories. Moscow maintains that only
"recognition of realities created as a result of World
War II...can serve as the foundation for the Soviet-
Japanese peace treaty."[71] The position of Japan on that
treaty is as follows:

> (The Soviet-proposed treaty) virtually means shel-
> ving of the territorial issue...Japan has adhered
> to a consistent policy that the conclusion of a
> peace treaty by resolving the northern territorial
> issue is indispensable to truly stable and lasting
> friendly relations between Japan and the Soviet
> Union.[72]

The suddenness and timing of the draft, and its
subsequent publication by Tass on 23 February 1978,
strongly indicated that it was another ploy to prevent
Japan from signing a PFT wth China. Also, by watching
Japanese reactions to the draft treaty, Moscow had a
litmus test of Japan's intentions. The draft treaty
consisted of 14 articles, and dealt with broad declara-
tions of peace, and exchanges in science, culture and
economics.

Not only certain omissions, but also some included
articles were unwelcome to the Japanese government. Article Three stated: "The USSR and Japan undertake not to
allow the use of their territories for any actions which
could prejudice the security of the other party."[73] The
Soviets interpreted this to prohibit the stationing of
US or any other forces on Japanese territory:

> This purely peaceful proposal by the Soviet Union
> was evaluated by militarist circles as a direct
> "threat" to the existence of the Japanese-American
> military "security treaty" in accordance with which
> U.S. military bases are located on Japanese terri-
> tory. Thus, in the heat of the attacks against the
> draft treaty, what was formerly kept quiet is ad-
> mitted--namely, the anti-Soviet orientation of Jap-
> an's military cooperation with the United States.[74]

The Soviets interpreted opposition to their proposed treaty to come from advocates of the Japan-China
treaty, who thought there would be a contradiction between the hegemony clause and Article Four of the Soviet
draft treaty: "The high contracting parties undertake
to refrain from any action encouraging any third party

126

to take aggressive actions against either of them." Moscow made it clear that the hegemony clause was an encouraging action, and may have calculated that Japan would be blocked from signing the treaty with China by Article Four of the treaty of neighborliness and cooperation.

Another dangerous clause, from the Japanese perspective, was Article Five, which called for immediate consultations in the event of a situation which endangered the peace. When the Soviet forces invaded Afghanistan in late 1979, the Soviets invoked a similar article in their treaty with Afghanistan as grounds for their presence.

The Soviets dismissed these criticisms as inspired by the PRC and its sympathizers.[75] An article similar to Article Three was included in the Soviet-Turkish declaration on neighborly relations of 17 April 1972, and did not turn that country into a Soviet satellite.[76] On the charge that the draft included Article Four in order to obstruct the Japan-China treaty, a Soviet commentator puckishly announced:

...It is strange to hear people say that this article reflects the Soviet intention to obstruct the proposed Japan-China peace and friendship treaty. If the Japan-China treaty is not intended to oppose the Soviet Union, one need not worry about Article Four at all.[77]

Nor was there any worry over Article Five, since "similar clauses can be found in many treaties and agreements," including those between some NATO countries and the USSR.[78]

The Japanese government viewed the treaty as without merit, and officially did not have the Foreign Ministry study it for a reply. Cabinet Minister Ushiba Nobuhiko said that its contents "are preposterous...it tries to treat Japan on the same level as its satellites."[79] Not only was it regarded as an offensive document, but publication in Soviet newspapers was considered a breach of diplomatic protocol.

If Moscow had hoped to coerce Japan into signing the treaty, or block the China-Japan treaty, or even arouse dissent within the government, it had badly miscalculated. Galina Orionova, a former researcher from the Soviet Institute on the US and Canada, described Soviet leadership attitudes:

In 1978 scholars from several institutions met in great secrecy to examine the threat posed by Sino-Japanese rappochement. They agreed that it was a mistake to continue treating the Japanese as inferiors, that they were not militarists and could not be denied their right to deal with China on

their own terms. The Party took no notice. The
Sino-Japanese treaty was signed, and the Japanese
officially protested against Soviet intrusion into
their affairs...[80]

The Soviets may have hoped that the Japanese would
find economic cooperation a sufficient inducement to
overcome reservations about other parts of the treaty
draft. With publication of the draft coming seven days
after the signing of the China-Japan Trade Agreement (16
February 1978), the Soviets were making a bid for Japan's cooperation before a permanent tilt towards China
occurred. Articles 7, 8, 9, 10, and 11 contained provisions which profferred Soviet-Japanese cooperation in
trade, science, technology, fisheries, culture, education, communications and other fields. If Japan wanted
economic advantages, the Soviets were expressing willingness to negotiate.
But as a Soviet diplomat in Tokyo forcefully told
this author, there could never be good economic relations without good political relations. Japan, he said
could learn from the example of West Germany. Since the
signing of the Soviet-GFR treaty on 12 August 1970,
rapid progress was made in bilateral relations, both in
politics and in economics.[81] The obverse of this was
that if Japan persisted in its "anti-Soviet course,"
Siberian development and other economic projects would
go to the West Germans and others who followed "realism"
towards the USSR.
Japan was experiencing an economic slump in 1977.
Industrial output and other indicators were lagging in
the opening months of 1978.[82] Consumer prices were
rising, and the strengthening of the yen was making
Japanese exports more expensive. To the Soviets, Japanese capitalists could bail themselves out by pursuing
better economic relations with Moscow. Japan was one of
the biggest three trading partners of the USSR, and over
100 trading companies were taking part in Soviet-Japan
trade by 1978.[83] The Japan government, however, preferred not to make cooperation with the USSR a pillar of
economic rehabilitation. In his policy speech to the
Diet on 21 January 1978, Fukuda pledged efforts to
achieve 7% economic growth, and to conclude a peace
treaty with China. These two promises were not unrelated, as we have seen.

THE NORTHERN TERRITORIES

The Kurile Islands (Chishima in Japanese) had long
been a frontier between Japan and Russia. The 36 Islands, spanning about 1200 kilometers, were ceded to
Japan in the Treaty of St. Petersburg (1875) in return
for part of Sakhalin. The Soviets claim that the treaty
was invalidated by Japan's "war of aggression" against

Russia in 1904, as well as by wartime agreements among the Allies and the San Francisco Treaty of 1951.[84] Roosevelt had offhandedly ceded the island chain to Stalin at Yalta,[85] but the Japanese government maintains that the four northern islands of Etorofu, Shikotan, Habomai, and Kunashiri are separate from the Kuriles and properly part of Japan. Soviet forces wrested the Kuriles and the northern territories from the Japanese in the closing weeks of the war, including the base at Hitokappu Bay, which had been used as the staging area for the surprise attack against Pearl Harbor.

Soviet possession of the islands has made life difficult for Japanese fishermen, who had long harvested the waters around the islands. Many Japanese inhabitants migrated to the main Japanese islands rather than live under Soviet occupation. Some of these exiles have formed a pressure group which continues to remind the government that their former homes are occupied by Soviet forces.[86]

In 1973, Prime Minister Tanaka visited the USSR and held talks with Brezhnev. The Joint Statement of October 10 made no direct reference to the northern territories, and only mentioned "outstanding problems." Asked whether "outstanding problems" included the territorial question, Tanaka answered, "there are no such things as outstanding problems which do not include the territorial problem."[87]

On 6 March 1978, the Soviet foreign ministry issued a verbal note which criticized Japanese authorities for "condoning an anti-Soviet campaign that demands the return of the southern Kurile Islands, which are Soviet territory." The note further stated:

We must point out that a continuous attempt to distort the significance of the 10 October 1973 Soviet-Japan statement is also fueling this retaliatory campaign over the Soviet islands. The Soviet Union has repeatedly explained its position on Japan's territorial claim, and the Japanese Government is fully familiar with the Soviet position. The Soviet Union confirmed its position as recently as January when Foreign Minister Sonoda visited Moscow. The Soviet Union told Sonoda that no unsettled territorial problems exist between the two countries and that the Soviet Union has never turned its territory over to any foreign country.[88]

The government of Japan found the contents of the note "completely unacceptable," and issued a rebuttal on 20 March:

(1) The USSR unlawfully occupies the four islands, and this poses a big obstacle to improving Japan-Soviet relations.

(2) Japan relinquished claims to the Kurile Is-

lands at the San Francisco Peace Treaty, but historical
and legal documents show that the Kuriles do not include
Habomai, Shikotan, Kunashiri, and Etorofu (Iturup) Islands.

(3) There is no reason for Japan to lose its inherent territory under the San Francisco Treaty.

(4) When Prime Minister Tanaka visited Moscow in
1973, it was confirmed that unresolved problems included
the four northern islands.

(5) Soviet criticism of statements in the Diet,
that the islands are Japanese territory, is unreason-
able.

(6) Demand for reversion is the general will of
the Japanese people.

(7) It is expected that the Soviet side will understand fully the Japanese Government's position, and
reach the decision quickly to conclude a peace treaty
through a package reversion of the four islands.[89]

In early 1978, the Party First Secretary of the
Sakhalin Region, P.A. Leonov, published an article entitled "Pearls of the Far East" referring to the Kuriles.[90] He called for large-scale development of Sakhalin and the island chain, and dismissed any notion of
"unsettled territorial problems." It was a plan for
further economic integration of the region into the
USSR, and urged Japan to accept the situation realistic-
ally.

The territorial issue remained frozen until 1978,
when Soviet forces reinforced the northern territories'
garrison, and made retrocession to Japan even more unlikely. In 1980, the Japanese Ministry of Foreign Affairs Diplomatic Yearbook declared:

> Regarding the basic issue of concluding the peace
> treaty between Japan and the Soviet Union by real-
> izing the reversion to Japan of the four northern
> islands, discussions were held at the first Japan-
> Soviet working level consultation in May 1979 and
> at the meeting of the Foreign Ministers of the two
> countries at the United Nations in September of the
> same year. But the Soviet side still failed to
> show a sincere wish for the solution of this issue.
> Instead, the Soviet Union further strengthened its
> military buildup on the northern islands, and it
> was learned that they had newly stationed troops on
> Shikotan Island.[91]

A subsequent pamphlet published by the Ministry of
Foreign Affairs (Japan) was more specific about the
Soviet buildup:

> It has been pointed out that, in recent years, the
> Soviet Union has been building up its military
> power in the Far East-Pacific region, as well as

130

in other areas. In January 1979, the Japanese
Defense Agency disclosed that the Soviet Union had
been deploying new military forces and constructing
new military facilities on Kunashiri and Etorofu
since around the summer of 1978.[92]

The deployment referred to here actually began in the
late spring of 1978, following Japan's rejection of the
draft treaty of neighborliness and cooperation, and at a
time when Japan had begun to move in earnest towards the
peace treaty with China. Much of the diplomatic and
military activity between Japan and the USSR will remain
secret for decades, until documents and memoirs reveal
inner communications. But on the basis of available
information, it appears that Soviet fortification of the
northern islands was a move to stop Japan from negotiating the treaty with China.
    Prior to 1978, a 1500-2000-man border guard force
was garrisoned in the northern islands. When the northern ice melted in late spring, Japanese and American
intelligence detected military movements around Etorofu.
The Japan government was not anxious to publicize the
moves, since negotiations with China might be affected.[93] Some suggested that the Soviet moves were also
directed against the US, but the greater fear was that
there was preparation for some future invasion of Hokkaido, using the northern islands as a staging area.[94]
Both possibilities were inadequate explanations of the
Soviet moves.
    The timing of the Soviet buildup coincided with
Japan-China negotiations and after sharp Soviet warnings
against the proposed treaty. In 1977, Soviet Ambassador
Polyansky lectured at the National Defense College in
Tokyo, and stated that his country would take countermeasures if Japan and China signed a friendship agreement containing the hegemony clause. Mr. J. Sassa,
Director of Education and Personnel of the JDA, told the
author that the government expected retaliation to be in
the form of withdrawing the ambassador. Thus, there was
some concern when Polyansky left Tokyo in July 1978.
    There was also heavy traffic in the Sea of Japan,
which prompted JDA Director General Kanemaru's remark in
the Diet: "Now the Japan Sea can be called the Soviet
Sea."[95] Nevertheless, the JDA official position was
that the naval movements were not to restrain China-
Japan relations. Official at the Foreign Ministry denied that Soviet movements were a "show of force"
against Japanese claims over the islands. They also
ruled out the possibility that Soviet exercises were an
expression of opposition to Japan's movement towards
negotiation of the treaty within China.[96] At the time,
in early June 1978, the movement of Soviet transport
planes (10 large Antonov-12's, each with a capacity of
20 tons of freight or 90 troops), and firing practice,

appeared to be practice maneuvers around Etorofu.

Chief Secretary Abe Shintaro charged that Soviet land and sea maneuvers were unlawful, but said that the government did not consider that there was a connection between the maneuvers and the China-Japan negotiations.[97] However, this was implausible because the USSR gave Japan advance notice of maneuvers in the "Southern Kuriles" the day after Tokyo proposed reopening treaty negotiations with China on May 31.[98] Abe could not officially link the maneuvers to the Japan-China treaty negotiations because his government's position was that the treaty did not concern any third country.

It was the second time since 1970 that the Soviets had conducted military practice around Etorofu. Japan lodged a protest with the USSR through its embassy in Moscow, calling for an immediate halt of the exercises. The main concern was possible damage to Japanese fishing boats and equipment in the area.

The Japanese government was forced to realize that this exercise was the first act of retaliation for moving forward on the treaty with China. But rather than admit this obvious connection, the government refused to confirm that the "exercises" had taken place. Ito Keiichi, director general of the JDA Defense Bureau, told a Diet committee on 8 June that the Agency had not yet confirmed the maneuvers. Press reports were based on judgments by General Kurisu Hiromi, Chairman of SDF Joint Chiefs of Staff, he said, but those did not represent the Agency's view.[99] However, another government source reported that landing maneuvers were taking place, under the overall direction of the Soviet Far Eastern Army Khabarovsk Military District. Ito said that the Agency had not yet verified whether landings on Etorofu had taken place.[100]

Within a few days, the government sought to play down the issue. Sonoda said that the reported maneuvers were not causing any strains in relations with the USSR.[101] The government planned no further protest, and viewed maneuvers around Etorofu as only usual firing practice and without political design. Sonoda said no ground troops were involved nor were there landing operations.[102] On 29 June, JDA Director General Kanemaru contradicted General Kurisu, telling the Diet that the chief of the Joint Staff Council was incorrect when he said that Soviet forces conducted simulated landing operations in the northern territories. Kanemaru's civilian subordinate, Ito, said that the Soviet operations occurred around Etorofu since 20 May, but Japanese intelligence could not determine whether these were for military exercise, or for deployment of Soviet units on Etorofu, or to build a military base.[103] He said that landing maneuvers were the least likely posssibility because of absence of supporting naval vessels.

Whether Tokyo was aware or not, the Soviet military

activity on Etorofu was directed at a major reinforcement of its garrison. The White Paper on Defense of 1979 recognized this and noted that:

> Since last summer (1978), for the first time in 18 years, the Soviet Union has been deploying ground forces of considerable scale, equipped with tanks and artillery of various types, on Kunashiri and Etorofu islands, an integral part of Japanese territory. The Soviets also seem to be constructing military bases on these islands. [104]

Nearly two decades earlier, in the summer of 1960, ground forces stationed on the two islands had been withdrawn, and half of the air defense planes removed in 1966. Since May 1978, that was reversed. Ground forces on the islands have been reinforced. Tanks, armored personnel carriers, artillery, anti-aircraft missiles, Mi-24 attack helicopters, and approximately 20 MiG-17 fighters were deployed on Kunashiri and Etorofu Islands. [105] The exact size of the Soviet units was not known definitely, but it appeared that nearly a division of ground forces was deployed.

As to reasons for the buildup, the Defense White Paper (1980) stated:

> It is not known for certain why the Soviet Union has deployed ground units on the northern islands. From the standpoint of global strategy of the Soviet Union, however, it seems to reflect the importance the Soviet Union attaches to the northern islands, the Kurile Islands and the Sea of Okhotsk and also efforts to build up and modernize Soviet forces in the Far East as a whole in recent years. It also appears that the deployment is also intended to produce political effects, such as forcing Japan to recognize the illegal occupation of the northern territories. [106]

With the intensification of the Soviet military buildup in the Far East, the strategic location of the northern territories has become more important. Etorofu, where the reinforcement has been most notable, lies further east than any of the main Japanese islands. From its air fields, Soviet plans can fly due south and patrol the Pacific waters off Japan. The Soviet base there can also defend the Soviet hold over the Sea of Okhotsk. There is a logistcal problem because of winter ice, but supplies are brought in from Petropavlosk, Vladivostok, and other Siberian bases. As the USSR continues to build its world fleet, it is expected that the islands will play a larger part in Soviet strategy in the north Pacific. If this materializes, the chances of reversion to Japan will become nil.

Thus the Soviet buildup on the islands served a
strategic interest - extending military power into the
north Pacific, and a political interest - forcing Japan
to recognize the irreversible loss of those territories.
The timing of the buildup, however, was most probably
calculated to penalize Japan for pursuing the treaty
with China. This coincidence, or linkage, was not officially recognized by the Japanese government. The Japanese position is that the treaty did not involve the
USSR, and so there were no connections. The Research
Institute on Peace and Security in Tokyo, however, saw a
linkage: "The Soviet Union probably intends...it as
political retaliation against the conclusion of the
Sino-Japanese Peace and Friendship Treaty, as well as a
discouragement of Japan's demand for return of the islands by putting them under firmer Soviet control."[107]
Another indication of the Soviet intention to use
the northern territorial issue to punish Japan occurred
in October 1978. A symposium between Japanese and Soviet experts was held in Tashkent. A certain Professor
Petrov, described as a person who participated in formulation of Soviet policy toward Japan, gave a statement
on various questions between the two countries. According to him, the Japan-China PFT was hindering the development of Japan-Soviet relations:

Before the signing of the Japan-China Treaty, Japan
had carried out a foreign policy which maintained a
balance, to a certain extent...However, with the
conclusion of the Japan-China Treaty this time,
Japan has clearly leaned toward China, and it has
taken the direction of developing Japan-China relations, with opposition to the Soviet Union as the
basis. It is by no means possible for us to understand Japan's attitude of speaking about the northern territory, despite such a situation. It is
clearly irrelevant for Japan, in view of the time
element, to bring up such a problem after its conclusion of the Treaty with China. [108](author's
emphasis added)

Petrov assigned all responsibility for worsened relations to Japan.
The territorial issue continues to aggravate relations between the two countries, and in 1981, 7 February
was declared "Northern Territories Day,"[109] in order to
keep the issue alive. Japan probably lost the islands in
the summer of 1978 with the treaty tilt towards China.

ANALYSIS

The USSR had two cards at its disposal in influen-
cing Japan's diplomacy towards itself and China: the
northern territories and the draft treaty of neighbor-

liness and cooperation. In order to understand why
Moscow proceeded as it did, we can draw up six possible
scenarios, ranging from "soft" to "hard," with reference
to effects on Japan. By late February, the USSR had
staked out initial positions on the territories and
draft treaty. As to possible consequences of altering
those positions, we can suggest the following: See
Chart One)

    Scenario One: (soft-soft) Here, the USSR gives
Japan part of what is demanded – retrocession of two islands and modification of the draft treaty to meet Tokyo's objections. Such a move would have distracted
Fukuda from pursuit of the treaty with China, and created a mood for listening seriously to Soviet proposals.
It would have made Sonoda's task of selling the China
treaty to the LDP more difficult because the prospect of
getting back the islands was opening up. Under these
circumstances, Japan would probably have negotiated
seriously with the USSR on the draft treaty. At the
very least, the Soviet "soft-soft" position would have
complicated Sino-Japanese treaty negotiations. However,
it was extremely unlikely that the USSR would so quickly
– and uncharacteristically – modify its initial bargaining position. Anyone in the Kremlin who pushed the
concessions – whatever the result – would be castigated
as giving away too much, and setting a bad precedent in
territorial questions – Soviet state doctrine is not to
bargain away areas under its control. (Perhaps Austria
after World Word Two and withdrawal of Soviet troops
from Iran are exceptions.) Therefore, the cost of concessions on the two variables were too high for the
USSR, and the results were not certain of inhibiting
Japan.

    Scenario Two: (soft-no change) This would have
distracted Tokyo somewhat from the China treaty because
there was sizable opinion in Japan, especially on the
left, that Article Three of the Soviet draft treaty
would be a blow against US forces in Japan. Article Four
could be interpreted as a negation of the hegemony
clause the Chinese were insisting on. Thus, for the USSR
to return two islands, while holding to the draft treaty
as published, would have upset the delicate consensus
Fukuda and Sonoda had achieved in favor of the treaty
with China. However, because of Soviet territorial doctrine, and the possible precedent this might create for
Chinese claims, this scenario too was unlikely.

    Scenario Three: (no change-soft) The northern ter-
ritories were more important than the issue of the draft
treaty, so the effect of this Soviet posture would not
be great. For the USSR to soften its stand on Article
Three of the draft treaty, however, could have alienated
socialists, who counted on Soviet support in their fight
against the US Security Treaty.

CHART ONE: Possible scenarios, with Soviet control of variables.

Scenario	Variable one: Northern Territories	Variable two: Soviet-Japan draft treaty (especially Articles 3, 4)
One	USSR returns 2 islands (soft)	USSR modifies draft to meet Japanese objections (soft)
Two	USSR returns 2 islands (soft)	No changes (soft)
Three	No change in USSR position: "already settled" (no change)	USSR modifications (soft)
Four	No change	No change
Five	Deploy troops (hard)	No change
Six	Deploy troops (hard)	Additional clause: "Japan recognizes territorial issue settled" (hard)

Scenario Four: (no change-no change) If the USSR continued its claim that there was no territorial issue between itself and Japan, and took no further action, while maintaining the draft treaty had to be signed without changes, it could be safely predicted that Tokyo's repulsion from Moscow would be sufficient to enhance the chances of the treaty with China. The USSR would maintain its principles of no changes in territorial status, of supporting the Japanese left in wanting the removal of US forces from Japan, and of opposing China's international united front. The disadvantage of this posture was that it virtually assured Japanese pursuit of negotiations of the treaty with China because no costs were imposed in doing so.

Scenario Five: (hard-no change) The reinforcement of the garrison forces on Etorofu in May and June of 1978 represented a significant hardening of the Soviet position, in the sense that not only would there be no discussion of any territorial issue, but these islands were turned into a security threat against northern Japan. The Soviets probably calculated that this move was raising the cost of the treaty with China, and would make Sonoda think twice about pursuing it. Now, Japan might even seriously consider the draft treaty with the USSR in order to get the troops out of the northern islands. We do not know what calculations the Soviets made in this move, but most likely, they were closely related to discouraging Japan from signing the treaty with China if it contained the hegemony clause.

Scenario Six: (hard-hard) In this final scenario in Soviet options, we can conceive of a situation of military reinforcements in the northern islands and an additional clause in the draft treaty stating the Soviet position that there are no territorial disputes between the two countries. Such severe moves would no doubt backfire, and accelerate Japanese perception of Soviet intransigence and threat. It would undercut the left as well, in its claims that if it came to power, it could more effectively negotiate on the territorial issue with the USSR. Such a treaty would foreclose any future discussions. Therefore, we must consider this last scenario as unlikely as the first.

With the above scenarios, the fifth appears as the closest to recent historical reality. In fact, an additional development was that after the harder line (reinforcement) on the northern territories, Moscow indicated willingess to modify the draft treaty, producing an additional scenario (hard-soft) not considered above. In practical terms, however, the results were not different from Scenario Five, because of the greater importance of the territorial issue.

The Japanese government, confronted with Scenario Five, minimized the hardening of the USSR posture in public, and in effect, acted as if it was facing

Scenario Four. Instead of debating the implications of
the move by Soviet forces, the government allowed wrang-
ling over questions of evaluations by civilian and uniformed intelligence. The question was isolated from the
treaty with China, and Beijing did not turn the Soviet
move into a propaganda affair to denounce the USSR for
its obvious hegemony. To focus Japanese attention on
the event would have underlined to Japan that the cost
of the desired Sino-Japan treaty could be permanent loss
of the northern territories as well as sizable increase
of Soviet military presence a few miles from its northern coast.

The Chinese periodically bring up the northern
territories as an example of Soviet hegemony, so their
omission in May and June of 1978, a golden opportunity
to illustrate their Soviet hegemony thesis, was puzzling
- unless seen in the above context. For example, on 3
March 1978, prior to the Soviet buildup, the Xinhua news
agency criticized the Soviet treaty draft given to Tokyo, as reiterated its continued theme: "Proceeding
from its policy of aggression and expansion as well as
its strategic need in contending for hegemony with the
United States, the Soviet Union has kept Japan's
northern territories in its firm grip."

Events worked to the advantage of Beijing: The
Soviet's tough stand on the islands, and deployment of
forces there, contrasted with China's claims to the
Senkakus. The comparison illustrated that the USSR was
a much greater threat to Japan than the PRC, and that
Soviet military power was behind its diplomacy. Soviet
behavior failed to intimidate Japan into either refraining from the treaty with China, or concluding the cooperation treaty with itself. The Soviet moves in the
northern islands, and the continued military buildup in
the Far East, have become major arguments by those who
want increased defense expenditures in Japan - a group
which included the Chinese communists.

Footnotes

     1. In September 1977, the government announced a
supplemental budget of 2 trillion yen for public works,
and the Bank of Japan cut the official discount rate by
0.75% in order to stimulate the economy. JTW, 10 September 1977, p. 2.
     2. Daily Report:USSR, 4 January 1978, p. M1 (Here-
inafter: DR:USSR).
     3. Ibid.
     4. DR:USSR, 14 August 1978, p. M1.
     5. Ibid., p. M3.
     6. DR:USSR, 6 January 1978, p. C1.
     7. DR:USSR, 21 March 1978, p. C1.
     8. DR:USSR, 19 April 1978, p. C3.

138

9.   DR:USSR, 12 May 1978, p. C3.
10.   DR:USSR, 13 June 1978, p. C1.
11.   Ibid., p. C2.
12.   DR:USSR, 26 January 1978, p. C3.
13.   Ibid.
14.   Peking Review, 19 April 1974, pp. 6-11.
15.   The Eleventh National Congress of the
Communist Party of China (Documents). (Peking: Foreign
Language Press, 1977), pp. 59-60.
16.   Ibid., p. 2.
17.   DR:USSR, 15 January 1978, p. C1.
18.   DR:USSR, 25 January 1978, p. C2.
19.   Eleventh National Congress, p. 57.
20.   DR:USSR, 25 January 1978, pp. C2-3.
21.   DR:USSR, 26 January 1978, p. C5.
22.   Ibid.
23.   DR:USSR, 30 May 1978, p. C7. See R. Bedeski,
State-Building in Modern China, pp. 117-121.
24.   San Min Chu I (The Three Principles of the
People).   Translated by Frank Price (Chungking:
Ministry of Information, Republic of China, 1943), p.
49.
25.   This was meant in the sense that capitalism
was divided between the first and second world.
26.   DR:USSR, 30 May 1978, p. C6.
27.   DR:USSR, 9 June 1978, p. M3.
28.   DR:USSR, 13 January 1978, p. C1.
29.   Documents of the First Session of the Fifth
National People's Congress of the People's Republic of
China (Peking: Foreign Languages Press, 1978), p. 103.
30.   Ibid., p. 101.
31.   Ibid.
32.   DR:USSR, 3 April 1978, p. C1.
33.   Fifth NPC, p. 113.
34.   DR:USSR, 3 April 1978, p. C2.
35.   Ibid., p. C4.
36.   DR:USSR, 12 May 1978, p. C1; 15 May 1978, p.
C1.
37.   DR:USSR, 15 May 1978, p. M1.
38.   DR:USSR, 25 May 1978, p. M3.
39.   Ibid.
40.   Ibid., p. M4.
41.   DR:USSR. 24 May 1978, p. C4.
42.   DR:USSR, 13 January 1978, p. C1.
43.   Asian Security 1980 (Tokyo: Research
Institute for Peace and Security, 1980), p. 89.
44.   Ibid., p. 104.
45.   DR:USSR, 12 May 1978, p. C2.
46.   DR:USSR, 18 April 1978, p. C1.
47.   NK, 10 January 1978, p. 1.
48.   DR:USSR, 22 February 1978, p. M1.
49.   NK, 11 January 1978, p. 2.
50.   NK, 10 January 1978, p. 1.
51.   NK, 11 January 1978, p. 2.

52. DR:USSR, 22 February 1978, p. M1.
53. Ibid, p. M2.
54. DR:USSR, 18 January 1978, p. M1.
55. Ibid., p. M2.
56. DR:USSR, 23 May 1978, p. M1.
57. DR:USSR, 23 January 1978, p. C2.
58. Ibid.
59. DR:USSR, 8 February 1978, p. M3.
60. DR:USSR, 21 April 1978, p. C4.
61. DR:USSR, 7 June 1978, p. M2.
62. DR:USSR, 7 June 1978, p. M2.
63. DR:USSR, 1 June 1978, p. M1.
64. DR:USSR, 6 June 1978, p. M1.
65. DR:USSR, 6 July 1978, p. M1.
66. DR:USSR, 12 July 1978, p. M1.
67. DR:USSR, 22 August 1978, p. M1.
68. DR:USSR, 23 August 1978, p. M1.
69. DR:USSR, 30 August 1978, p. M1.
70. Ibid., p. M2.
71. DR:USSR, 16 June 1978, p. M3.
72. Japan, Ministry of Foreign Affairs, Diplomatic Bluebook (1980 edition) (Tokyo: Foreign Press Center), p. 51.
73. Text of treaty draft in DR:USSR, 23 February 1978, pp. M1-3.
74. DR:USSR, 6 March 1978, p. M1.
75. DR:USSR, 8 May 1978, pp. M1-2.
76. DR:USSR, 18 April 1978, p. M4.
77. Ibid.
78. Ibid.
79. TS, 24 February 1978, p. 1.
80. Nora Beloff, "Escape from Boredom: A Defector's Story," Atlantic Monthly 246:5 (1980), p. 45. Research and interpretations from various institutions apparently carried little weight with the Party: "...documents which constantly flood in (the Central Committee) from all the rival academic institutions find their way straight into the wastepaper basket." p. 45.
81. DR:USSR, 22 May 1978, p. M2.
82. DR:USSR, 3 April 1978, p. M2.
83. DR:USSR, 17 January 1978, p. M2.
84. Swearingen, p. 189.
85. John J. Stephan, The Kuril Islands (Oxford: Clarendon, 1974), p. 155.
86. AS, 26 August 1978, p. 3.
87. Swearingen, p. 196.
88. DR:USSR, 8 March 1978, p. M1.
89. YS, 21 March 1978, p. 2.
90. Summarized in TS, 3 February 1978, p. 1.
91. Bluebook, p. 51.
92. Japan's Northern Territories (Tokyo: Ministry of Foreign Affairs, Japan, 1981), p. 19.
93. SK, 17 June 1978, p. 1.
94. Ibid.

95. MS, 29 June 1978, p. 2.
96. Daily Report: Asia and the Pacific, 7 June 1978, p. C1. (Hereinafter DR:AP.)
97. DR:AP, 8 June 1978, p. C1.
98. Ibid.
99. DR:AP, 8 June 1978, p. C1.
100. DR:AP, 9 June 1978, p. C1.
101. DR:AP, 14 June 1978, p. C1.
102. DR:AP, 16 June 1978, p. C2.
103. DR:AP, 29 June 1978, p. C1.
104. Defense of Japan 1979 (Tokyo: Japan Defense Agency, translated by Mainichi Daily News, 1979), p. 37.
105. Defense of Japan 1980 (Tokyo: Japan Defense Agency, translated by the Japan Times, 1980), "Diagram 10," p. 57.
106. Ibid.
107. Asian Security 1980, p. 43.
108. SK, 7 October 1978, p. 1.
109. DR:China, 12 February 1981, p. D3.

7
The Sino-Soviet Conflict Widens

Concerning the Soviet buildup on the northern islands in the summer of 1978, two possible explanations of Soviet motives may be offered. First, it was a Soviet maneuver to force Japan to reconsider closer ties with China, and to go slow in negotiating the peace treaty. Neither the governments of Japan, the USSR, nor the PRC, endorses this explanation, but circumstantial evidence points to its plausibility. The timing of the move was soon after the Sino-Japanese LTTA and the decision of the Fukuda government to go ahead with negotiations on the peace treaty. It was also a strong signal to both Japan and China that the USSR would not surrender territory.

It was no simple matter to move thousands of troops and their equipment, and a decision must have been made months before. On a visit to the Soviet Far East in April 1978, Brezhnev probably gave the final go-ahead to military commanders in the area. The Soviet decision to reinforce Etorofu necessarily affected relations with Japan. Tokyo's rejection of the neighborliness and cooperation treaty may have indicated that a show of force was needed to bring Japan back to the realization of Soviet power.

A second explanation is that reinforcement of the northern territories was part of a general strengthening of Soviet Far East forces, and Etorofu was designated to play a greater role in the fortification of the Sea of Okhotsk. For a number of years, the USSR has been transferring new weapons into the region, and increasing naval operations in the Pacific. Part of this deployment was directed against the PRC, and also to reduce US superiority in the Pacific region.

In any conflict involving the PRC, the US and the USSR, Japan would be an affected party. To the extent that Japan was used as an American staging area or forward base against the USSR, it would become involved in a US-Soviet conflict. This was the implication of the US-Japan Security Treaty which leftist and pacifist

forces emphasized. Conservatives, on the other hand,
stressed the US contribution to Japan's defense, a situation which created security dependence which was unacceptable to nationalists. Pointing to the Soviet buildup in the Far East generally, and the 1978 deployment of
troops on Etorofu locally, the pro-defense groups argued
for greater self-defense efforts against Soviet military
threats.

The defense dilemma was further exacerbated in
1978-79: (1) Soviet strategic and tactical forces were
strengthened in the Far East, and posed a threat against
Japan. (2) Japan and China became linked by the PFT
containing the hegemony clause which China and the USSR
agreed was anti-Soviet, although Japan rejected this interpretation. (3) US strategic interest in the Far East
was secondary to the European theater, as expressed in
the withdrawal of ground forces from Korea. (4) China
was building an international united front against "Soviet hegemonism." This was to include NATO, the US, and
Japan if possible. (5) Vietnam moved towards the USSR
through participation in COMECON and a treaty of cooperation during 1978. Expulsion of refugees and border cla-
shes with China erupted into the short war of February
1979. (6) The Soviet takeover of Kabul in late 1979,
contrasted with American indecisiveness in Iran, and
illustrated the Soviet will to act belligerently, while
the US administration was still torn by self-doubts.

Each of these developments raised questions about
Japan's security. The Chinese felt vindicated in their
charges against Soviet hegemonism by the Afghanistan
affair, but the Japanese government would not admit this
as a general proposition about Soviet behavior, as Beijing would have preferred. However, the "counter-attack"
against Vietnam, shifted some of the blame to China as
becoming less "peace-loving" than originally claimed.
The US was seen as a declining superpower, and therefore
less dependable as a guarantor of Japanese security.
Under these conditions, demands were heard for significant bolstering of Japan's self-defense forces.

THE SOVIET MILITARY BUILDUP IN NORTHEAST ASIA

The timing of Soviet moves in strengthening the
northern territories was linked to Japan's urgency in
negotiating the treaty with China. But the move was
also a part of general upgrading of Soviet forces in
Northeast Asia which had been in progress since 1969,
when Soviet and Chinese troops clashed on the Manchurian
border. By 1977, 25% of Soviet conventional forces were
deployed east of Irkutsk - a region containing only 10%
of Soviet population. In 1972, Soviet army divisions on
the Sino-Soviet border numbered 43, and were considered
to be in a low state of combat readiness. In 1973, the
Soviets prepared to make the large army presence

permanent, with the building of roads, barracks, and
training grounds.
A 1979 study[1] of Soviet forces in Northeast Asia
considered them to be defensive. The presence of 12,000
men trained in amphibious operations and a growing naval
presence in the Sea of Japan was not seen as having
offensive potential against Japan.
Growth of Soviet naval power was also noted in the
Brookings study by Johnson and Yager.   Since the US
blockade of Cuba in 1962, the USSR has been building its
ocean-going navy. Previously, the Soviet Union had been
largely a land power, with its vessels used mostly for
coastal patrol. In April 1970, 20 surface ships and 12
submarines of the Far East fleet participated in the
Soviet worldwide naval exercise, "Okean."   Five years
later, "Okean II" (or "Vesna") saw four Soviet task forces operate in the Pacific. Another indication of Soviet
naval expansion into the Pacific has been the development of Petropavlovsk, on the Pacific side of the Kam-
chatka peninsula, as a major naval base. The disadvantage of Soviet bases on the Sea of Japan, such as Vladivostok, is that ships can be blockaded at three choke
points: the Straits of Soya, Tsugaru, and Tsushima.
The disadvantage of Petropavlovsk is that it must be
supplied by air or ship.   These geopolitical realities
have led the Soviets to focus on anti-submarine warfare
(ASW) in the region, and to build up its own submarine
force. The Pacific submarine fleet accounts for about
one-third of all Soviet submarines.[2]
How have these developments affected Japan? How
has the Japanese defense establishment perceived the
Soviet military buildup? To answer, we can examine the
annual defense reports published by the Japan Defense
Agency since 1976. The 1977 report stressed the need to
maintain a rough balance of power in the region between
the two major military superpowers. The 1977 report,
Defense of Japan, reiterated that strategic mutual deterrence between the US and USSR had been achieved.
However, the US naval and air superiority in conventional forces was decreasing, due to a quantitative decline
of US forces, and a marked expansion of Soviet forces.[3]
The 1977 defense report cited four reasons for the
Soviet arms buildup (drawing from a report by the US
Department of Defense):

(1) To disintegrate the unity among the Western
powers through the exercise of political pressure;
(2) Expanding Soviet influence in the Third World;
(3)   Neutralizing the military advantage of the
Western powers and increasing the influence of the
Soviet Union in areas of political East-West confrontation; (4) Reordering the military balance to
provide advantages to the Soviet Union in arms
control negotiations with the West.[4]

The Sino-Soviet border and the Korean peninsula continued to be areas of high tension, and a "confrontation atmosphere" due to the existing opposing military structures. A degree of stability was present in Northeast Asia because of mutual deterrence in the region.

However, trends favored the Soviet Union in naval affairs: The US Chief of Naval Operations, Admiral James L. Holloway, told Congress on 2 February 1976 that the US had lost the control it once had over the Sea of Japan: "At present, any operations that the US Navy would want to conduct in the Sea of Japan," he testified, "would be with the sufferance of the Soviets."[5] The Defense Agency estimated over 300,000 Soviet troops in the Far East, naval tonnage at 1,250,000 and around 2,000 military aircraft.[6] By early 1980, the corresponding figures were 350,000 troops, 1,520,000 tons and 2,060 aircraft.[7] One consolation to the US and its allies was that China and the USSR were no longer a linked threat against the West. Since 1972, a situation termed "tripolarization" had emerged in Northeast Asia. (This terminated in 1978 with the US-PRC normalization, as will be examined later in the next chapter.)

Japan has been especially concerned about the qualitative improvement of Soviet naval and air power in East Asia. Geography has been the island nation's best defense against hostile land forces. In recent years, the Soviet Far Eastern naval and air forces have been receiving advanced weapons, including Backfire Bombers and Kiev class light aircraft carriers.[8] This permitted the USSR to interfere in remote regions.[8] The crash of a Soviet "spy satellite" reminded Japanese of another dimension of the security question - development of outer space as a future battleground.[9]

The 1978 report considered it "difficult for the Soviet Pacific fleet to destroy the (US) Seventh Fleet's sea control mission, due to the latter's open sea air capability provided by aircraft carriers and its substantial submarine force for self-defense." Even so, "Soviet aircraft...are considered capable of attacking Seventh Fleet ships with standoff missiles (capable of striking warships from positions outside such ships' air defense umbrellas)."[10] Thus, the American defense umbrella over Japan was in danger of neutralization by the Soviet military buildup.

The next annual defense report saw further concern over Soviet military improvements in the Far East. US defense expenditures had stagnated in the past decade, according to the 1979 defense report, while Soviet capacity to expand its political influence had steadily improved. While earlier reports noted US and Soviet mutual deterrence postures, there were signs that the USSR was moving towards a nuclear capacity to win rather than deter a nuclear war.[11] Greater Soviet emphasis on the Far East was occurring for two reasons: First, a new stage in the Sino-Soviet dispute was emerging in the post-Mao years. After Mao's death, the Soviets refrained from provocative acts or language, hoping rapprochement with the new leadership would come about. Beijing's hard line was made final at the Fifth NPC, and both states resumed their confrontation. As noted earlier, this confrontation now affected non-communist countries. China involved NATO, the US and Japan in building an international united front.

The second reason for increasing Soviet attention to the east was the desire to develop Siberia. It was a storehouse of natural resources, and development of these would be a needed boost to the Soviet economy.

The JDA was becomong more concerned about the outbreak of conventional war - which US-USSR mutual deterrences could not stop. The Soviets had improved their chemical warfare capabilities, while ground forces were reformed or reorganized every few years, so as to be able to engage in war at any time.[12] Another anxiety of the JDA was the Backfire Bomber, described as "a variable-geometry medium bomber with a maximum speed over Mach 2 and maximum unrefuelled range of about 5,700 kilometers."[13] With its air-to-ship missiles, and low-altitude strike capability, the Backfire was an attack weapon against aircraft carrier task forces. Because of this, and its use in blocking sea transportation, the Japanese are particularly concerned: "In the event such high performance bombers are deployed in the Far East, it would be necessary to focus attention on air defense measures and securing of sea lanes in waters surrounding Japan."[14]

These Backfires were deployed in the Far East, and gave heightened Japan's concern about security. The 1980 defense report stated the new situation:

> The buildup of both the Soviet ground forces in the Far East and the Soviet Pacific Fleet has been remarkable in the past several years, and the military situation surrounding Japan has become even more difficult due to such factors as the deployment of Backfire bombers and SS-20 intermediate range ballistic missiles in the Far East and the use of bases in Vietnam.[15]

The 1980 report was particularly sobering, because for the first time, it included a section on instability in the Middle East. The Iranian revolution, US helplessness over the hostages, and Soviet invasion of Afghanistan underlined Japan's dilemma of dependence on the region's oil, and American military incompetence in light of the abortive rescue operation. Moreover, the USSR was "in a position to stage separate operations on several fronts by keeping massive military forces in areas ranging from Europe to the Middle East and the Far East."[16]

A new type of ship was added to the Soviet Far Eastern Fleet in 1979 - the Kiev-class aircraft carrier. It is smaller than US carriers, and carries about 40 VTOL (vertical take-off and landing) multipurpose fighters. It also has ASW helicopters, various types of missiles, and excellent command, control and communications facilities.[17] The JDA saw deployment of the Kiev-class carrier in the Far East to mean that, "though in a limited sense...the Soviet Pacific Fleet is now possessing a capability to provide air cover for its warships operating on the high seas far from the Soviet coasts, enhancing its ability of land power projection."[18]

The Minsk was the first Kiev-class carrier to deploy to the Far East. It was to demonstrate Soviet naval power, but itself could not alter the balance of naval power. The US had 13 carriers to 2 in the Soviet navy. The Minsk presence in the Pacific was important because it enhanced Soviet ASW. Hostile submarines could close off the several straits which enclosed the Seas of Japan and Okhotsk, so the Minsk could carry out countermeasures in wartime.

Japan had little to fear from the Soviet naval buildup as long as American military power remained credible and superior and the US-Japan treaty was intact.[19] Ironically, a Japanese corporation had contributed to Soviet naval capability in the Far East. The All-Soviet Ship Import Corporation placed an order with Ishikawajima-Harima Heavy Industries to build a super-large floating dock. The dock was to have a lift capacity of 80,000 tons.[20] Because existing docks at Vladivostok had a 30,000 ton capacity which was sufficient for 8,000 ton Kestra II cruisers, the largest ships operating in the Soviet Far East at the time, the only plausible reason for the order was the intention to deploy the Minsk - the 40,000 ton aircraft carrier.

The dock was built and towed to Vladivostok in November 1978, much to the embarrassment of the Japan government. MITI had approved the contract, assuming that the dock would be used for general ship repair. Japan ship-building companies were in a depression, so the 13 billion yen order was welcomed.[21] It was regretted that the government did not even extract a promise for peaceful uses.[22] The company maintained that it was not a weapon, but US and JDA officials were shocked because it made Minsk deployment possible.

In his "Foreward" to the 1980 defense report, JDA Director General Omura Joji took note of the sense which the Soviet military buildup had aroused among Western countries. Japan, he wrote, must consider its defense from the standpoint as a member of the international community. He thought that the problem of Japan's defense had come to an important turning point in the 1980s, and asked rhetorically:

Could this not be said so when we look at the fact
that the age in which Japan could enjoy its peace
and security by excessively relying on the US
strength is over and that the defense problem has
become taken up as a major issue in Japan-US relations?[23]

Although he was concerned primarily with US-Japan
relations here, Omura was referring to a totally new
situation in the postwar period. The oil shocks of the
early 1970s had demonstrated Japan's energy vulnerability. Japan was now concerned about a new source of
vulnerability - military security. The period of Soviet
military buildup coincided with the American post-Vietnam trauma and stagnation of defense preparations. It
was becoming obvious that American military superiority
was under challenge by the Soviets. The US as well,
recognized the decreasing disparity between its forces
and those of the USSR. In response, US leaders requested
Japan to contribute more to its own defense.
    The Soviet military buildup in the Far East, seen
through the eyes of the Defense Agency, was becoming a
serious threat to Japanese security. On the surface, it
would appear that Japan had ample reason for concern.
The Soviet reinforcement of the northern territories
confirmed this threat.
    But before passing judgment on Soviet actions in
the Far East, it is necessary to examine Moscow's perspective, or at least that which is public. Here it becomes apparent that the USSR, by late 1977, perceived a
new potential threat on its eastern flank. Soviet media
claimed that a resurgent Japanese militarism, encouraged
by the US, and possibly joining with the Chinese "revanchism," posed a clear danger to the Soviet state. Soviet
observers saw a linking up of NATO, Japanese "militarism," the PRC, and the United States in the broad international united front proclaimed at the Fifth NPC in
Beijing. The Siberian maritime front was one of the weak
flanks on Soviet frontiers, and had to be strengthened.
Both China and Japan had outstanding territorial claims
against the USSR, and it was perhaps only a matter of
time before they joined in common cause to demand retrocession.
    In examining the claims, counterclaims and activi-
ties of the four states dominating Northeast Asia, a
common cliché becomes tragic truth: each party claims
its own actions are defensive, while those of the adversary are expansionist and offensive. Nowhere is this
more true than between Japan and the USSR. Russian confrontation with Japan began in the late ninteenth century and culminated in the Russo-Japan war of 1904-5.
After world war one, Japan deployed troops in Siberia.
Despite a nonaggression pact during the second world
war, Japanese and Soviet armies engaged in skirmishes,

and the Soviets captured the Kuriles in the closing days
of the war. With such a historical background, it is not
surprising that Moscow viewed any expansion of Japan's
military capability, especially accompanied by anti-
Soviet sentiments, as a threat to Far Eastern interests.
     Soon after Sonoda left Moscow in early 1978, the
Soviet media took up the theme of revived Japanese militarism. Tass saw the "Japanese Army" as one of the
strongest in Asia, with its up-to-date weapons, and more
than 260,000 men. The Soviet estimate of SDF strength
is more than 20,000 men larger than JDA figures.[24] Tass
blamed the US for pressuring Japan to achieve "qualitative perfection" in defense forces, as well as the big
Japanese companies which manufacture weapons.[25] Japan's
plans to purchase advanced planes from the US, such as
F-15 fighters and P-3C anti-submarine aircraft, signalled to the Soviets the Japanese intention to expand
military strength.[26] In addition, the JDA was preparing
emergency legislation to broaden powers in event of war.
These and similar steps, according to Pravda, indicated
that "military circles are attempting, not always publicly but methodically and persistently, to expand their
influence in the political life of the country."[27]
     The strengthening of the SDF paralleled the expan-
sion of the "military alliance" between the US and Japan, with the Pentagon demanding that Japan play a larger
role. Defense cooperation would inevitably draw Japan
into US military actions, Pravda reported.[28] Japan's
defense activities clearly contravened the constitution
because the SDF is

          fitted out with the latest military equipment,
     which is far from being of a defensive character.
     It has tanks, heavy artillery, missiles and air-
     force. The country has 2,450 military bases and
     installations. From 1960 to 1970, Japan's military
     spendings trebled from 160,000 million to 569,500
     million yen a year.[29]

     Certain psychological taboos were also broken in
Japan, and this the Soviets saw as a dangerous development. General Kurisu's article on the argument that
offensive power is the best defense, was seen as one
example of this trend.[30] Business circles were portrayed
as favoring military buildup as a way to cure the reces-
sion underway in Japan.
     In the government, the old reluctance to name any
hypothetical enemy was replaced by identification of the
USSR as the most likely attacker.[31] Kanemaru, JDA Director General, was portrayed by Tass as "scaring the
Japanese people with the prospect of a Soviet attack for
one definite objective: to justify Japan's enforced
militarization," as well as to strengthen stronger US-
Japan defense relations.[32] Tass pointed out that

Kanemaru also favored signing the Treaty of Peace and
Friendship with China, containing "a clause directly
aimed against the Soviet Union." Thus, "the point of
the strategic plans of the Japanese militarists is aimed
at the Soviet Union. At present, apparently, the Japanese military leaders would like to use Peking as their
own secret weapon."[33]

Japan's rejection of the proffered treaty of neighborliness and cooperation, gravitation towards the PRC,
and defense expansion program probably signified to the
Soviet leadership that a potential threat was brewing in
eastern Siberia, and that little additional diplomatic
leverage over Japan would be lost if a more forceful
posture was taken. In early April 1978, Leonid Brezhnev
visited the Soviet Far East. Accompanying him was Ustinov, the USSR minister of defense, and Admiral Gorshkov.
Gorshkov was the driving force behind the modernization
of the Soviet fleet and its transformation into a formidable extension of his nation's military power.

In Vladivostok, Brezhnev, his group, and Pacific
Fleet commanders watched a naval exercise involving
opposing forces. Brezhnev remarked that seamen "had
fought skillfully against submarines, surface vessels
and airplanes." A unit commander replied that the unit
"is implementing with determination the demands of the
USSR Constitution to reliably defend our socialist fatherland and always be militarily prepared to insure an
immediate rebuff to any aggressor."[34]

On his return to Moscow, Brezhnev gave an account
to the central party. Some of his visit had been concerned with inspection of economic enterprises in Siberia, especially exploitation of natural resources.[35] In
the statement on Brezhnev's Siberian visit, the military
implication was that his meetings with Soviet soldiers
had significance in "further improving the military and
political training of the personnel of the Soviet Armed
Forces."[36] Such a task, however, did not require the
presence of military heavyweights Ustinov and Gorshkov,
so it is safe to assume that the inspection visit considered far more serious issues, including what to do
about the northern territories, and the reorganization
of the Siberian military districts which followed the
visit.

To the Soviets, Kanemaru was the arch-conspirator
in Japan's remilitarization and grand strategy. In July,
Tass called him "this emissary of Japan's militarist
circles" as he estabished contacts with NATO headquarters in Brussels, and then went to Washington to strengthen Japan-US military cooperation. His circumnaviga-
tion, Krasnaya Zvezda (Red Star) claimed, was linked to
new military outlays and calls to equip the SDF with
nuclear weapons.[37] In a television broadcast, the head
of the JDA said that military preparations must be conducted with the USSR as the assumed enemy. General

Kurisu was another alleged militarist in the eyes of the USSR. His outspoken comments on the need for greater defense was proof that the Japanese military wanted greater autonomy and influence.[38] His removal by Kanemaru as chairman of the Joint Staff Council, however, was seen as mere camouflage for military preparations. Kanemaru was branded as a militarist, and his endorsement of the China-Japan treaty was thus prima facie evidence of its anti-Soviet nature.

Thus, Soviet and Japanese mutual images reinforced the expectation of armed expansion on both sides. Each increment of defense was seen as offensive by the other. The beneficiary of this development was Beijing, where Soviet-Japanese confrontation was a means to reduce Soviet military pressure.

THE VIETNAM FACTOR

Soviet reinforcement of the northern islands' garrison indicated hardening of diplomatic attitudes, as well as an escalating Soviet military presence in the north Pacific region. The next Soviet moves - in Southeast Asia - posed a much greater threat to Japan's economic lifelines. Ray Cline, an official of the CIA, interpreted events this way:

> President Jimmy Carter at the end of 1978 began touting the PRC as a friendly, peace-loving quasially of the United States, just preceding its plunge into war with Vietnam early in 1979. The result of the Chinese attack was that the Soviet Union increased its presence - and influence - in Vietnam by moving into former American air bases at Danang and former American naval facilities at Cam Ranh Bay. The sea lanes of Southeast Asia are now much more vulnerable to Soviet interruption than before, and both Japan and South Korea are more liable to Soviet pressure because of their dependency on oil and other trade commodities than reach them via these sea lanes. How could the United States have better assisted our enemies at the expense of our friends in that part of the world?[39]

The Vietnam case is cited by Cline to illustrate his thesis that "strategic coherence has been almost totally lacking in the Carter administration." It is not entirely correct, however, to see the Soviet military presence as a response to the Chinese attack against Vietnam. Nor was Carter's abetting Chinese intentions a major factor in the eventual Vietnamese invitations to the Russians. This is not to deny Cline's thesis about the lack of strategic coherence, nor to disagree with the results of the Chinese incursion as endangering Japan and the ROK.

It is probable that Sino-Japanese negotiations and conclusion of the 1978 treaty encouraged a tighter Soviet-Vietnam relationship. This parallel diplomatic activity was unrelated in the eyes of Japanese diplomats during the summer of 1978, when Vietnam entered COMECON. Japan had made aid commitments to Hanoi, and Japanese companies were discussing oceanic drilling for oil with the Vietnam government.[40] Even when China cut off aid to Vietnam in July, the Fukuda government expressed intentions to continue its own assistance. Vietnamese Foreign Vice Minister Phan Hien visited Tokyo in July and pledged that Vietnam would follow an independent line between Moscow and Beijing. He was highly critical of China and expressed hope for US-Vietnam normalization.[41]

When Sonoda announced that China had suspended aid to Vietnam, he indicated that this might bring the Sino-Soviet confrontation into Southeast Asia.[42] Nevertheless, the foreign minister maintained that there was no connection between the aid suspension and China-Japan negotiations. In September Deng Xiaoping expressed annoyance at continued Japanese aid to Vietnam - a country described as a "small hegemonist."[43]

In the growing tension in Indochina, Japan sought to maintain a balanced presence. In addition to a program of 10 billion yen in aid to Vietnam, Japan discussed economic cooperation with the Pol Pot government in Kampuchea as well. (The Japanese ambassador to China was concurrently ambassador to Kampuchea and visited the country in early September.)

The signing of the USSR-Vietnam treaty on 3 November 1978 was officially viewed in Japan as a move to aid in Vietnam economic reconstruction.[44] The Foreign Ministry hesitated to conclude that Vietnam had abandoned its independent line, and indicated that the treaty seemed weaker than other similar kinds of treaties with African and Asian nations.[45]

The treaty contained one article with military implications:

> The two parties signatory to the Treaty shall exchange views on all important international questions relating to the interests of the two countries. In case either party is attacked or threatened with attack, the two parties signatory to the Treaty shall immediately consult each other with a view to eliminating that threat, and shall take appropriate and effective measures to safeguard peace and the security of the two countries. (Article 6)

The Japanese Foreign Ministry admitted that the treaty probably had the intention of countering China.

The Japan government did not admit the obvious possibility, however, that the Soviet-Vietnam treaty was a countermove against the Japan-China treaty, signed 53

days earlier. The Nihon Keizai was more blunt, and in
an editorial, saw Article Six as indicating a military
alliance.[46] The draft Japanese-Soviet friendship and
cooperation treaty, published in Izvestia, also provided
for mutual consultations in emergency.

The Soviet Union seems to hold the position or
principle that a friendship and cooperation treaty
should 'primarily' provide for a kind of military
alliance. It can be thought that the Soviet Union's
opposition to the conclusion of a Japan-China peace
treaty had its background in such a position.[47]

The Foreign Ministry preferred to stress the aspect
of economic cooperation in the Soviet-Vietnam treaty,
but Nihon Keizai saw other reasons:

The Soviet Union has been endeavoring to conclude
friendship and cooperation treaties with those
nations in important strategic positions. Conse-
quently, these treaties, when viewed by third nations, strongly reflect the Soviet Union's own
world strategy, rather than the intention of helping the economic and social development of these
nations or extending aid for the maintenance of
their security.[48]

Further linkage of Vietnam and the Japan-China
treaty was provided when Polish Premier Jaroszewicz
visited Fukuda in November. The premier said he understood Japan's peaceful intentions in the Japan-China
treaty, but "China interprets the Treaty as anti-USSR,
and is trying to extend the effects of the Treaty all
over the world." He also criticized China as "trying to
take a hegemonistic policy toward neighboring countries,
such as Vietnam."[49]

To the PRC, the Soviet treaty with Vietnam was
clearly a military alliance, especially coming on the
eve of "a Soviet-backed attack waged by Vietnam on Kampuchea."[50] This treaty and the one concluded between
the USSR and Afghanistan were interpreted as part of
"the Kremlin's southward push" towards the Indian Ocean.
China characterized Soviet strategy as follows:

Success in making a breakthrough to the Indian
Ocean would enable the Kremlin to turn eastward to
meet halfway its advance southwestward from its far
eastern territories. This would pave the way for
penetration into the smaller countries in Southeast
Asia and the Asia-Pacific region in general and
control over the sea lane linking the Indian Ocean
with the west Pacific. It is intended to undermine
the U.S. position in the west Pacific, threaten the
oil supply route to Japan and encircle China. In

the other direction where the Kremlin's emphasis
lies, this would facilitate its move to the west to
consolidate with its gains in the Middle East and
Africa, and so place under its control the passages
from the Indian Ocean to the Mediterranean and to
Europe around the Cape of Good Hope.[51]

Ironically, the Chinese accepted the legacy of the "dom-
ino theory" from the US, which had tried and failed to
bolster support for war against Vietnamese communism by
referring to the threat to the rest of Southeast Asia.
The Chinese invoked the far more extensive threat of
Soviet world adventures. A few days prior to China's
"counterattack" against Vietnam, Renmin Ribao proclaimed:

> With the fall of Phnom Penh, the specter of "domi-
> noes" is again present in Asia. People have an-
> xiously asked: The Soviet-Vietnamese hegemonists
> have brazenly captured Kampuchea by force today;
> where will they strike tomorrow?

> The lords of the Kremlin are major players of domi-
> noes. They have toyed with one sovereign state
> after another like dominoes, toppling one today and
> annexing another tomorrow. They also tried to make
> a sudden breakthrough over an extensive area so as
> to turn all countries into their vassals or protec-
> torates. Their game table is enormous, covering
> the whole world, including land and seas. They have
> advanced on the Horn of Africa, stained the shores
> of the Red Sea with blood, staged coups d'état in
> South Asia and backed subversives in the Persian
> Gulf. They have used mercenaries and armed bandits
> in large-scale wars in central Africa and engaged
> in neocolonialist deals in a big way under the ban-
> ner of supporting national liberation. They use
> colored people to fight colored people and let
> others make sacrifices while they enjoy the fruits
> and become "overlords." Wherever they have suc-
> ceeded, they have used so-called "friendship" trea-
> ties as shackles to tie down the territory and sov-
> ereignty of others. Every domino they have toyed
> with or toppled is stained with the blood, tears
> and suffering of countless people.[52]

The next few months after the Soviet-Vietnam treaty
witnessed rapidly escalating tension in the region. The
JDA noted Soviet ships making port calls at Cam Ranh
Bay, and became concerned that Soviet naval presence in
the region could strangle Japan's oil shipping lines.[53]
Vietnam was approximately half way between Japan and the
Mideast, where 80% of Japanese oil originated. With the
US navy distracted in the Mideast and Africa, Japan's

security could be endangered. If Cam Ranh Bay became a
Russian naval base, it would solve a perennial problem
of refuelling for operations in the region.
     The Chinese saw global and regional geopolitics be-
hind Soviet moves in south and southeast Asia. Renmin
Ribao quoted Mackinder and Mahan to support China's
claim that control of the south Asian "crescent," from
the Red Sea to the Strait of Malacca, would enable the
USSR to control the seven seas and the world.[54] The
Soviets and their Cuban clients were engaged in a pincer
movement from the Horn of Africa to Vietnam, as well as
in naval deployment in the Red Sea, Persian Gulf, and
Indian Ocean. With access to Vietnamese air fields and
ports, Soviet air and naval forces could link its Indian
and Pacific operations, and pose threats to shipping
around Southeast Asia, With bases in Vietnam, the USSR
could close in on the Malacca Strait, and strangle Japan's shipping from the Middle East.
     Japan was still providing economic aid to Vietnam
in 1978. Sonoda pointed to this when the Soviets criticized Japan for leaning towards China.[55] As Vietnam
moved closer to the USSR and launched its attack on Kampuchea, it became increasingly difficult for Japan to
maintain its aid program. Vietnamese Deputy Prime Minister Nguyen Duy Trinh, concurrently foreign minister,
visited Tokyo in mid-December. Earlier, Japan had indicated its intention to continue aid after the Soviet-
Vietnam treaty. The Vietnam foreign minister stressed
that his country's autonomous orientation would not
change. The treaty with the USSR would contribute to
economic reconstruction, but Vietnam remained a member
of the non-aligned movement,[56] a statement greeted with
skepticism.
     Trinh also held talks with Sonoda, who stated that
ASEAN anxieties about Vietnam made Japanese aid to Vietnam difficult.[57] Sonoda also was anxious about the possible Sino-Soviet confrontation in the Indochina peninsula. The results of the talks were released on December
19: Japan would extend 4 billion yen in non-reimbursable
aid and 10 billion in reimbursable aid during the next
fiscal year. In addition, 150,000 tons of Japanese rice
was to be loaned in consideration of the food shortage.
Japan would not comply with Vietnam's request for aid on
projects until Tokyo had ascertained that its policy of
autonomy and nonalignment would continue.[58]
     Before the year was out, Vietnam invaded Kampuchea
and pushed Pol Pot out of Phnom Penh. As the head of a
regime responsible for the slaughter of hundreds of
thousands of his countrymen, his forcible removal from
the capital brought more relief than outrage. Vietnamese
sponsorship of Heng Samrin, however, was not based on
humanitarian considerations. The new rulers of Kampuchea
ousted the Chinese clients, and installed a government
which was ultimately dependent on the USSR through

155

Vietnam. In response, the Japanese government froze the
scheduled economic aid and also the relief rice. This
decision cost Vietnam 36 billion yen over four years.[59]
On 23 March 1978, Hanoi had closed around 30,000
private businesses in Vietnam, most of which were owned
by ethnic Chinese.* This decision, and growing tensions
between China and Vietnam set off the exodus of ethnic
Chinese from Vietnam. Tensions grew worse, and on 16
June China withdrew its ambassador from Hanoi. It is
possible that Brezezinski's visit to China in May also
played a role in stiffening China's attitude. His account of US security goals was depicted as "perhaps providing indirect encouragement to Beijing for an increasingly militant stance toward Hanoi."[60]
China reduced aid to Hanoi in mid-June, and suspended it completely on 3 July, following Vietnamese entry into COMECON. Negotiations convering the 1.7 million
Chinese living in Vietnam broke off in late August.
Vietnam hoped to normalize relations with the US, and
dropped its claim for economic aid from Washington. The
US, however, was in no hurry to normalize relations with
Hanoi for a number of reasons, including: (1) Vietnam's
forcible expulsion of hundreds of thousands of citizens;
(2) the closer relations between Hanoi and Moscow; (3)
lack of progress in locating US servicemen who were
unaccounted for since the end of the Vietnam war; and
(4) Vietnam's continued expansionism in Indochina.
On Christmas 1978, 12 Vietnamese divisions invaded
Kampuchea. It was ostensibly undertaken by the Kampuchean National United Front, led by Heng Samrin, to drive
out the Pol Pot regime. By 7 January 1979, the Kampuchean capital was taken, and the defeated forces retired
to mountains and rural areas to conduct guerrilla warfare against the Vietnamese and their collaborators.
The fall of Pol Pot was a setback for the Chinese, who
were unable to protect their Kampuchean allies. Vietnam
was already closely linked to Moscow, and dominated
Laos. Hanoi's goal appeared to be an Indochinese federation under its own control, proclaimed Chen Chu, Beijing's ambassador to the UN.[61]
While the Vietnam-Kampuchea dispute had been sim-
mering, Sino-Vietnamese relations continued to deteriorate. From the situation of close friendship during the
war against the US, relations worsened almost immediately after the war ended. The two countries disputed the
Paracel and other islands groups. By November 1977, the
PRC called Vietnam a "minor hegemonist." The 480-mile
border between the two countries was demarcated by bar-
bed wire and other barriers, while border incidents

*This account of events leading to and including the
Sino-Vietnam conflict is a summary of Asian Security
1979, pp. 95-126.

156

increased: over 100 in 1974; over 400 in 1975; 900 or
more in 1976; 752 in 1977; and 1108 in 1978, according
to Chen Chu.[62]

From early January 1979, the Chinese moved troops
towards Vietnam and on 17 February, launched an attack
on the full length of the border. The total Chinese
forces amounted to about 320,000 men, and were under
command of Xu Shiyou, who later served as minister of
defense. The actual attack was commanded by Yang Dezhi,
and was supported by about 700 fighter aircraft. Vietnamese forces were scattered prior to the attack - 12
divisions in Kampuchea, 3-4 in Laos, and only 5-6
against China. The Chinese campaign lasted 27 days, and
accomplished the capture of the provincial capital of
Lang Son, on the road to Hanoi. Vietnamese forces were
withdrawn from Kampuchea to meet the Chinese attack, but
no counteroffensive was launched. By March 16, the
Chinese withdrew their forces.

One result of the short war was that the Soviet
Union increased its naval presence in the Vietnamese
area, bringing logistical support to their allies, and
deploying ships in the South and East China Seas. China
demonstrated that it was a major regional power and
would intervene to help its Kampuchean ally, although
this was not the official reason for the Chinese
attack.[63]

China was risking that the USSR would not intervene
by launching a countermove, but took precautions nevertheless. A "top level war alert" was announced when the
fighting started, and a general mobilization order was
issued in Guangzhou.[64] Civilians living along the Sino-
Soviet borders in Heilongjiang and Xinjiang were evacu-
ated more than 30 kilometers from the frontier, even
before Chinese troops entered Vietnam.[65] Soviet aid to
Vietnam was limited, and no further action was taken
against China.

The Chinese attack was more an embarrassment than a
surprise to the US. US intelligence had indicated China's military concentration on Vietnam's borders in
early February 1979.[66] Approximately 10 army divisions,
more than 150 aircraft, many tanks and military vehicles
were poised for a showdown against Vietnam. A US official considered that if China made an attack, it would
be similar to the 1962 China-India border incident.
China would attack in a blitz 25-50 kilometers into
Vietnam, then withdraw. The final decision on the attack
would probably come when Deng returned from Washington.
The US government officially opposed any military attack
along the border, and feared that the Chinese action so
soon after Deng's visit it would appear that a joint US-
China decision on the war was made.

Japan's government asked both China and Vietnam to
solve their border dispute peacefully, and asked third
countries, especially the USSR, to refrain from any

action which would cause further deterioration of the Indochinese situation. Foreign Minister Sonoda told a Diet hearing that the government had proposed a cease-fire.[67] The Japan Foreign Ministry claimed that it was "conducting positive diplomacy on such a scale as unprecedented in postwar history for the settlement of an international dispute."[68]

The Tokyo Shimbun was less enthusiastic about Gaimusho efforts however: (author's emphasis)

> We appreciate such a diplomatic posture, but we cannot appreciate the Foreign Ministry's ability to judge the situation. The Foreign Ministry made a mistake in formulating prospects as to the revolution in Iran, and also, its judgment on the situation in Cambodia was too optimistic, even though leaders in nations concerned were double-tongued. In regard to the China-Vietnam dispute, the Japan-China Treaty triggered it, in a certain respect, that is, the Japan-China Treaty gave birth to the Soviet-Vietnam Treaty, which caused Vietnam's military intervention in Cambodia, and this brought about Chinese forces' advance into Vietnam. The Foreign Ministry did not fully perceive these chain reactions. The Ministry should probably self-reflect severely on its way of collecting and analyzing information.[69]

The Chinese incursion into Vietnam shattered many illusions about the PRC being a peace-loving nation. Sonoda's claim that the Japan-China treaty strengthened peace and stability in the region was shaken. Even worse, the short war activated the military potentiality of the Soviet-Vietnam treaty. While China took the risk that the USSR might attack in retaliation, the resultant Soviet submarine and other naval port calls in Vietnam may be an even more destabilizing development in the long run.

If China had demonstrated its will to oppose Vietnamese "hegemony" and save its ally Kampuchea at risk of war, it also helped to expand Sino-Soviet conflict to areas heretofore uninvolved. Japan, by August 1978, had acquiesced in an anti-hegemony treaty, and was feeling Soviet pressure as a result. With the short China-Vietnam war, Soviet air and naval presence was extended to Southeast Asia, posing a new threat for Japan and ASEAN as well. China has claimed that these developments merely proved the hegemonistic nature of the USSR. From another perspective, however, it seems that expanded Soviet activities have served to diffuse the Soviet threat to China and arouse other countries' hostility to Moscow. The result has been to project the Sino-Soviet dispute into a world-wide confrontation.

China's united front diplomacy has been highly

successful, and leaders in Japan, Western Europe and the US seem hardly aware of what has happened. China has modified its institutional structure to modernize the country and also to accommodate the requirements of non-communist industrial countries for trade and joint investment. Although legitimated in Marxist-Leninist terms as a temporary united front, the current policy of the PRC is also a modern form of "using barbarians to control the barbarians." In the current case, if suspicions between the USSR and non-communist countries can be stirred up, China will benefit.

In early March 1979, two Soviet warships entered the military port at Danang for water, fuel, and rest.[70] These were the first Soviet warships to call at Vietnamese ports since the establishment of the Socialist Republic of Vietnam. The Russians had long coveted a port of call in Southeast Asia, since the navy had no transit bases between Aden and Vladivostok. Soviet aid to Vietnam and the Chinese attack in February 1979 produced the long-awaited opportunity. The situation was even more dangerous for Japan, because US military strength was distracted by events in the Middle East, and unlikely to oppose Soviet activities in Vietnam.

The JDA viewed Soviet activity with anxiety. According to US information, the Soviets were building a communications base and an aviation control tower at Danang - which had been the largest US base abroad during the Vietnam war.[71] With access to Danang, the USSR could repair warships, further develop operations in the Pacific and Indian Oceans, and deploy reconnaissance planes from the air base. It was also feared that Soviet Backfire bombers could be moved there in an emergency.

Japan threatened to suspend all aid to Vietnam if it was made into a Soviet base.[72] The Vietnamese ambassador to Japan stressed that the Soviet presence was essential for stability in Southeast Asia.[73] China's warning of a second possible counterattack pushed Vietnam into further dependence on their Soviet ally. The Japanese ambassador to Vietnam saw Hanoi's dependence on the USSR increasing in rough proportion to the Chinese threat.[74] The Vietnam position was that "there are no Soviet bases, but for the purpose of defense from the Chinese threat, its using of bases is being recognized as a temporary measure." Vietnam, according to Ambassador Hasegawa in May, had not concluded an agreement on the use of the bases. He thought that if a second war were to start, Vietnam might hand over the bases to the USSR.

In May 1979, JDA Director Yamashita visited China and talked with Vice Minister of Defense, Su Yu. Both expressed concern about the strengthening of Soviet forces in the Far East, and especially the Soviet use of Vietnam ports and bases.[75] Su Yu indicated that the USSR continued to deploy large numbers of military forces on

the Sino-Soviet border, and that the Soviet warship
calls at Cam Ranh Bay are more dangerous for Japan than
for China. From the Soviet perspective, such discussions
probably implied a de facto military relationship between the two countries, although Yamashita avoided
direct reference to the "Soviet threat."

Besides the possibility of Vietnam becoming a Soviet base in Southeast Asia, Japan expressed concern over
Vietnamese expulsion of hundreds of thousands of refugees and the continued presence of Vietnamese troops in
Kampuchea.[76] On the refugee issue, a report by the US
State Department stated that Vietnam had collected $120
million in exit fees from the expellees - a sum which
coincided with the amount of foreign currency reserves
in Vietnam.[77]. Vietnam had concluded that the 1.5 million Vietnamese of Chinese descent were potential sub-
versives, and thus had to be expelled.

In August 1979, Japan announced that aid to Vietnam
would be resumed, because the outflow of refugees was to
be held down - a precondition for the resumption on
which Hanoi agreed.[78] From the 54,781 refugees of June,
the outflow dropped to 17,769 in July 1979. China and
ASEAN opposed aid resumption, but Sonoda thought that
aid channels have Japan an opportunity to take diplomatic leadership in Indochina diplomacy.[79] Japan also
hoped to mediate between Vietnam and the US and to establish diplomatic relations between them. An aid package of $50 million was hardly likely to buy the influ-
ence Sonoda wanted, but at the ASEAN conference in Bali,
Sonoda stated that Japan's aid to Vietnam would be a
lever for Asian peace and stability.[80] The Pol Pot
government, ASEAN and China thought that even non-military aid was a form of support for Vietnamese military
activities, and tried to convince Japan not to resume
the aid.

Neither Japanese aid nor sincerity had much effect.
The JDA confirmed that the Soviet navy had granted eight
warships to the Vietnam navy since the Soviet-Vietnam
treaty.[81] These ships were limited to coastal guard,
but could be useful against small Chinese ships which
had been supporting Pol Pot. Moreover, the linking of
the Soviet and Vietnamese navies would be a further
threat to Japanese shipping in the region, according to
the JDA.

A greater threat to Japanese ships was the Soviet
submarines which began calling at Vietnamese ports in
the spring of 1979. The US indicated that medium-sized,
Fox-class subs were regularly visiting Cam Ranh Bay.
The first visits were reported at the time of the Sino-
Vietnam war. Cam Ranh Bay became the only port of call
between Vladivostok and Sri Lanka for Soviet subs.[82]

CONCLUSION

The Christmas 1979 invasion of Afghanistan opened up a new front in East-West confrontation. The Soviet takeover in Kabul outraged much of the world, and set off temporary sanctions by the US and its allies. To China, it was simply the latest validation of the hegemony thesis of Soviet behavior. To many in Japan and the West, the Soviet invasion was the prelude to southward expansion into the Middle East. History may show that it was none of these - that it was simply a desperate attempt by the Soviets to prop up its influence in a Marxist regime, or an isolated opportunity to install a more dependable client.

Whatever the actual reasons, the Afghanistan incident was a convincing display of Soviet military might and will which demonstrated a capacity to act with overwhelming force anywhere along the border. It had a sobering effect on many who had previously ignored the implications of the Soviet eastern military buildup.

This military buildup had achieved considerable momentum in Asia during the second half of the 1970s, as noted earlier. Now, with access to ports in Vietnam, the Soviet fleet could target missiles into China from all directions. It could challenge the US fleet in the Pacific and Indian Oceans in the near future, and it could blockade Japan's shipping lanes. These three states posed the greater potential threat to Soviet Asia, and so they could be expected to be targets of the Soviet military machine in event of war.

However, the Soviet Foreign Ministry and Defense Ministry were working at cross purposes. In Asia, it was in Moscow's best interest to prevent a military alliance among the US, the PRC, and Japan. Territory, treaties, and trade were the most effective instruments which Soviet diplomacy had at its disposal to negotiate with Japan, but these proved little match for what China offered. Whatever flexibility Soviet diplomats may have had in the territorial question, it was cancelled with the 1978 military reinforcement of the northern islands. The Soviet unilateral closure of discussions on the territory issue ruled out a peace treaty. With Soviet intervention in Afghanistan, trade between Japan and the USSR nearly came to a halt. Furthermore, the Soviet land, air and naval buildup in the Far East has tightened the US-Japan security relationship, and stimulated greater Japanese willingness to strengthen its defenses. Soviet military activity has also made Sino-US military cooperation a greater possibility.

In undertaking to explain the motivations for the Soviet buildup in East Asia, four possible reasons can be mentioned: first, Moscow needs to defend its Central and East Asian territories against possible Chinese revanchism. Border skirmishes continue, and China

continues to claim territories now inside the USSR. The
Soviets fear that war over these lands is a future possibility. Second, Japan is overcoming its past subordi-
nation to the US economy. This may someday be translated
into military power which could be dangerous to Soviet
Far Eastern territory. Most dangerous would be a triple
entente against the Soviet Union. The Soviet military
buildup can thus be interpreted as preemptive defense
against future contingencies, and a demonstration to
Japan that it cannot rearm or ally with China and the US
without incurring high costs to itself.

Third, the Soviet buildup merely reinforces a territorial status quo in Asia against Chinese and Japanese
claims. With superior military forces in place, neither
country will lightly risk military adventures against
Soviet territories. Moreover, the presence of Soviet
forces increases the cost to the Chinese of undertaking
actions against Soviet allies. Had the Chinese continued
their "counterattack" against Vietnam by attempting to
take Hanoi, Soviet armor thrusts into Xinjiang or Heilongjiang were within the realm of possibility.

Fourth, the Soviet buildup strengthens the worldwide strategic position. Naval presence in the ocean
perimeters of Asia gives the USSR greater capability
against the US than was possible earlier. It also allows
the Soviets to show the flag more frequently and to
assist clients and allies in the third world. In this
sense, the Soviet military buildup is part of the larger
ongoing struggle between the USSR and the US.

In light of these reasons, the Japan-China treaty
was a factor in the Soviet buildup. The treaty of 1978
was both a contributing cause and an effect of Soviet
security strengthening in the Far East. This is not to
assign exclusive responsibility either to the Soviet
buildup or to the China-Japan treaty as a cause for
increased tensions in East Asia. Both developments
created dispositions which resulted in higher levels of
tension. Soviet mistrust of Sino-Japanese collaboration
and of US-Japan defense cooperation, disposed the USSR
to greater anxiety over its Far Eastern possessions.
Japanese anxieties over Soviet intentions in the region
no doubt disposed Tokyo to take a harder line on defense
matters. Thus far, Japan has exercised self-restraint
both in its relations with China, and in expansion of
defense forces. If this self-restraint dissolves, we
may see even higher levels of tension in the region.

Relations between Japan and the USSR have never
been amicable for an extended period, although there has
been trade and other economic cooperation. At the beginning of the 1980s, we can identify several sources of
contention between the two states:

The major reason has been the Japan-China treaty
itself. Despite disavowals by Japan that it is not
directed against any third country, the USSR sees it as

a strengthening of the anti-Soviet line of China. Japanese assistance to China's modernization is characterized as ultimately assisting military buildup.

The second reason for declining relations has been the issue of the northern territories. Both sides have hardened their position, and the Diet passed resolutions condemning the USSR for its military buildup. In 1981, the government declared 7 February to be "Northern Territories Day," to keep the issue alive. The USSR has said it will never return the islands.

A third reason has been the increasing sense of Soviet military threat. Overflights (nicknamed the "Tokyo Express") increasingly test Japan reactions and defenses, while the incident of a Soviet submarine violating Japanese waters in September 1980 heightened Japan's concerns. Increased activities of the Soviet navy in the international waters around Japan, and in Southeast Asia have stimulated anxieties about the country's vulnerability. The JDA has identified the USSR as the most likely aggressor against Japan, and argues that defenses must be expanded to meet specific threats.

A fourth source of friction between the USSR and Japan has been the problem of fisheries. Japanese resent that agreements must be renegotiated every year. Increasing use of fishing grounds for military maneuvers has restricted activities in a vital sector of Japan's food economy. Occasional seizure of Japanese fishing vessels and coercion of crews into espionage activities has produced more ill-feeling.

Finally, the Soviet intervention in Afghanistan has created a new burden on Japan-Soviet relations. Japan joined the US in trade sanctions and in boycotting the Moscow Olympics. A pending visit by Soviet parliamentarians was "postponed" by Japan, and visits by Soviet officials were severely restricted. Trade declined, and Japan Air Lines requested permission to allow a cutback in flights to Moscow because of declining passenger traffic.

If better diplomatic relations between Japan and the USSR must await conclusion of the peace treaty, the prospects in the early 1980s do not look promising. In November 1980, a Japanese-Soviet round-table conference was held in Moscow. Japan's delegation raised objections to Soviet intervention in Afghanistan and the military buildup of the northern territories. In another session, the Soviet side submitted a proposal to improve Soviet-Japan relations in three stages: reduce friction in various areas; discuss and conclude a treaty of good neighborliness and cooperation; and finally, a peace treaty.[83]

Concerning Japan's objections to the draft, the Soviet side maintains that it is only a draft, and can be altered through diplomatic discussions. In the aftermath of Afghanistan, Japanese distrust of the USSR has been heightened, and it is unlikely that modification of the treaty will lead to Japanese acceptance - even for preliminary discussions. Without some spirit of mutual trust and mutual advantage, which the Japanese perceived in relations with China in 1978, a Japan-Soviet friendship treaty is not likely to be concluded.

The Japanese Foreign Ministry and other sectors were not enthusiastic about signing a friendship treaty with the Soviets. Similar treaties had been signed with Afghanistan and Vietnam. On 12 January 1980, Brezhnev stated that the USSR forces has entered Afghanistan in response to the terms of the treaty with that country.[84] Quite naturally, the Japanese became skeptical about signing a similar treaty. Article Four of the draft treaty was similar to the emergency consultation clause in the Soviet-Vietnam treaty. With classic understatement, Foreign Minister Okita, on 10 January 1980, said: "The logic is strange that the Soviet Union can enter other countries because there are treaties of good neighborliness, friendship and co-operation, concluded with them. Japan, on its part, must study the Afghanistan problem and learn lessons from the results of the studies."[85]

To these more recent difficulties can be added the historical burdens of mutual distrust, as well as cultural-psychological incompatibility. The two nations developed and industrialized in the late nineteenth century, and found themselves in competition for power in Northeast Asia. The Russo-Japanese War, Japan's intervention in Siberia after world war one, expansive Japanese militarism in Asia, and Soviet mistreatment of Japanese prisoners of war have left scars not easy to erase. The USSR is consistently selected as the least liked country in popular opinion polls.

The Japanese embraced modernity and its material benefits. The Russians have had it thrust on them, and its impact has been more in areas relevant to military than to consumer uses. The Japanese have had a long history of religious diversity, with mutual accommodations of Shinto, Buddhism and innumerable sects. The Russian church saw itself as the "third Rome," and the last bastion of pure Christianity. The tsar was the chief guardian of the faith. Both societies are derivative from older civilizations.[86] The Russians lack natural frontiers around much of its periphery, with the result that invaders found the state easy to penetrate once defenses were defeated. On the other hand, there have been few natural barriers to Russian expansion. The Japanese are accustomed to limited space and natural boundaries for many centuries. They had no problem of integrating conquered peoples since the Ainus, and so do not have to devise an artificial citizenship such as "Soviet."

The Japanese and Russians have little except their humanity and proximity in common, and it is this latter which has been the source of conflict for a century. As Japan emerges from its decades of recovery from the war, and from under the US shadow, is the prewar rivalry in East Asia to be revived?

Much will depend on US actions in the East Asian region. Soviet activities have contributed to a Japanese disposition to rearm, but other variables are also relevant. In particular, US rapprochement with the PRC will make the USSR even more concerned about Far Eastern security. Because the US and Japan are linked by a security treaty, Japan will be intimately affected by US foreign policy. Both of these aspects will be examined before we focus specifically on Japan's defense question.

Footnotes

1. Stuart E. Johnson, with Joseph A. Yager, The Military Equation in Northeast Asia (Washington, D.C.: The Brookings Institution, 1979).
2. Ibid., p. 14.
3. Defense of Japan 1977, p. 7.
4. Ibid., pp. 17-18.
5. Ibid., p. 21.
6. Ibid., p. 22.
7. Defense of Japan 1980, p. 261.
8. Defense of Japan 1978, p. 17.
9. Ibid., p. 28.
10. Ibid., p. 37.
11. Defense of Japan 1979, p. 9.
12. Ibid., pp. 20-22.
13. Ibid., p. 36.
14. Ibid., pp. 36-37.
15. Defense of Japan 1980, p. 6.
16. Ibid., p. 11.
17. Ibid., p. 54.
18. Ibid.
19. SK, 1 August 1979, p. 9.
20. YS, 8 January 1978, p. 2.
21. TS., 11 November 1978, pp. 8-9.
22. YS., 28 September 1978, p. 1.
23. Defense of Japan 1980, "Foreward."
24. As of 31 March 1978, the actual strength of the SDF was given as 239,982. Defense of Japan 1978, p.213.
25. DR:USSR, 24 January 1978, p. M3.
26. DR:USSR, 25 January 1978, p. M3.
27. DR:USSR, 6 February 1978, p. M1.
28. Ibid., p. M2.
29. DR:USSR, 21 February 198, p. M3.
30. DR:USSR, 1 March 1978, p. M2.
31. DR:USSR, 6 April 1978, p. M1.
32. Ibid.
33. Ibid.
34. DR:USSR, 7 April 1978, p. R1.

35. DR:USSR, 17 April 1978, p. R1.
36. Ibid., p. R2.
37. DR:USSR, 3 July 1978, p. M4.
38. DR:USSR, 2 August 1987, p. M1.
39. "The Future of U.S. Foreign Intelligence Operations," in The United States in the 1980s, eds. Peter Duignan and Alvin Rabushka (Stanford, CA.: Hoover Institution, 1980), pp. 486-487.
40. NK., 23 March 1978, p. 6.
41. AS., 9 July 1978, p. 1.
42. YS., 4 July 1978, p. 1.
43. SK, 8 September 1978, p. 6.
44. TS, 5 November 1978, p. 2.
45. AS, 8 November 1978, p. 2.
46. NK, 7 November 1978, p. 2.
47. Ibid.
48. Ibid.
49. NK., 16 November 1978, p 2.
50. DR:China, 3 January 1979, p. A9.
51. Ibid., p. A10.
52. DR:China, 23 February 1979, p. A15.
53. SK, 18 November 1978, p. 1.
54. DR:China, 29 June 1979, p. C2.
55. S, 16 December 1978, p. 2.
56. YS, 18 December 1978, p. 7.
57. YS, 16 December 1978, p. 1.
58. YS, 20 December 1978, p. 2.
59. MS, 10 January 1979, p. 1.
60. Asian Security 1979, p. 96.
61. DR:China, 26 February 1979, p. A23.
62. Ibid., p. A24.
63. DR:China, 21 February 1979, p. A5.
64. Ibid., p. A9.
65. DR:China, 27 February 1979, p. A4.
66. AS, 3 February 1979, p. 1.
67. DR:China, 27 February 1979, p. A4.
68. TS, 19 March 1979, p. 4.
69. Ibid.
70. TS, 10 March 1979, p. 4.
71. MS, 26 March 1979, p. 2.
72. AS, 11 April 1979, p. 2.
73. NK, 21 April 1979, p. 2.
74. SK, 21 May 1979, p. 3.
75. AW, 19 May 1979, p. 2.
76. YS, 10 June 1979, p. 2.
77. MS, 24 July 1979, p. 2.
78. NK, 15 August 1979, p. 1.
79. Ibid.
80. YS, 29 July 1979, p. 2.
81. YS, 10 October 1979, p. 2.
82. MS, 5 October 1979, p. 1.
83. DR:China, 24 November 1980, pp. D4-D5.
84. NK, 13 January 1980, p. 2.
85. Ibid.

86. Marius Jansen, "On Foreign Borrowing," in Albert M. Craig, ed., Japan: A Comparative View (Princeton, N.J.: Princeton University Press, 1979), pp. 18-48.

8
U.S.-China Rapprochement and Japan

When President Nixon announced his intention to visit Beijing in early 1972, the Japanese government considered itself a victim of "Nixon shock." When Carter announced normalization of relations with the PRC on 15 December 1978, it was a "Carter shock." The latter move had been expected, but again Tokyo had not been accorded the normal trust due to an important ally. In any event, normalization of relations between the US and China was a major watershed in international relations. Michael Oksenberg, who was on the staff of the National Security Council during the Carter administration, considered the China connection "perhaps the single most successful foreign policy the United States has pursued" for nearly a decade."[1]

In establishing links between the wealthiest country and the most populous one in the world, the US-PRC rapprochement has undoubtedly been successful. But whether the terms of the arrangement, the timing and the expectations in certain quarters of the US will be most conducive to peace and stability in the East Asian region is another question.[2] The terms of normalization required the US to sever official defense and diplomatic relations with Taiwan, although Congress subsequently passed the Taiwan Relations Act, restoring more links than Beijing or Carter wished the US to have.[3] As to timing, it came when negotiations over SALT II were nearing fruition, and may have been used to prod the USSR into moving more quickly in making concessions. Also, the normalization announcement came less than a hundred days after the China-Japan PFT, which the USSR had denounced as anti-Soviet. With Japan's strong links with the US and an increasing tilt towards China, US normalization with Beijing appeared to complete the strategic triangle in the Far East which Moscow held with grave suspicion.

There was also an expectation in some quarters that cultivation of the Chinese connection could be an important counterweight to the USSR. By supplying arms to

168

Beijing, helping in modernization of the Chinese armed
forces, and encouraging China to stand firm against
Moscow, this persuasion saw two main goals achieved at
minimal cost to the US. First, China would be incorporated into the Western network of states which encir-
cled the USSR. By holding down Soviet troops on the Mongolian and Siberian fronters, the Chinese were preventing greater concentrations against NATO and elsewhere.
By increasing the capability of Chinese forces, greater
diversion of Soviet forces could be accomplished. Secondly, maintenance of the Sino-Soviet conflict was in
the interest of the non-communist world. The Sino-Soviet
alliance in the 1950s was considered to be the major
threat to world peace by the US, and a danger to the
independence of nations on the perimeter of the two communist giants. Breakdown of the alliance into two rival
camps of communism did not immediately enhance peace and
security in the Far East, but it did reduce the perceived threat of their cooperative relationship. With the
demise of Mao and the emergence of Deng Xiaoping and his
pragmatists, the possibility of a pro-US, pro-NATO and
anti-Soviet China was a strategic windfall for the West.
To nurture this situation was sufficient reason to normalize relations and sell modern weapons to China.

The first phase of Carter's new Asian strategy
consisted of the pullout of US forces from South Korea,
and the doctrine of optional presence. Because of a new
reassessment of North Korean capability, and of domestic
pressures in the US, the administration did not carry
out the withdrawal. But the thinking behind this plan
indicated to Asians that the administration wanted disengagement from extensive commitments in the Far East.
The second phase began in 1978 and depended on China
playing an anti-Soviet role. Whether the administration
was responding to the opportunities and domestic pressures, or had worked out an overall strategy to deal
with post-Vietnam Asia, is not clear.

Both aspects of the new Asian strategy exercised
important effects on Japan. The US abrogation of the
Mutual Defense Treaty with Taiwan made Japanese wonder
which defense commitment would next be scrapped. A report that the US government was to examine the effects
of ending the defense agreement with Japan was highly
discomforting. Tokyo could not protest American derecognition of Taiwan, since it had done so six years earlier. But Japan did not have a defense treaty with
Taibei, so the US action was more serious. Also, Taiwan
was mentioned in numerous agreements between the US and
Japan as within the "scope of the Far East," so at the
very least, some technical diplomatic questions had to
be answered.

To Japan, the US-China rapprochement had even more
serious questions with regard to defense matters. As a
junior member of the US-Japan defense pact, Japan could

conceivably be involved in future conflicts with the US
- including those encompassing the US, China, and the
USSR. Whether Tokyo approved or not, a de facto triangle
involving itself, the US and the PRC was emerging in the
region. US global interest may have been enhanced by the
Chinese tilt, but Japan would become more vulnerable.
The USSR could--and did--exert local coercion on the
weakest side of the triangle, and Japan could do very
little in retaliation, as was demonstrated in the case
of the northern islands.

Japan's close alignment with the US had been a
source of many postwar benefits. But for Japan, it has
also been a factor which reduced autonomy in diplomacy.
As long as advantages far outweigh costs, the relationship will continue to be agreeable from Japan's point of
view. After Japan's pro-China tilt of 1978, the US-PRC
rapprochement, Soviet invasion of Afghanistan, and the
end of SALT II détente, the Japanese have found themselves taking an anti-Soviet position. Perhaps the logical outcome of these tendencies will be a remilitarization of the Japanese nation--if it is only the logic of
international security which determines defense policy.
Numerous other variables--such as the constitution, domestic opinion and party system, and economics--also help
to decide defense policy, so Japanese full rearmament is
not inevitable.

In this chapter, we shall examine the Sino-American
rapprochement and its impact on Japan. The main points
of this normalization process are: (1) The PFT probably
accelerated Carter's agenda of normalization; (2) it occurred in a context of cooling US-Soviet relations; and
(3) it has increased the plausibility of a US-China-
Japan triangle against the USSR.

CLOSING THE US-CHINA-JAPAN TRIANGLE

The US and Japan had improved relations with the
PRC during the 1970s, beginning with the Nixon visit
which resulted in the Shanghai Communiqué. Japan went
further in September and established full diplomatic
relations with Beijing--while abrogating formal relations with Taibei. The retention of Japan-Taiwan commercial links was not affected, in an arrangement which had
been hinted in conversations betwen Komeito Chairman
Takeiri Yoshikatsu and Premier Zhou Enlai.[4] Chinese
flexibility on this question was conveyed by Takeiri to
Tanaka, and possibly facilitated normalization in 1972.

Because of the existence of the US-Republic of China (Taiwan) Mutual Defense Treaty, the Taiwan question
was a much greater obstacle in US-PRC normalization. By
1978, Washington was willing to accede to Beijing demands that the Mutual Defense Treaty be abrogated. At
least four reasons can be cited for President Carter's
surrender on the Taiwan issue:

First, the commercial value of trade with China was a major attraction. American allies were reaping significant benefits from their ties with China as the country entered its program of four modernizations. The China-Japan Long Term Trade Agreement was a major instance of rapid penetration of the China market which produced anxiety in US business circles that American corporations would be frozen out. A flourishing trade was not prevented but the US anticipated that commercial connections would be far greater after normalization.

Second, the question of Taiwan security was not seen as a major issue in 1978. The PRC did not have the naval and air capacity to take the island by force. A major military mobilization would be necessary to accomplish "liberation" of Taiwan, with the result of impeding other areas of economic modernization. If the PRC sought to blockade the island, significant damage to Taiwan's foreign trade would occur. But such action could also undo the growing contacts with the US and Japan. US forces had been withdrawn from Taiwan, and PRC policy under Deng's leadership was to seek unification peacefully. The Japanese formula of recognizing Beijing, while carrying on trade and other relations with Taiwan, offered a realistic alternative to status of non-recognition. In addition, the new Carter Asian strategy of avoiding automatic intervention in Asian conflicts was at odds with the US-ROC defense treaty. Thus, post-Vietnam "realism" considered the defense commitment to Taiwan as an anomaly.

Third, the initial, almost indifferent, attitude of the administration towards Soviet and Soviet clients' expansion in the third world was under revision by early 1978. Détente was not delivering its earlier promise of reduction of tensions as the USSR continued arms expansion and penetration of developing areas. In this context the "China card" looked increasingly attractive. Links with a strongly anti-Soviet PRC was considered a prudent countermove which required not a single US soldier to be moved. A pro-China tilt would be a clear signal to the USSR to halt its international misdeeds.

Fourth, US public opinion was increasingly supportive of recognizing the PRC. Time seemed ripe for a dramatic move in foreign affairs which could also help Carter's popularity. Finally, it was perhaps possible that normalization with China could prod the USSR to be more agreeable to concluding the SALT II agreement.

In retrospect, the normalization which began on 1 January 1979 did not live up to more optimistic expectations. Trade with China has grown considerably, but economic retrenchment caused China to cancel contracts and reduce foreign purchases. Many Western firms encountered major obstacles and disappointments after initial euphoria.

Despite US derecognition of Taiwan, the island remains a prosperous and energetic society--along with Singapore a showcase as an alternative Chinese society to the "revolutionary" mainland. Beijing has not given up its option of taking Taiwan by force, and the US continues to supply weapons to Taibei. The US suffered a loss in credibility among Asian allies after the abrogation of the defense treaty, but this has been minimized by continued informal arrangements--to the chagrin of Beijing.

As to the China card, this may be dangerous for the US in the long run. It has exacerbated Soviet anxieties in the Far East over the prospects of a US-PRC-Japan combination against USSR power. Stalemated in Europe and threatened in East Asia, Moscow might be tempted to become more active in the Middle East. The Soviet naval forces may also be expected to expand as a countermove against perceived encirclement.

The shift in views on China from the Ford to the Carter administrations can be seen in Defense Department Reports to Congress. In January 1977, Secretary of Defense Donald H. Rumsfeld noted that:

> Peking is gradually developing an intercontinental and sea-based ballistic missile capability. Accordingly, we must take this into account in the design and deployment of U.S. strategic nuclear forces. In addition, we must be aware of Peking's conventional capabilities. Allies in Asia are necessarily sensitive to the regional power of the PRC and cannot ignore the possibility of local conflicts which could affect their interests, and ours. [5]

One year later, a new administration saw the PRC not as a growing military threat, but as a potential counterweight to the USSR.

> Effective relations with the People's Republic of China (PRC) are important not only because China is a strategic counterweight to the Soviet Union, but also because such relations will strengthen the interest of the PRC in regional stability. Accordingly, the normalization of U.S.-P.R.C. relations in accordance with the principles of the Shanghai Communiqué remains a major goal of this administration. [6]

Further in the same report, Secretary of Defense Brown noted that the course of the PRC remains uncertain: "Despite hopeful prospects, we cannot wholly ignore the PRC for purposes of force planning. Sino-Soviet relations could improve." [7] He also indicated the sensitivity of American Asian allies to the PRC's regional

power, and echoed his predecessors concern that local
conflicts could involve the interests of the US. Brown
reserved his deepest concern for the Sino-Soviet rivalry, which could go as far as nuclear exchanges. Noting
this rivalry, he made a statement which would have less
credibility one year later: "The United States has not
encouraged or taken sides in this antagonism." [8]
   The rationale for the shift toward the PRC was present in administration defense planning. In April 1978,
the President's Special Advisor on National Security,
Zbigniew Brzezinski, visited the PRC and gave evidence
of the US intention to nurture the China connection
against the USSR. Secretary of State Cyrus Vance had
gone to Beijing in August of the previous year as Carter's first emissary to the PRC, but came away with
little success.
   The Brzezinski visit was to reconfirm American commitments in Asia, and to explore a coordinated US-China
strategy toward the USSR. [9] The inclusion of weapons and
security specialists in the group indicated the nature
of the visit, while the Chinese hosts appreciated Brzezinski's anti-Soviet sentiments, which reflected growing
American irritation at Soviet advances in Africa.
   But if Brzezinski's visit to China was intended to
reassure American allies, it was not a completely convincing gesture. Washington still adhered to the withdrawal policy from South Korea, while criticisms of
human rights violations there, the Philippines and elsewhere, were seen to undermine the stability of those regimes. Only Congressional refusal to approve appropria-
tions for the transfer of US equipment to South Korean
forces was seen as inhibiting American withdrawal. [10]
Carter's stress on European security in his State of the
Union message, and in the National Defense Report, further indicated where his priorities lay. Under these
circumstances, US rapprochement with China might be
interpreted as a substitute, rather than a confirmation
of continued Asian commitment.
   A pro-China, anti-Soviet stance was enunciated by
Brzezinski in Beijing. He expressed "US resolve to counter hegemony, either on a global or regional scale." [11]
Then he listed "three basic beliefs" which indicated a
close concurrence of Sino-American goals: First, US-
China friendship was extremely important to world peace.
Second, a secure and powerful China will be in US interests. Third, a powerful and confident America, dealing
with world problems, will be in the interests of China.
On his return from Beijing, Brzezinski stopped in Tokyo
and explained to Fukuda that the Chinese hoped for an
early conclusion of the PFT. He also conveyed the view
that there was basic Chinese support for close US-Japan
relations based on the security treaty.
   The historic visit to the PRC established the strategic structure which preceded and influenced US-China

normalization. Brzezinski's trip signalled the cooling of the Carter administration's attitude towards the USSR, and as a diplomatic cue, it indicated the possibility of Sino-US cooperation if Moscow did not restrain its penetration of Africa. There was no evidence that the Soviet Union was intimidated by this, but may have been alarmed that a triangular relationship of the US, China, and Japan was forming in East Asia. Such alarm undoubtedly contributed to the closer cooperation between Vietnam and the USSR.

Fukuda was not expecting normalization so soon, and was caught by surprise when the announcement came. Already nervous over US withdrawal from Korea, many Japanese did not welcome the abrogation of US commitments to Taiwan.[12] When Fukuda went to Washington for summit talks with Carter in May 1978, established policy lines were merely confirmed.[13] The two leaders agreed that the PFT and promotion of US-PRC ties were important for stabilization of Asia. More important to the two nations was the Japanese trade surplus with the US and other matters of trade and defense.[14]

The administration itself was not united on whether to proceed with normalization, although by June, James Reston was suggesting that Carter might accept China's conditions for normalization as early as 1979.[15] The Secretary of State and the Director of National Security Council disagreed over how to deal with the USSR. Brzezinski's hardline comments against the Soviets were not welcomed by Vance, who considered the latter's visit to China an unnecessary challenge to the USSR. Chinese officials were exultant at the sympathetic understanding their views received from the President's special advisor.

Strategic considerations were not the only reasons for US-PRC rapprochement. The absence of regular diplomatic channels was an anomaly, but not an impenetrable barrier between the two governments. More important, Japan, NATO countries, and France appeared to have a competitive advantage in dealing with China because of diplomatic relations. Because the US was restrained by Taiwan, Carter decided to cut the gordian knot which had prevented normalization.

The Japanese Foreign Ministry was caught by surprise by Carter's December announcement to normalize relations with Beijing (16 December, 0430 Tokyo time). Later, Foreign Minister Sonoda claimed that Japan had contributed to US-China normalization.[16] The move was another major accomplishment for Deng Xiaoping, and strengthened his hand in carrying out reform programs initiated since 1977. In November, he had told Takeiri, that after relations between China and the US were normalized, he was ready "to go where Marx is."[17]

The timing of the announcement was kept secret by Washington in part because of the probability of prema-

ture press leaks. But the implications of the move were
clear to the JDA, which generally was cautious about the
various diplomatic moves of its government and of the
US. The JDA saw the US strategy as one of withdrawing
from the ROK and Taiwan, and to counter the USSR with
NATO and the PRC. Thus, normalization indicated an accelerated withdrawal from Asia.[18] It was expected that
the US long-term strategy was to have China confront the
USSR on land, and itself maintain a balance with the
USSR using the Seventh Fleet and nuclear missiles.
   Nihon Keizai portrayed China's ultimate aim as reconciliation with the USSR. To accomplish this, China
needed equality in economic and military power to face
the Soviet Union. This would be acquired by getting cooperation of advanced industrial nations. In other
words, the US and PRC were using each other for strategic purposes. Under these circumstances, Japan's own
interests were not necessarily served, and so a more
autonomous defense policy ought to be pursued.
   China's leap from the defunct treaty with the USSR
to a triangular relationship with Japan and the US was a
major decision intended to serve China's own national
interests. China's national strategy was to form an
anti-Soviet front which would remove direct Soviet pressure.[19] In this respect, Deng Xiaoping's "China first"
foreign policy was remarkably successful in 1978. After
the first year in the presidency, Carter appeared willing to join the anti-Soviet front, at the expense of
de-recognizing Taiwan.

SINO-AMERICAN RAPPROCHEMENT AND JAPAN'S SECURITY

   The Chinese shift from decades of strident anti-US
foreign policy to one of increasing trade, diplomatic,
and cultural intercourse reflected domestic changes
within the communist regime. A more moderate and pragmatic line in Beijing was experimenting with greater material incentives, limited dissent, foreign investments,
and more emphasis on technical education--all of which
were anathema during Maoist days. In this way, the rapid
development of contacts with the US, Japan and Western
Europe was part of general reorientation of the Chinese
state. This reorientation has not reduced the likelihood
of Soviet war against the PRC, but represents an end to
isolation from the major power centers in order to iso-
late the present major enemy - the USSR.
   One explanation of the Sino-Soviet rift is that the
Chinese and Russians are engaged in life-and-death
struggle over control of the Eurasian heartland through
protracted struggle. It can also be seen as a device by
China to reinforce the unity of the nation. As Franklin
Houn has pointed out, the existence of an external enemy
has long been useful in China for governments to maintain central control.[20] Without the existence of poten-

tial foreign invasion, centrifugal forces would probably
have much greater strength, and could erode central control.

Another explanation has been that the Chinese are
turning to the West and Japan for assistance in modernization so that in future decades, Beijing can deal with
the USSR as an industrial and military equal -a relationship not necessarily in the best interests of the
industrial democracies.

The attitude of the US and its allies is that their
short-term and long-term interests vis-à-vis China coincide. The expansion of trade, and encouragement of an
anti-Soviet China, are considered to be major benefits
which will grow and endure over future decades. The industrial democracies do not consider it likely that they
may be serving the strategic interests of China's "broad
international united front" against Soviet hegemonism--a
situation which would signify entry into the Sino-Soviet
dispute from which they had been heretofore aloof.

These possibilities do not necessitate an explicit
strategic plan on the part of Beijing to have the West
and Japan fight its holding action against Moscow. But
developments since 1976 indicate that the Chinese are
utilizing the recent "China fever" for long-range strategic purposes - and their leaders would be remiss if
they did not take advantage of these opportunities.

Chinese political thinking and the development of
its political institutions are the products of a three
thousand year evolution, if we take the foundation of
the Western Zhou dynasty as the starting point. Feudal-
ism, in the Western and Japanese sense, was eliminated
in the Qin empire, although fragmentation and regional-
ism have remained during periods of central weakness.
Thus, the tendency towards centralization has been a
long-term trend in Chinese state development. This
centralization reached its highest refinement during the
Ming and Qing dynasties, but appeared in danger of destruction with Western intervention in the nineteenth
century. In order to reconstruct the central state, and
adapt the more successful models from abroad, the Chinese polity has undergone several transformations since
1900, including constitutional monarchy, parliamentary
republic, de facto federalism, nationalist party dictatorship, and communism.

These foreign-derived solutions were attempts to
answer the challenge of modern fragmentation and vulnerability to foreign invasion. Throughout this century,
there has been a combination of political imitation and
improvization, in the search for institutions to provide
central control and modernity. The patronage of the USSR
in the 1950s was reciprocated by institutional imitation
- which was facilitated by the Leninist organizational
base of the Chinese Communist Party. A nationalist reaction against Soviet intrusion and chauvinism encouraged

the building of domestic institutions based on Yanan experiences, and China's special conditions of agricultural predominance. This nativism, populism and sinocentrism reached its extreme form in the Cultural Revolution.

With the ascendancy of Deng Xiaoping after the death of Mao, a new foreign model for China appeared implicit in the reforms: some democratic elements, a large dose of legal system, greater attention to market dynamics, and massive infusions of foreign capital and technology, added up to an attempt to replicate numerous developmental schemes of other contemporary nations. The vision was no longer one of a Chinese imitation of the Soviet Union, but of the societies of Hong Kong, Singapore, Japan, and even Taiwan, on a massive scale. The visions of Soviet and Maoist socialism were attempted and found to be unworkable.

If the working models were already in place, it was a short step to recognizing that China would also do well to move one step further, and readjust foreign policy to suit new realities. The step of collusion with the US carried risk of alienating domestic factions and revolutionary allies, but the potential gains were proportionately great. China's aid to Vietnam and other revolutionary movements had not prevented the latter from siding with the USSR. In other parts of the world, the anticipated upsurge of "oppressed peoples" had gone the same way as Marx's anticipated proletarian revolution in industrial societies. Thus, reduced emphasis on revolutionary alliances as a major prop of Chinese foreign policy was not expected to bring major disaster.

In joining with the US against the USSR, China was not compromising its principles. The notion of a united front allowed tactical compromises to achieve long-range goals. One major theoretical "adjustment" was necessary, however. In the heyday of Maoism, superpower rivalry between the US and USSR was seen as the main threat to world peace. After US withdrawal from Vietnam, the US sought withdrawal from the rivalry which had led to involvement in Vietnam. If that intention materialized into full-blown isolationism, China would be left bearing the brunt of Soviet pressures. The theory of superpower rivalry leading to war was replaced by the view that Soviet hegemony leads to war.

US military power was balanced by Soviet power, but American will had declined. Ideologically, China could not formally approve American capitalism or "hegemony," but pragmatically the US had to be encouraged to resist the USSR. The struggle of opposites maintained a stable world. The encouragement of US opposition to Soviet expansion was a necessary price to pay for hegemonist balance.

The strategic logic of Sino-US collaboration was sensible from the standpoint of enhancing China's security. At a more emotional level, there was also receptivity in China to the US and Japanese connections. Despite decades of enmity, there has remained a reservoir of goodwill in China towards the two countries. Many scientists and educators, now in their sixties and older, had studied in Japan and the US. Despite propaganda against Japan and the US, millions of Chinese had remained informed of developments in the two countries--including the steady economic growth while their own country had stagnated during the Cultural Revolution.

Since 1976, a new generation of Chinese is being exposed to non-Soviet versions of modernity. This will create new tensions between themselves and their revolutionary predecessors, as well as with those who remain at home. It is possible that this new generation of students sent abroad can become harbingers of non-Maoist change in China's future. Their impact, however, will most likely be in the middle and managerial levels of society and economy, rather than in the central organs of the state and party.

The suspension of relations between the PRC and the US (as well as Japan) for nearly three decades was unnatural and unfortunate. No two nations had affected China's prewar modernization as greatly as the US and Japan. Soviet influence, except as occasional supporters of militarists such as Feng Yuxiang or revolutionary groups, was sporadic. After 1949, the US chose to support the Guomindang on Taiwan, and earned Beijing's enmity until that support was withdrawn. A large part of Japan's cultural heritage originated in China, and close affinities have existed between the two societies. Japanese expansion at China's expense has been officially forgiven, and the two countries look forward to renewed intimacy. Japan is important for capital and technology transfer to China in its program of modernization.

From the Chinese standpoint, there is much that can be learned and imitated from Japan, as the second major economic power in the world. But Japan itself--as a modern economy--is derivative of the US. The US occupation imposed a democratic constitution, broke up old-style zaibatsu, initiated land reform, revised the educational system and generally created ·the structures within which the postwar "Japanese Miracle" could take place. Then, American technology, management techiques, and consumer products were introduced, mass-produced and refined, until in many cases, the imitation became superior to the original and displaced it. In this sense, modern Japan is not an alternative model to the US, but rather a variant adaptation. From the standpoint of modernization, China may learn from both "teacher" and "student."

These considerations argue that there is a natural affinity among China, Japan and the US which was artificially interrupted during the Maoist years by quarrels between Beijing and Washington. Getting these relations back to "normal" is therefore a goal of US foreign policy, and useful as a means to restrain Soviet expansion.

Aside from the consideration that any claim to natural affinity as the basis of international alliance must be viewed with suspicion, the above argument ignores a more long-lasting relationship of China--that its inner Asian frontier has been the source of invasion and conflict for at least three thousand years. The Soviet menace is merely the present manifestation of a perpetual menace. From the Chinese standpoint, the USSR-Eurasian threat has undertaken a global strategy, and China must respond in kind. To enlist the US and Japan against encroachments by the USSR has been the quickest way to checkmate that threat. The anti-Soviet strategy does not necessarily serve US or Japanese interests, particularly if the new Asian entente provokes a belligerent Soviet counterresponse.

When the US announced intentions to normalize relations with the PRC, the Japanese Foreign Ministry could only offer supporting statements in public. Within the walls of the Gaimusho, however, there was concern over the "Carter Shock" - nonconsultation and the abrogation of the Defense Treaty with Taiwan. As the US's major ally in Asia, Japan was concerned with the consequences of normalization on Japan's own security. The trend towards normalization was evident in later 1978, so it was no complete surprise. But three major questions remained regarding its effects on Japan's security: First, how would US-China rapprochement affect peace and stability in Asia? Second, to what extent would the US cooperate in China's military modernization? Third, now that the US had abrogated the treaty of defense with Taiwan, and with the tendency to pull US forces out of East Asia, would a power vacuum appear in the region?

1. Sino-US Rapprochement and Asian Security

Regarding the first question, we have already examined the probability that the Japan-China Treaty heightened tensions in the region. With the inclusion of the US into China's united front strategy, the new polarization between Soviet forces and China-Japan-US was reviving international tension in East Asia. Even while Brzezinski was in Tokyo after leaving Beijing, for example, Chinese leaders were stepping up their verbal criticisms of Vietnam. China's attack against Vietnam, soon after Deng's visit to the US, met relatively little criticism from the US, indicating acquiescence. [21]

Carter resistance to Soviet challenges stiffened during 1978. By May of 1978, Carter was adopting the notion of linkage in US-USSR relations. At a NATO conference the US urged a 3% annual increase in defense spending to counter recent Soviet advances. [22] Brzezinski called Soviet acts in Africa a violation of détente, and

wanted the US to stand and face the USSR or face a state
of world anarchy.[23] On 7 June, Carter addressed the Naval Academy at Annapolis and stated that détente is reciprocal, decrying Soviet provocations.[24]
    Washington hawks pointed to Soviet action in Asia
as well as in Africa. The military buildup of the northern territories, Soviet increased presence in Vietnam,
and expanding naval presence in Asian water were causing
concern among Asian nations allied to the US.[25] Carter
was pressing the USSR to choose between cooperation and
confrontation.[26] The SALT II talks were the minimum
necessary effort to prevent unlimited development of
nuclear arms. However, no framework was established to
deal with problems of US-Soviet competition in the third
world.
    Rather than establish a new set of structures, US
hawks preferred to recoup some of the losses suffered
during the post-Vietnam era of withdrawal. The US should
not drift into separation from Asia, and should move to
a more positive diplomacy. The quickest result, some argued, would come from rapprochement with the PRC--shar-
ing Beijing's anti-hegemony stance.[27]
    The most immediate effect of Sino-US normalization
may have been to strengthen China's attitude towards
Vietnam. At the time of the announcement of normalization, the Vietnamese foreign minister was visiting Tokyo, and the Japan Foreign Ministry informed him of the
contents of the announcement.[28]
    The China connection with the US did not remove Ja-
panese doubts about US diplomacy in the region, and that
its defense power was falling behind the USSR. The US
National Defense Report (early 1979), pointed out that
Soviet increases had decreased American military predominance. The bright spot was that:

> The possibility of the Soviet Union's launching a
> large-scale attack in two regions (Asia and Europe)
> in the world has decreased further, due to the im-
> provement of Sino-US relations, besides the worsen-
> ing of the Sino-Soviet confrontation.[29]

    Also, with Sino-US normalization, the US no longer
needed to hypothesize a Sino-US military conflict. From
this view, US military planning had been relieved of a
local worry, Taiwan, which had stalemated the USSR in
Asia and Europe. This would have been an important benefit of Sino-US rapprochement. If the stabilization of
the Korean peninsula is also considered a benefit of
growing intimacy of China and the US, then normalization
was a significant and inexpensive increment to US security and world stability.
    Subsequent events, however, raise doubts about such
a conclusion. China's attacks against Vietnam increased
the latter nation's dependence on the USSR, and possibly

strengthened the Soviet foothold in Southeast Asia. Nor can the Soviet adventure in Afghanistan be isolated from global strategic considerations, since it brought Moscow's troops only a Pakistan away from the Persian Gulf. What appeared as a US checkmate of the USSR in early 1979, may now be counter-checkmated by new expanded presences.

Japan's views of Carter diplomacy by early 1979 saw a string of failures, except for the brief success with the Camp David agreement between Egypt and Israel. The US lacked a world strategy, and instability was increasing, according to Mainichi.[30] Unwilling to face the USSR in Africa, suffering the loss of a major ally in Iran, and acquiescing in the China-Vietnam war, US foreign policy was further eroded by the Vance-Brzezinski rift. Carter's pre-inaugural ideas on defense proved to be impractical, and he shifted from a liberalist to the middle-of-the-road position.[31]

Slowly Washington attempted to retake the initiative against the USSR, while maintaining discussions on the SALT II treaty. Negotiations concluded in May 1979. Brezhnev desired to separate relations with the US and the Sino-Vietnam conflict.[32] At the Vienna summit talks Carter and Brezhnev signed the SALT II agreement, which confirmed the existing situation of US and Soviet nuclear armaments.[33] It was the first face-to-face meeting between Carter and Brezhnev, although Carter's term was well into its second half.

The Nihon Keizai hoped that SALT II would end or reduce the dangerous nuclear competition between the two superpowers.[34] The two leaders also agreed to hold periodic summit talks. However, the US failed to get Soviet cooperation for Mideast peace settlement, or cooperation on Vietnam and Kampuchea. Even with greater cooperation, the two leaders could not handle all global problems bilaterally. The treaty, which was not ratified by Congress, had other problems. Arms inspection was considered inadequate, and it did not cover conventional weapons such as IRBM, Minsk carriers, and the Backfire Bomber. These were of major importance to Japan's security.

The fate of SALT II became a hostage to US-Soviet relations. US distrust of the USSR was further fanned by disclosure of 3000 Soviet combat troops deployed in Cuba. Although Carter and Vance said there was no threat to the US, their presence prolonged Cuban deployment in Africa and assisted in Soviet intelligence activities in the Caribbean region.[35] The USSR, however, denied the presence of a combat unit.[36] The result was to fan support for a harder line against the Soviets, and to increase the difficulty of Senate approval of the SALT treaty.

2. US-China Military Cooperation

The US had been the leader in restricting arms sales to the PRC. COCOM restrictions provided the major mechanism for allied cooperation. In June 1978, US policy showed indications of change. The US was preparing to revise the interpretation of COCOM guidelines on transferring technology to the PRC, so that aid to China could check the USSR.[37] Europe and Japan were enthusiastic to export technology to China and welcomed such changes. US industries were also encouraged by loosening of restrictions.

On 9 June, the US government approved for export to China certain aerial geological survey equipment. Using infrared guidance systems, the equipment had not been approved for export to the USSR because of a "danger of being used for military purposes."[38] But in the case of the PRC, it was "not technology for military uses." A month before, the US government had denied a Michigan firm permission to export similar technology to China. The government claimed that the new decision was due to a reexamination of the technology, but it was apparent that there was a division of opinion in Washington on how to proceed with the China connection. In any event, the decision to export was preliminary, and needed COCOM approval.

The US was examining aid to China's military modernization as part of its anti-Soviet strategy. With a stronger Chinese military power, the USSR would be forced to strengthen its forces in the Far East--possibly at the expense of the European theater.[39] In November, the US relaxed restrictions on the export of tactical weapons to the PRC, although still restricting large computers and precision machinery. The US would not export weapons to China, but would allow allies to reach an independent decision on their own course of action.[40] Brzezinski indicated that a stronger Chinese army would contribute to stability in international relations. The Arms Control and Disarmament Agency, however, held an opposite view--that the export of weapons to China could harden Soviet attitudes and damage negotiations on strategic weapons.

After initial enthusiasm over normalization subsided, a cooling period set in after the Chinese attack against Vietnam. Vice-President Mondale visited the PRC in August 1979 and returned relations to their original momentum.[41] During his visit, the US agreed to extend $2 billion to China in loans over the next five years. In a speech at Beijing University, Mondale issued a strong warning against the USSR. "The US regards any nation, which weakens and isolates China, as a nation which takes a position running counter to American interests."[42] The New York Times revealed defense plans of further military relations with China.[43]

The administration was cautious not to depend on China. After the China-Vietnam war, the US became concerned about involvement in regional disputes, although the strategic relationship was further solidified by Defense Secretary Brown's visit to the PRC. No US Secretary of Defense had visited the USSR, so Brown's visit to the PRC took on added significance.[44] Soviet Defense Minister Ustinov has been invited to the US but declined.

Tokyo was a usual stopover on high-level exchanges between the US and PRC. Usually, they provided opportunities for formal discussions and consultations. Japan had become the middle ground between the US and China. Such a role could not support Japan's claims that it was following omnidirectional diplomacy. From the Soviet perspective, Japan was a major, though silent, partner in the anti-Soviet coalition in East Asia. Brown's visit to China in January 1980, plus Ohira's visit the month before, further strengthened the impression of a quasi-military alliance among the three nations. As the weakest link, Japan was bound to feel Soviet pressure.[45]

The Brown visit occurred in the wake of worsening US-Soviet relations. It was not directly related to events in Afghanistan, but the latest Soviet move was obviously of great concern to the US and PRC. From China's standpoint, the Soviet intrusion presented a new threat to the western borders, and also threatened China's ally, Pakistan. The administration, already distracted by the hostage situation in Iran, became anxious over the latest Soviet thrust toward the Mideast. Under these circumstances, the China factor appeared even more attractive as a means of augmenting US global strategy. US weaponry was still prohibited to China, but military-connected technology, such as special steel plate manufacturing for tank armor, was offered.[46]

The Brown visit ended any pretense of American equidistant diplomacy between the USSR and PRC. The US Defense Department estimated China needed from $41 to $63 billion in aid for its military modernization. It was agreed that the US would supply a Landsat D inspection satellite to China. This had military applications, but was not a weapon.[47] The US clearly considered China a deterrent power against the USSR, but drew the line at providing weapons.

US policy was based on three principles: First, the international order was based on the stability of East-West relations, primarily between the US and USSR. Second, to prevent limited wars, the US found it necessary to ally with China to restrain the USSR. Third, this will reduce the possibility of aggression in Asia.[48] The flaw in these principles was that it was equally possible for the US-China alliance to provoke the USSR into further adventures.

3. Taiwan and Japan's Security

The PRC maintained three conditions had to be met if the US wanted to establish normal relations with itself: abrogation of the US-Taiwan Treaty, US withdrawal of its troops from Taiwan, and severing of diplomatic relations between Washington and Taibei.[49] These conditions had been rejected by previous US administrations because of long-standing commitments and the need to defend an ally against continued mainland threats to "liberate" the island by force. As late as 1978, PLA leaders were declaring the possibility of using force against Taiwan.

To facilitate normalization, the Carter administration acceded to Beijing's conditions, although unofficial relations were maintained with Taiwan. Congress passed a special "Taiwan Relations Act" in 1979, largely to prevent Carter from further eroding US interests in Taiwan. The PRC has not abjured the use of force in attempting to convince Taiwan to reunify with the mainland. Deng indicated that China could not bind its own hands regarding the use of force, or else Taiwan would not listen: "If one of our hands is bound in regard to the Taiwan problem, that will come to impede a peaceful formula. There will also be the possibility of their assuming the attitude of fearing nothing."[50] With the Chinese attack on Vietnam as the background, Deng indicated his country would not wait forever if peaceful persuasion did not work.[51]

Beijing's pursuit for peaceful unification after normalization relieved the Japanese government.[52] China insists that it is an internal affair. Japan continues to maintain a flourishing economic relationship with Taiwan. Reunification by force would not be easy, given Taiwan's 330,000-man army, 180,000 ton navy, and formidable air force.[53] Some concern was raised in Japan that Taiwan might move towards the USSR to counteract loss of US military ties, but any such move would have been more provocative than helpful.

From the Japanese standpoint, abrogation of the US-Taiwan Defense Treaty removed a potential source of conflict between the US and PRC. Foreign Minister Sonoda indicated that with Sino-US normalization, it was unlikely than an armed dispute would occur in the Taiwan Straits area.[54] Although Beijing had not renounced force, the administration expected that the PRC would not attack Taiwan. The continued strength of Taiwan's armed forces, PRC distractions in carrying out modernizations, and the greater security threat of the USSR-- all made an attack against Taiwan unlikely. Moreover, if mainland forces did launch an invasion against the island, the US would have to restudy its relations with China. In the context of Carter's desire to avoid US involvement in foreign conflict, however, such reexamination would probably exclude the use of American forces to assist Taiwan. Congress retained the option of exporting modern weapons to Taiwan, over the objections of Beijing, as an additional guarantee against Chinese intimidation.

CONCLUSION

Thus far, we have examined the international environment of the PFT. Our conclusions can be summarized as follows:

1. Carter's decision to withdraw US ground forces from South Korea exercised a potentially destabilizing influence on Far Eastern security. In the context of the administration's "Europe-first" strategy and post-Vietnam isolationism, the withdrawal from South Korea indicated a lessened American commitment to Asian security.

2. For a number of reasons, the Fukuda government opened negotiations with Beijing over the PFT. Among these reasons are included: uncertainty about the US posture in East Asia; the successful LTTA in February 1978; Japan's desire to give definite expression to the notion of "omnidirectional diplomacy"; domestic enthusiasm for a special relationship with China; the possibility to pressure Soviet concessions on the northern territories; and the pragmatic thrust of Chinese domestic and foreign policy after Mao's death.

3. Deng and Hua wanted a treaty with Japan largely to build its diplomacy of an international united front. This was evident from Beijing's active diplomacy on the Soviet periphery among small nations. The greatest attention was given to Japan and the US. Japan agreed to the anti-hegemony clause with public reservations, but China treated Japan as a new ally. The USSR accepted the Chinese interpretations, and strengthened the Etorofu garrison in anticipation of the Japan-China treaty

4. The USSR opposed China's united front, Sino-Japan cooperation, and US enthusiasm for the China card, and met the Chinese challenge in three ways: building up military and naval forces in the Far East; COMECON and treaty relations with Vietnam; and the buildup in the northern territories.

5. As the US normalized relations with the PRC, Japan was drawn more closely into the anti-Soviet triangle. While the new US-PRC relationship was welcomed publicly in Japan, privately, there were concerns over US-Japan competition over the China market. Although Carter reversed the withdrawal scheme, American involvement in Asia still remained a lower priority. The China card was a substitute for that involvement, not a signal for reentry. Also, cutting ties with Taiwan was a further means of reducing political and military involvement in East Asia.

The result of the above developments was to leave

Japan's national security in greater doubt than at the beginning of the Carter years. Japan's shipping lanes around Southeast Asia became vulnerable to Soviet presence in Vietnam.

The problem is not that the USSR has become more "hegemonistic" in recent years towards Japan, but that the USSR sees itself confronted by a US-China-Japan combination in the Far East. This leads to a most delicate situation for the Japanese in matters of defense. Now Japan perceives a greater Soviet threat than a few years ago. Because of the present triangular relationship, an expanded Japanese defense capability would be seen as a net increase to the total power of the US, PRC, and Japan combination. Japan's omnidirectionality was compromised with the 1978 PFT and cannot be easily resurrected. Japan may perhaps minimize damage to its neutrality in the Sino-Soviet quarrel by refraining from further moves towards large defense buildup.

This prescription is more easily given than carried out. In the remaining two chapters, we will examine certain salient factors of Japan's defense policy. The government now faces a new international environment, and must decide in the next few years how to confront it. From the Japanese perception, the Carter years were a period of fumbled diplomacy and declining military strength vis-à-vis the USSR. How these events affected the vital American-Japan Security Treaty will be examined in the next chapter.

Footnotes

1. Michel Oksenberg, "China Policy for the 1980s," Foreign Affairs 58:2, p. 304.
2. Edward N. Luttwak, "Against the China Card," Commentary 66:4 (1978), pp. 37-43.
3. See Carter's comments, Toronto Globe and Mail, 28 August 1981, p. 13.
4. Author interview with Komeito spokesman, 19 February 1981.
5. US Department of Defense, Report of the Secretary of Defense, Donald H. Rumsfeld to Congress (Washington, D.C.: Government Printing Office, 1977), p. 13.
6. US Department of Defense, Annual Report Fiscal Year 1979 (Washington, D.C.: Government Printing Office, 1978), p. 23.
7. Ibid., p. 29.
8. Ibid.
9. SK, 25 May 1978, p. 2.
10. MS, 2 May 1978, p. 5.
11. NK, 26 May 1978, p. 2.
12. YS, 27 April 1978, p. 1.
13. NK, 5 May 1978, p. 2.
14. JTW, 13 May 1978, p. 1.

186

15. MS, 28 May 1978, p. 5.
16. MS, 17 December 1978, p. 2.
17. AS, 30 November 1978, p. 4.
18. NK, 17 December 1978, p. 2.
19. SK, 7 July 1978, p. 6.
20. Chinese Political Traditions (Washington,
D.C.: Public Affairs Press, 1965), p. 29.
21. NK, 7 April 1979, p. 3.
22. SK, 2 June 1978, p. 6.
23. NK, 3 June 1987, p. 5.
24. SK, 9 June 1978, p. 6.
25. TS, 9 June 1978, p. 4.
26. YS, 9 June 1978, p. 5.
27. MS, 26 May 1978, p. 5.
28. AS, 17 December 1978, p. 2.
29. NK, 3 February 1979, p. 2.
30. MS, 2 March 1979, p. 5.
31. SK, 25 February 1979, p. 2.
32. AS, 10 May 1979, p. 2.
33. TS, 20 June 1979, p. 4.
34. SK, 20 June 1979, p. 12.
35. NK, 10 September 1979, p. 5.
36. AS, 15 September 1970, p. 5.
37. NK, 12 June 1978, p. 2.
38. YS, 10 June 1978, p. 2.
39. YS, 19 June 1978, p. 4.
40. AS, 11 November 1978, p. 1.
41. AS, 29 August 1979, p. 2.
42. NK, 10 September 1979, p. 5.
43. AS, 4 October 1979, p. 1.
44. SK, 4 October 1979, p. 1.
45. YS, 18 November 1979, p. 1.
46. NK, 13 December 1979, p. 1.
47. SK, 11 January 1980, p. 10.
48. MS, 17 March 1980, p. 2.
49. NK, 26 October 1978, p. 2.
50. MS, 27 February 1979, p. 4.
51. YS, 15 January 1979, p. 2.
52. Various schemes for reintegrating Taiwan with
the mainland are cited in NK, 30 December 1978, p. 2,
and AS, 19 October 1979, p. 4.
53. NK, 17 December 1978, p. 2.
54. MS, 21 December 1978, p. 2.

9
Japan's Security
and the United States

The broader Sino-Soviet dispute, and the US-China rapprochement in an anti-Soviet context are developments which created pressures on Japan towards rearmament. Japan's new ties with the PRC stimulated the USSR to perceive a new threat in the east. With these changes, the US-Japan Security Treaty no longer addresses a Chinese threat, and today has largely anti-Soviet implications only. The present chapter examines the US-Japanese link, with emphasis on security relations, in order to evaluate Japan's potential for remilitarization.

After the end of world war two, Japan's peace and stability allowed economic reconstruction and growing prosperity. This peace contrasted with the conflicts in the region - civil war in China, the Korean war, and the Vietnam war. From the late nineteenth century until 1945, Japan had been a major expansionist and military power in East Asia, but military defeat and the nuclear holocausts at Nagasaki and Hiroshima were experiences which led to postwar pacifism.

Out of postwar domestic revulsion against war, reinforced by American occupation reforms, Japan vowed never to repeat the experience of the war. Military forces were dismantled, and the 1947 constitution revoked all means of aggressive war potential. Civilian reindustrialization was facilitated by the absence of defense claims on the national product, and Japan's industries were able to rebuild with the most advanced technology available. A broad national consensus and a favorable international setting combined to produce the so-called "Japan miracle."

Not only did Japan benefit from favorable domestic factors such as a skilled and disciplined work force and growth oriented government policy, but postwar occupation by the US and its allies formed a vital link with the Western world. The US occupation facilitated the peace constitution, land reform, parliamentary institutions, free labor unions and a US stake in the revitalization of Japan. While conservatives and socialists both

188

express discontent with institutions imposed by a foreign army of occupation, it is debatable today whether
the diverse elements in Japanese politics could agree on
an alternative set of arrangements. Conservatives emphasize moral education, the right of self-defense, and
patriotism. Radicals stress welfare, reduced scope for
private industries, and neutrality in world affairs to
the extent of dismantling the Self Defense Forces and
abrogation of the US-Japan Security Treaty. Unless one
or the other wing of Japanese politics achieves major
predominance, the postwar institutions will probably
remain in place.

The US linkage has been vital in the postwar Japanese state. Trade and investment between the two countries have produced prosperity and occasional friction.
In the realm of defense, the US and Japan signed a Treaty of Mutual Cooperation and Security in 1960. Many Japanese opposed the treaty, and mounted massive demonstra-
tions against the government in Tokyo to prevent its
signing. It was renewed in 1970, and its twentieth anniversary passed uneventfully in 1980. The treaty is
opposed by the left because they argue that Japan could
be involved in a war not of its own making. In a Soviet-
US war, for example, Soviet missiles might be launched
against US bases in Japan.

The mainstream and conservatives argue that the
treaty helps provide a nuclear umbrella for Japan in a
time of international tensions, and has allowed Japan to
concentrate economic resources in non-military sectors -
a fact which has contributed to the nation's high rate
of economic growth. Unlike NATO, the US-Japan treaty is
not a true alliance. The US is obligated to come to
Japan's aid in the event of an attack against Japan -
but the reverse is not true. Japan can stay neutral in
any conflict involving the US.

The effects of world war two have lingered in Japan
for over 35 years. Japan's sense of war guilt toward
China may have been responsible for generous terms in
the 1978 PFT. A second effect has been the occasional
revival of irredentism toward the northern territories.
Soviet behavior in attacking Japan in the last weeks of
the war and annexing the Kuriles contrasted to American
administrative retrocession of Okinawa in 1972. In this
respect Japan's position contrasts with the West German
accommodation to postwar territorial reality. A third
effect of the war is the "nuclear allergy" - which finds
expression in the three non-nuclear policies of the
Japanese government: non-use, non-manufacture, and non-
deployment of nuclear weapons. Fourth is the postwar
institutions of the US occupation, while a fifth has
been the galvanizing effect on a generation of Japanese
who survived the war and lived through the occupation.
This generation is responsible in large part for the
concentrated efforts which produced the Japan economic

miracle.   With   their   retirement,   many   are   questioning
whether   their   younger   successors   can   carry   on   with   the
same   intensity   of   commitment.

Through   the   postwar   period,   Japan's   foreign   policy
has   proceeded   from   the   assumption   of   strong   ties   with
the   US   -   the   dominant   military   power   in   the   Pacific   region.   With   the   Carter   presidency,   however,   the   US   entered   a   crisis   of   confidence.   The   American   failure   to   defeat   the   Vietnamese   communists   produced   a   psychological
and   institutional   angst   which   affected   a   wide   range   of
security   commitments.   Moreover,   the   USSR   was   engaged   in
a   steady,   long-range   military   buildup   in   Asia,   directed
against   China   and   the   US,   but   which   would   inevitably
affect   Japan.

In   withdrawing   US   ground   forces   from   South   Korea,
Carter   promised   that   US   commitments   to   the   defense   of
Japan   were   unaffected.[1]   Without   an   understanding   with
North   Korea,   there   was   no   certainty   that   the   withdrawal
would   not   invite   a   second   Korean   war.   Sonoda   hoped   that
China   would   act   as   a   restraining   force   on   Pyongyang.   We
have   seen   how   tensions   in   East   Asia   intensified   during
1978   and   1979.   US   intentions   appeared   firm,   but   the   will
and   capacity   to   fulfil   previous   security   commitments
were   weakened.   Apparent   US   helplessness   over   Iran   and
the   abortive   rescue   mission   for   the   hostages   suggested
an   American   "giant   with   feet   of   clay."

As   the   USSR   increased   its   military   presence   in   the
northern   territories   and   Vietnam,   Japan's   vulnerability
was   underscored.   American   strategy   placed   priority   on
defense   of   Western   Europe,   and   the   Middle   East   was   becoming   a   troublesome   region   for   vital   US   oil   supplies.
Under   these   conditions,   crisis   in   the   Far   East   would   not
receive   the   attention   it   would   have   in   earlier   years.   As
Carter   was   building   bridges   to   China,   he   expected   regional   stability,   and   hoped   to   avoid   US   involvement   in
another   Vietnam-type   conflict.

This   was   of   little   consolation   to   the   Japanese,   who
saw   the   Soviet   threat   increasing   in   the   summer   of   1978.
The   1978   PFT,   with   its   hegemony   clause,   brought   Japan
into   the   Sino-Soviet   conflict   despite   Tokyo's   protests
of   peaceful   intentions.   Since   the   summer   of   negotiation,
Japan's   defense   establishment   has   been   moving   toward   a
higher   profile.   Old   inhibitions   and   doubts   about   the
role   of   Self   Defense   Forces   are   dissolving   in   direct
proportion   to   the   perception   of   the   Soviet   threat   to
Japan.   This   process   has   not   been   discouraged   by   the   US,
partly   in   hope   that   an   increased   defense   capacity   by
Japan   will   augment   US   forces   -   especially   as   American
forces   are   challenged   by   growing   Soviet   power,   or   as
they   are   deployed   to   support   US   Rapid   Deployment   Forces
or   other   mobile   troops   in   the   Mideast.   The   US   has   also
encouraged   Japan   defense   increases   as   a   way   of   easing
the   trade   deficit   -   to   make   Japan   take   more   responsibility   for   its   own   defense,   buy   US-made   weapons,   and   pos-

sibly become less competitive in exports.

With Soviet threats to Japan, the Japanese left has lost some support for its opposition to defense preparations. A number of preliminary steps have been taken which remove some previous restrictions on the Self Defense Forces. While this trend hardly means a remilitarization or rearming of Japan, it could result in an expanded role for the Self Defense Forces in the future. As the US focuses more on Europe and the Middle East, Washington welcomes this development.

During the 1978-80 period, major changes occurred which may call for a redefinition of the US-Japan relationship.[2] In particular, US concern with Soviet threats in other parts of the world may leave Japan vulnerable. This led to US pressures for Japan to assume more of the burden for its own defense. Under these demands, and with the realization that the US defense umbrella was losing some of its certainty, Japan's defense officials spoke out for stronger defense measures. As the Soviet Union moved its most recent and advanced weaponry to the Far East, the previous assumption that Japan's Self Defense Forces only had to prepare against limited, small-scale invasions, came under close scrutiny. The Soviet invasion of Afghanistan demonstrated that non-alignment was no guarantee of sovereignty.

Although changes have occurred in defense thinking, certain legal and political barriers inhibit a rapid buildup of defense capability. First, the constitution stipulates limits on Japan's defense forces. Second, opposition parties in the national Diet critically question and oversee the Defense Agency, challenging any expansion in its role. Third, public opinion, although demonstrating greater acceptance of the SDF and the US-Japan Security Treaty, moves slowly in overcoming its inhibitions. Fourth, some parts of the business community want greater defense spending in order to save weak industries, but perhaps the general feeling was that government investment in arms was not prudent economic policy. Finally, there is recognition that military expansion will possibly provoke the USSR into further countermeasures. The emergence of Japan as a military power could also create friction with ASEAN countries. These barriers may be expected to inhibit a rapid expansion of the defense establishment, but much depends on international configurations - especially the US-Japan defense relationship.

JAPAN'S SECURITY AND THE US-JAPAN TREATY

In an examination of Japan's sovereignty, two contradictory principles are predominant. First, the so-called "Peace Constitution" with its renunciation of war clause can be considered a noble experiment in pacifism. In addition, Japan has demonstrated that pacifism can be profitable if human and material resources are directed towards peaceful pursuits. The trauma of war, and the benefits of peace have strongly reinforced Japan's commitment to its present course.

The second principle has been reliance on the US defense umbrella to shield Japan from possible enemy attack or intimidation. The US deploys troops in Japan, and uses Japanese ports as bases or ports of call for naval ships. If Japan is attacked, US forces would go into action after joint consultations.

These two principles have coexisted in the past two decades in uneasy accommodation. Proponents of the first principle argue that the treaty is a mortal threat to the peace constitution, that US forces are stationed in Japan to carry out aggressive activities against socialist countries, and that the presence of US troops makes Japanese cities the targets of nuclear attack in time of war. Proponents of the second principle argue that it is the presence and credibility of US forces which allow Japan the luxury of minimal armaments and that the treaty gives Japan a free ride at the expense of US taxpayers - or more accurately a cheap ride.

Since 1978, the efficacy of neutrality as a Japanese option has been delining. Although the Soviet buildup is largely directed against China and the US, Japan's friendship and anti-hegemony treaty with the former, and security treaty with the latter, make Japan a likely target of intimidation. Indeed, it is not so much that neutrality of Japan has failed, but that it was never given a chance to succeed. Nor, in the circumstances of the 1980's, is it likely that Japanese neutralism will have much opportunity to be practised.

The Soviet fleet was an increasing threat to US Pacific power in 1978, and Defense Secretary Brown requested a greater Japanese role to cope with this threat. In an emergency, the US navy could secure central Pacific shipping lanes which connected Hawaii, Guam, Australia and Southeast Asia. The US requested that Japan secure the branch lanes to Japan itself.[3] Such an emergency mission would require a strong antisubmarine capacity. The US navy wanted Japan's Maritime Self Defense Force (MSDF) to shoulder the role of partner in Japan's defense. Nevertheless, Brown considered the US naval strength superior to the Soviet strength, despite its buildup in the western Pacific.[4]

Under the Carter administration US pressure on Japan to increase defense spending became stronger, because of Japan's rising affluence, low defense spending and the growing Soviet threat.[5] JDA Director General Yamashita later cited the increasing Soviet emphasis on the Far East. While he noted doubts that the US might be unable to come to Japan's assistance in an emergency, he also indicated that the Defense Agency would continue to consult and cooperate in defense matters with the US.

He cautiously called for constant study of the changing situation, and hoped to avoid a panic.[6] But by 1979, Japan's defenses were clearly a matter of serious concern.

The JDA was reported to request a second US nuclear aircraft carrier for the Pacific fleet.[7] (The USS Midway, with its home port at Yokosuka, was the oldest US carrier, built in 1945.) Yamashita denied that the request was made, but such a latent wish probably existed in the JDA, which was increasingly concerned about the Soviet buildup.[8] Another indication of Japanese concern over the Soviet buildup was the statement by Air SDF Chief of Staff Takeda that negotiations were being held with the US to have B-52's participate in joint training exercises. Aircraft carriers were also considered to be used as targets in the exercises.[9] This training expansion was deemed necessary to prepare against hypothetical intruders, such as the Soviet Backfire bombers and Minsk carriers.

The 11th Japan-US security consultations were held in Hawaii, from 31 July to 2 August 1979. The last consultations had been held more than a year and a half before, and the defense situation had changed considerably in the interim.[10] Yamashita had earlier visited the ROK - the first JDA Director to do so while in office - and voiced grave concern over the Soviet buildup. The Foreign Ministry, however, hinted that it was dangerous to overemphasize the Soviet threat, thus indicating a difference in opinion.

The 1979 report on defense (Japan) described the Soviet buildup, and emphasized the relative decline in US strength. While admitting the Soviet danger, US officials pointed out the weaknesses of Soviet Far East Forces, such as long and vulnerable lines of support and communication, and choke points such as straits. There was a danger of Japanese overreaction to the Soviet buildup, and Brown did not consider the Soviet garrisons in the northern territories to be an overwhelming threat.[11] Former director of the Arms Control and Disarmament Agency, Paul Warnke, considered that Soviet military expansion had been directed against China. He also thought the establishment of close Sino-Japanese, and Sino-American, relations, along with East European instability, were causing considerable Soviet anxiety.[12]

Events towards the end of 1979, however, made the Japanese more anxious about their own security. The assassination of Park Chung Hee in Seoul set off a year of instability in South Korea. Japan became a reluctant partner in the US economic war against Iran, and Soviet willingness to use its military might was demonstrated in Afghanistan.

Because of concern in Japan that US predominance in Asia was weakening, leading members of the LDP met to create a "Japan Security Problem Research Center." The prospectus stated that

> the military balance in Northeast Asia, where the
> US enjoyed predominance, has completely collapsed,
> due to the multiplier effects caused by America's
> separation from Asia and the strengthening of Sov-
> iet Far Eastern military forces; and that when
> changes in power relations, brought about by the
> competition in economic power between the US and
> Japan are taken into consideration, a third revi-
> sion of alliance relations between the US and Japan
> will be unavoidable. [13]

This and other expressions of concern at the apparent decline of US interest in Asia were met by denials
from the US. [14] The Mondale and Brzezinski visits were
meant to demonstrate continued US concern for the region. But in the plan to withdraw US forces from South
Korea, US reassurances that Japan had a specialplace in
its strategy downplayed South Korea (and Taiwan) as
important to Japan's security, or that US ground forces
in the Korean peninsula played an important deterrent
role there. [15]

Brzezinski's speech of 27 April 1978 was also intended to reassure Asian leaders of the US commitment.
However, he indicated that the alliance and cooperative
relations based on the US-Japan Security Treaty were not
to be guaranteed automatically. He hoped that Japan
would play a larger role in its own defense. [16] As with
the Nixon and Ford administrations, Carter would not
take on the responsibility for maintaining governments
unwilling or unable to defend themselves.

On the Japan side, further doubts were expressed
about the ability of US forces to aid Japan in an emergency - especially if crises in Europe and the Middle
East erupted simultaneously. Yamashita said that such a
situation was unlikely, and continued to express faith
in the US-Japan security structure. [17] Uniformed personnel, however, were less certain and sought improvements
in the security structure. For one thing, there was no
unified command in an emergency, as in NATO or the Republic of Korea. [18] In addition, the MSDF and US Navy had
different communication systems, which precluded combined fleet operations in an emergency. A sizable proportion of SDF officers had studied in the US, and the
American military system was the most familiar foreign
model. By late 1978, 49 generals of a total of 89 had
studied in the US. [19]

Asahi reported that many uniformed officers doubted
whether US forces would come to the aid of Japan in
times of emergency: At a meeting of the Defense Cooperation Subcommittee in the spring of 1978, SDF officers
sought clarification of the strength of US forces which
would aid Japan in an emergency. The US side was reluc-

tant to answer this request, and Japan's National Defense Council initiated efforts at greater coordination for specific plans.

Japanese defense officials were concerned that the growing US problems in the Middle East could cause a permanent diversion of forces to that region. Ground SDF Chief of Staff Nagano was assured that the US would make efforts to divert naval forces from the Mediterranean to the Middle East rather than from the Seventh Fleet, which was responsible for the security of Pacific.[20] Reports that the US Navy would create an Indian Ocean fleet were denied by the US Chief of Naval Operations, Admiral Hayward. Such a fleet would have to borrow some ships from the Seventh and other Fleets.

Japan also counted on the US nuclear umbrella for defense, although many citizens had severe reservations about US deployment of nuclear weapons in or around Japan. Kissinger's speech in Brussels (1 September 1979) on the credibility of a US nuclear umbrella for NATO had implications for Japan as well.[21] The former secretary of state indicated that the US could not be expected to commit nuclear suicide if the USSR attacked Western Europe. That is, there was a limit on how many guarantees the US could give NATO without risking its own self-destruction. No US president would launch an ICBM attack against the USSR to defend Western Europe at the risk of US destruction. Such a strategic guarantee to NATO was in fact a suicide pact for the US. By extension, the US would not provide such guarantees to Japan.

The so-called swing strategy of the US received considerable attention in Japan after coverage in the Washington Post (8 October 1979).[22] According to this strategy, a crisis in the NATO region would cause the US to reassign a number of naval ships from the Pacific to Europe. It was suspected that the US had carried out this strategy for the previous 25 years, while keeping it a secret from Japan. Defense Secretary Brown minimized the study, describing it as one of several staff studies, and not representing current US policy.[23] He also indicated that "swing" operates both ways. During the Vietnam war, the US moved ten aircraft carriers to the west Pacific waters from Europe.

Paul Warnke, one of the most knowledgeable Americans in superpower armaments, did not see a Soviet threat to Japan.[24] He considered the modernization and buildup of Soviet forces in the past ten years as largely directed against China. With the US and Japan leaning towards the PRC, Soviet uneasiness was increasing. The USSR was a threat to world security, but Warnke also believed the US had important military and technological superiority over the Soviets. He considered Kissinger's statements irresponsible, because the US possessed a number of deterrents at different levels. Warnke also saw no evidence of any physical threat to Japan from the

USSR. The deployment of forces in the northern territories was for political, not military, purposes.

Some of the friction between the US and Japan came from the fact that US strategy was global in scope, while Japan was concerned only with the home islands in defense considerations. Through Japan's participation in major economic and summit conferences, development aid programs, and the responsibilities that came with the status of being an economic world leader, the country was becoming more internationally-minded. One aspect of this has been the Japanese anxiety over any shift of US naval forces. A US task force was created to cruise the Indian Ocean after the Soviet incursion in Afghanistan.[25] This force thinned out naval defenses in the Far East, but also enhanced Japan's security by securing the sea lanes from the Persian Gulf to Japan. This became was even more important with the expansion of Soviet naval activity in Vietnam waters.

One manifestation of the swing strategy under Carter was the Rapid Deployment Force (RDF). American strategy had reduced preparations from an earlier potential to fight 2.5 wars to 1.5 wars. When the RDF was introduced in early 1980, it was assumed that US bases in Japan might be used as relay or supply bases. This, it was feared in Japan, would cause the country to become further involved in US global strategy, and could cause strains in the US-Japan security relationship.[26] The Security Treaty called for mutual consultations in emergency situations, and using bases in Japan for global strategy was precisely what pacifists opposed.

The Japanese government supported the RDF, and claimed there was no problem in using Okinawa bases. For the RDF to be moved to the Middle East from Japan bases was not combat action, and therefore not an object of prior consultation. Furthermore, Japan could not restrict the action of US forces after they had left Japan.[27] The Japan Socialist Party (JSP) opposed this linking of US bases in Japan with possible military action in the Persian Gulf - a region the party considered peripheral to the Far East. The government, however, maintained that the Gulf was in fact vital to Japan's security, because much of the nation's energy came from the region.[28]

The US agony over Iran and Afghanistan was shared in part by Japan. Reluctantly, Tokyo joined the boycott of oil purchases over the hostage issue. The US could do little about Soviet aggression in Afghanistan, but Japan would cooperate as much as possible with the US - but not to the extent of greatly increasing defense expenditures.

The main expression of the US-Japan Security Treaty was deployment of US military forces on bases throughout Japan. As the SDF expanded in size and capability, small-scale joint maneuvers were carried out. Officers

were sent to the US for training, and considerable weaponry was of American manufacture. No large-scale joint
maneuvers of the US and Japanese forces, such as "Team
Spirit 78" took place, although US forces on Okinawa
were included in the operation.[29]
    Joint naval maneuvers began in the late 1960s, with
training in anti-submarine warfare. The first joint air
maneuvers took place in November 1978. Although the US
had wanted joint ground maneuvers with Japanese forces,
none had taken place as of early 1981. Closer integration between US and Japanese forces has been facilitated
by US training. ASDF pilots were proposed to be trained
in the US, beginning in 1979. It was also proposed that
the number of SDF students sent to the US be doubled in
order that communication be improved between the military of the two countries.[30]
    In 1980, Ohira decided to allow the SDF to partici-
pate in the multinational maneuvers of RIMPAC around
Hawaii. These maneuvers included US, Canadian, Australian and New Zealand naval forces, and occurred every
two years. The JDA defended its decision by maintaining
that the exercise was designed to train naval forces for
combat, and was not intended for joint defense. The distinction was crucial because Japan did not have defense
treaties with the other nations involved, except for the
US. According to JDA Counsellor Sassa, in testimony
before the Diet, there had been 83 instances of US-Japan
joint maneuvers, and RIMPAC participation was considered
training at a higher level. About 700 Japanese MSDF
personnel participated.[31]
    Opposition party members were highly critical of
the decision. The SDF was escalating its scope of training, and some feared that once the taboo against joint
maneuvers involving nations other than the US had been
broken, it was possible for SDF forces to conduct joint
maneuvers with any country (including the ROK)[32] - with
which Japan did not have a security treaty: all in the
name of training. The opposition was also suspicious of
the manner in which the decision was announced - by the
MSDF Chief of Staff. A Yomiuri editorial rhetorically
asked if it would not have been better for the civilian
head of JDA to announce it.[33]
    The decision to participate in RIMPAC was an excep-
tional step by the SDF. Ohira had decided in favor of
participation shortly before he left for the US.[34] In
1976, the US had urged Japanese participation in RIMPAC
and the JDA was reported to have accepted. Foreign
Ministry officials apparently discouraged participation,
and prevailed.[35] Public opinion had changed since that
time, and the MSDF was even able to fire its missiles in
training. The opposition parties had become more flexible, as evidenced by the JSP visit to the US. With the
formulation of the defense guidelines, more definite
procedures of cooperation had been clarified. Japan's

participation in RIMPAC was also useful as evidence that Japan was not settling back for a "free ride" in defense at the expense of the US.

In the RIMPAC exercise, each nation maintained independent command of its own forces. Japanese ships test-fired anti-submarine torpedoes, while live rounds of ammunition were fired. Australian fighter planes provided the hypothetical enemy in the operation. The emphasis was on electronic links and communications-- counterweapons, computers and missiles. It was also an opportunity for MSDF ships to fire their cannons at full charge - a rare opportunity on Japanese firing ranges because practice areas in Japan are limited in size. [36]

SDF officers favored such an exercise as an opportunity to learn from other forces and to discover inadequacies which might otherwise be ignored. The open spaces of the Pacific Ocean provided ranges for firing and maneuver lacking around Japan. The JDA defended RIMPAC participation against critics. Ex-MSDF Chief of Staff Uchida suggested that those who opposed SDF training were like people who thought that fire-fighting training causes fire. [37] Japanese forces would learn from other countries and combat skills would be upgraded. In a historical perspective, it was also useful to avoid the isolation of Japanese military forces which was so prominent in the prewar period - and which was a factor in the ultranationalism of imperial military forces.

CONSTITUTIONAL ISSUES

Article Nine of Japan's postwar constitution states:

1. Aspiring sincerely to an international peace based on justice and order, the Japanese people forever renounce war as a sovereign right of the nation and the threat or use of force as a means of settling international disputes.

2. In order to accomplish the aim of the preceding paragraph, land, sea, and air forces, as well as other war potential, will never be maintained. The right of belligerency of the state will not be recognized.

During the Carter years, Japan's vulnerability to external attack and the Soviet threat to Japanese security provided arguments for the SDF to increase its capability. Article Nine seemed to prohibit any such expansion, and the Cabinet stood between opponents and proponents of expanded defense capacity.

Each departure from existing practices by the SDF has been subject to controversy. When the decision to participate in RIMPAC 1980 was announced, questions were raised whether these exercises were designed to enhance collective self-defense. These questions raised serious doubts about the constitutionality of Japanese participation. According to the JDA, RIMPAC participation consisted only of training for self-defense, and was legal under Article 5 of the Defense Agency Establishment Law.[38] The government's position was:

> Japan can conduct joint training even with those countries which do not maintain a security treaty with Japan, when the training aims solely at improving combat techniques, and is not to lead to the exercise of the collective right of self-defense in a way to assist in the defense of other nations, in accordance with Japan's policy of exclusively for defense.[39]

Carter's State of the Union Message and the US National Defense Report in early 1980 relayed a sense of quasi-wartime emergency to Japan - the "keystone of security in the Far East." It was a label the government had to reject, however, if it meant integration into a strategy of collective security. In the new international period of tensions, both the US and PRC did not disguise their hope that Japan would take a stronger defense posture.[40]

Legality was not the only source of the fierce opposition to expanded military activities. In Okinawa, for example, there had long been opposition to US military bases. The reversion of the island to Japan's sovereignty was accomplished in 1972, with considerable support from pacifist elements on Okinawa. The civilian population had suffered casualties of around 200,000 in April 1945, when US forces attacked and defeated Japanese defenders.[41] When landing maneuvers of US forces began on 18 August 1979, many who had survived the war were reminded of their experiences. The maneuvers involving 40,000 US troops, 26 ships and 280 planes were the first such operations since reversion seven years earlier.

Okinawa contained 53% of the US base area in Japan, and bore much of the brunt of the US-Japan treaty. The "Fortress Gale" maneuvers in August 1979 were carried out as a training operation for elements of the Seventh Fleet and Okinawa marines. Protests erupted from city assemblies, rallies, and even the conservative governor.[42] Many Okinawans remained ambivalent because, although the sound of guns and plans brought back war memories, the economy still needed US forces. US bases contributed an estimated 100 billion yen annually, compared to 130 billion yen from tourism. There were 50 American military facilities, occupying 13% of the land area. Much of the land rented from owners for military purposes was not suitable for other uses, and therefore brought extra income.

Another instance of the dependence-suspicion dilemma of American-Japanese relations was the question of nuclear arms. Japan has been the only nation to have been the victim of nuclear weapons, and its citizens understandably do not want these weapons as a matter of principle. This has created suspicion towards the US, whose forces sometimes carry nuclear weapons. When Navy Secretary Claytor testified in Congress that the Japan-based carrier, Midway, may have a nuclear role, it causes a furor in Japan – even though he indicated it had no such role at the time.[43] There has been continued suspicion that US planes carried nuclear weapons, but it has been US policy not to refer to the location of such weapons except in NATO or South Korea. Despite this "nuclear allergy," Japan depends on the US for providing a "nuclear umbrella." The constitution does not specifically prohibit nuclear weapons for self-defense, but it is unlikely that Japan will radically alter its three principles in the next few years.

Japan's postwar pacifism has also been reinforced by international opinion. ASEAN, South Korea, and China – as well as the US – do not want Japan to pursue a program of major rearmament. They might agree that larger defense forces are desirable, but not beyond some limit whereby Japan's economic power is translated into major military power.

Japan and West Germany are occasionally compared as examples of defeated nations which rebuilt their war-damaged economies to become major world economic powers. The similarity ends there, as West Germany has become a staunch member of the Western alliance, with a formidable military force. Moreover, having lost much territory and suffered division between east and west, the German people have more reason to hold revanchist grudges against the USSR than do the Japanese.

In the case of West Germany, Warsaw Pact threats and military pressure have been fairly consistent since the war. West Germany did not include a peace clause in its constitution, relying more on a federal system to balance the central government as a means to prevent totalitarian revival. Also, Germany's geopolitical position in central Europe means that the country can never be isolated from the tensions which exist in the region. Finally, many citizens have fled from East Germany and amply understand the differences between democracy and communism. Political and economic freedom have to be defended, and neither isolation nor pacifism are seen as realistic alternatives to maintaining a strong army.

In Japan, the nation has been isolated by its geography from conflicts on the Asian mainland. Japan became involved in war prior to 1945 because nationalism, militarism, and imperialism expanded Japanese forces into Asia and the Pacific basin. By having Self Defense Forces maintain a minimum capability of defending against "limited, small-scale invasion," the Japanese state seeks to prevent a repeat of historical militarism or expansionism.

The policies of pacifism and isolationism have a certain viability if the Tokugawa period (1603-1867) is taken as the model for contemporary Japan. For over two and a half centuries peace reigned in the country with only occasional disruption. Although it is impossible today for Japan to maintain the same isolation, non-involvement in international conflicts can preserve the peace and prosperity which was lost during the war years.

While Japan's economy was developing after the war, and its democratic institutions were acquiring permanence and legitimacy, the US defense umbrella provided protection for the delicate new growths. Until the mid-1970s, Japan could rely on US indulgence in its special institutions of the peace constitution and minimal defense force. After Vietnam, however, many Americans opposed continued involvement in East Asia at previous levels, especially as Soviet and various threats emerged in other regions. Moreover, US sympathy for Japan's minimal defense efforts was eroded by economic success which posed direct threats to US industries, especially in autos, steel and electronics. Increasingly, Japan was accused of getting a free ride in defense matters.

US PRESSURE ON JAPAN TO EXPAND DEFENSES

Until the mid-1970s, American administrations had generally accepted Japan's special situation with regard to defense. Prior to 1977, the US saw the region as a major theater of conflict and threats from communism, but China's post-Mao pragmatism reduced US anxieties about the region. With regard to Japan, it was sufficient to nourish and protect the most stable Asian democracy and America's major Asian trading partner. By the early 1970s, Japan was becoming a major economic competitor with the US. By the close of the decade, many Americans considered the decline in their auto, steel and other industries as directly related to Japan's rapidly expanding success in those very fields.

Many suggested that American shouldering of Japan's defense burden was becoming inappropriate, and that Japan must carry more of that burden itself. During the fiscal year 1978, JDA Director General Kanemaru said the defense budget was 1.9 trillion yen, or 0.9% of the GNP.[44] In his talks with Brown in June, he indicated that Japan would cooperate with the US in defense--but could not promise any budgetary increases.

In early November, Ambassador Mansfield addressed the defense question and claimed that the US never applied pressure on Japan to share in regional military power.[45] He noted tensions in the region, but warned against an excessive strengthening of Japan's defense capability. Mansfield was taking a middle ground between those in the administration who were pushing for greater Japanese defenses, and Japanese reluctance to recognize tensions. The US dollar was weakening against the yen, and the Soviet threat appeared more formidable and capable of applying pressure at many points, so the US urged Japan to bear a greater share of defense costs.

US Representative Richard C. White, Democrat member of the House Armed Services Committee, summarized some American dissatisfaction over Japan's reluctance to increase defense expenses:

> In regard to the argument that Japan is taking a free ride, if the American people look squarely at the present situation, such a reaction will come to the fore, automatically. If we look at the world, we will realize that Japan is a big industrial country. As to trade with the US, Japan enjoys a surplus balance. Moreover, the US takes on the greater part of the responsibility for defending Japan. The US, however, suffers from a deficit in its trade accounts, and the people are seeking a curtailment in the annual expenditures. Japan may say that there are Constitutional restrictions in the country, but the times have changed.[46]

White argued that an expanded defense role would be in Japan's own interests because of the vulnerability of the nation's shipping lanes:

> The first point to which I want to call your attention is that Japan does not live in a dream world. If the Japanese people are to consider, as a reaction to their terrible experience during World War II, that they can live in their islands peacefully in the future, too, and that they can maintain the present situation permanently, without possessing any large-scale military power, the day may come when Japan will no longer be a great nation. In my opinion, Japan is one nation which contains weakness within itself above all other nations in the Far East. The reason is that Japan depends upon sea lanes for shipping, to too great an extent. In order to maintain Japan's greatness as present and to ensure the supply of raw materials, Japan must sail out, in a positive way, to the oceans, not making defense efforts within its country alone, and it must, thus, defend its sea lanes for shipping. Today, the concept on self-defense does not stop at the edge of the sea. The self-defense of today is to have power, which will enable us to advance our

national self-defense efforts, in a positive way,
to outside our country, to such an extent as to
hold back an attack to be made by an enemy.[47]

Finally, increased Japanese defense power was needed to hold back Soviet naval power, and would be welcomed by other nations:

> Japan's military power in the 1940s and that at
> present are different. At that time, Japan had
> transport airplanes and aircraft carriers, and with
> the support of these, Japan waged the war of ag-
> gression. However, at present, we are hoping that
> Japan will possess war potential for its defense,
> and that it will be used for holding down the ad-
> vance of Soviet military power into the Pacific
> Ocean. If it becomes clear that Japan's self-
> defense efforts are directed solely at a threat
> from the North, nations in Asia will also welcome
> it.[48]

The occasion of White's visit to Tokyo was a symposium of American and Japanese legislators. American Con-
gressmen stated the necessity of increased Japanese defense measures.[49] The Japanese Foreign Ministry had
conducted a public opinion survey in the US. According
to this Gallup survey, 54% of the respondents classified
as intellectuals replied that Japan should increase military expenditures for defense. Japanese legislators
heard their American counterparts criticize Japan as
able to have developed its economy because it had made
no efforts in defense. In defense spending, Japan spent
only $55 per capita compared to $700 per capita in the
US or $95 in Taiwan. The view in the US was that Japan's
defense efforts did not correspond to its economic affluence.

Nihon Keizai found dissatisfaction over Japan in
the US, especially over economic relations. Japan's GNP
was about half of the US's, and per capita income was
nearly equal.[50] The Japanese were accused of diverting
economic power from defense to strengthening competitive
export power. The government in Tokyo claimed that a
large-scale increase in defense expenditures would upset
the military balance in the region - a development which
might stimulate greater Soviet buildup in the Far East,
and thus was not necessarily in American interests. It
was a valid argument, as was evident from the Soviet
response to the Sino-Japan Treaty of 1978.

Some blame for American difficulties in economics
was directed against Japan. But it was not accurate to
see Japan as the source of a decline in international
competitiveness of American products, increasing dependence on foreign oil, domestic inflation, and low savings rates (around 5% of US disposable incomes). Japan's

high savings rates (22% of disposable incomes), govern-
ment-business cooperation, relative labor-management
harmony, realistic adaptation to higher energy costs by
domestic price increases, and other factors had avoided
many of the US problems.[51] The truth was that Japan was
out-competing its American mentor by retaining and ref-
ining lessons and institutions which dated back to the
first postwar decade.

Japan's economic success was attributed to many
factors, including protectionism, low investment in public welfare, "workaholism," etc. In this sense, US pressure on Japan to expand defense expenses was related to
US economic distress, and an attempt to equalize the
terms of competition.

The question of expanding Japan's defense capability posed several problems. The US economic situation
was probably a temporary dilemma which could be solved
by more enlightened policies. Once US inflation was
brought under control, after industry was encouraged to
modernize plant and machinery, and a rational energy
policy was introduced, American competitiveness would be
reasserted. Likewise, the Soviet threat was in part a
result of Carter's and Congress's reluctance to take
measures to resist that threat until 1978. The problems
were not overwhleming, and could be solved.

For these reasons, the Japanese government was
reluctant to surrender to US pressures, and tended to
temporize. When Prime Minister Ohira held talks with
Carter in 1980, he promised to look into the matter of
accelerating defense increases. The US interpreted his
polite - but noncommittal - response as an agreement to
speed up defense increases. For the Japanese, defense
buildup was not simply a matter of diverting funds from
one item to another, or printing more money to cover
deficits incurred by increased spending. Defense is a
delicate constitutional question, and for Ohira or any
prime minister to obey a US demand could conceivably
result in the collapse of the government. A political
party in name, the LDP is more a coalition of factions -
some of which only tenuously support the government, as
the non-confidence motion of May 1980 proved.

Moreover, the "economic miracle" in Japan may be a
very delicate phenomenon, and to tinker too roughly with
civilian and defense spending could result in weakening
the economy, with serious implications for America's
major ally in East Asia. Japan held a major trade surplus with the US, and US industries and unions advocated
protection from Japanese competition.

With the abortive rescue operation in Iran in 1980,
more inadequacies of US forces became evident. This, and
anxiety over the Mideast, intensified US pressures on
Japan to increase defense spending. Chairman Stennis of
the US Senate Armed Services Committee (6 February 1980)
stated: "The strengthening of Japan's sea and air de-

fense power is most important in guaranteeing the security of the Western nations and the whole world. Japan claims that it is bound by various restrictions. However, the US too, has restrictions."[52]

The Japanese government sought to rebut such criticisms by making larger contributions to its defenses. Financial prudence required the government to increase taxes, float bonds and reduce other expenses in order to increase defense power. Foreign Minister Okita indicated his government's willingness to reach the symbolic limit of one per cent of GNP, but doubted that the goal could be reached quickly.

Another step to offset US criticism has been to increase foreign aid to those nations facing a Soviet threat. In particular, Pakistan and Turkey have received increased aid. A further action was for Japan to increase its share of expenses in maintaining US bases in Japan.

The US Defense Department suggested that Japan should make even greater efforts in 1980. Defense Secretary Brown requested greater defense expenditures, saying that the Soviet invasion of Afghaistan had created an entirely new situation. With the USSR poised against the Middle East, Japan's oil supply was threatened. Brown also rejected arguments that financial difficulties excused Japan from greater defense efforts. All countries, including the US, faced economic problems, and Japan had to understand that without security, there could be no financial stability.[53] The Carter government was losing patience over Japan's reluctance to take measures to provide more of its own security. As US forces might be diverted to other regions, Japan was expected to play more of a role in the defense of sea lanes north of the Philippines and west of Guam.

Although US pressure created difficulties for the Japanese government, it also reinforced certain latent domestic sentiments that increased defense spending would be politically useful. As an economic superpower, Japan's international power was not commensurate with its productive accomplishments. Japan was seen as a ruthless exporting dynamo, but niggardly in defense. Compared to the NATO members, Japan was not upholding its international responsibilities. Some Americans and Japanese argued that a militarily stronger Japan would have more influence in the international community.

The flaw in this argument was that a rapid diversion of economic resources into arms could erode the other factors which had produced Japanese economic strength. As a result, a stronger defense posture would be achieved at the expense of a proven mix of trade, manufacturing, and domestic stability, leaving Japan no better off than before. Given the context of the de facto triangle of the US, the PRC and Japan, the USSR would probably respond to Japanese defense increases with its own military pressure.

The US wanted Japan to increase expenditures in line with its own intended annual increase of 4.5% per year for the next five years. NATO members also intended to increase their defense spending by 3% annually in the same period.[54] The US expected Japan to increase capacity for anti-submarine operations, and Japan ordered 45 P-3C Orions for this purpose. Other weapons were also planned, including destroyers, mine-sweepers, and anti-submarine helicopters. The US expected Japan to improve its capacity to block the three straits of Soya, Tsugaru, and Tsushima against the Soviet navy if necessary.[55]

The US was facing difficult times, and Washington was venting impatience against Japan. Auto imports made continued inroads at the expense of US manufactures. When Vance and Okita met in Paris in December 1980, was Japanese trading companies continued to do business with Iran despite sanctions over the hostage taking,[56] and Japan subsequently restrained such activity. As a symbol of support for US sanctions against the USSR, Japan bought 2-300,000 tons of US grain to offset losses due to the embargo. Japan also joined the US in boycotting the summer Olympic games in Moscow.

For reasons already noted, Japan could not respond quickly to US pressures to increase defense. Moreover, the administration itself was divided over important issues, as Vance's resignation indicated. US foreign policy in East Asia under the Carter administration was not a model of consistency, so it was unwise for Japan to respond enthusiastically to the latest mood in the wake of Afghanistan. If the US made formal requests to increase defense spending, Japan was unlikely to alter its constitutional and economic structure over what might prove to be a temporary crisis. With an Upper House election in a few months, and a possibility of LDP loss of the majority in the Diet, Tokyo was hardly in a position to hand an explosive issue like defense to the opposition parties in the coming campaign. Ohira had requested Hua Guofeng to restrain his statements when he visited Tokyo in May 1980, so as not to create any problems for the LDP in the election. It was also necessary for the US State and Defense Departments to exercise the same moderation in requests over defense expenditures.

When Ohira visited Carter in May 1980, defense discussions were not scheduled. Nevertheless, Carter mentioned to Ohira that the US hoped Japan would advance its attainment of the Medium Term Operations Estimate (MTOE) from five to four years. Ohira's reply was non-committal but the US interpreted it as agreement. The speedup of this had been requested by Brown to Okita in March, and Carter's mention was the first presidential reference to the matter.[57]

Ohira could understand US concern over the direc-

tion of international events, as well as the US desire
to push Japan into greater cooperation against the Soviet threat. He maintained that there was no promise to
increase defenses. But opposition spokesmen claimed the
talks took place in an atmosphere of agreement over Japan increasing defense expenditures steadily and significantly.[58] In other areas besides defense, US and
Japanese interests did not coincide exactly. Far more
dependent on Mideast oil, Japan could not afford to
alienate the dominant Arab powers.

Institutional differences between Japanese and
American political systems meant that the prime minister
of Japan did not have the same political power as the
president of the United States. Both were heads of government, but the prime minister was far more constrained
in his ability to carry out policy. Cabinet government
and Diet politics were riddled with distinct factions,
which sometimes operated as quasi-political parties. The
government bureaucracy, especially the Ministry of Finance, exercised further constraints over what the prime
minister could deliver. The opposition parties provided
a third source of constraint, and through questioning
and maneuvering in the Diet, they could create further
difficulties for the government. Fourth, the electorate
itself has a major stake in government. Issues such as
conscription, nuclear power and defense spending are
watched very carefully as areas which could affect livelihood. Finally, the mass media exert a major influence
over public opinion, articulating and coordinating the
above restrictions on the prime minister. As a result,
if Ohira desired to make major changes, it was a slow
process.

US-JAPAN SECURITY COOPERATION

Under the Status of Forces Agreement (SOFA) between
the US and Japan, the US was responsible for expenses of
its forces. By 1978 this had risen to about $1 billion,
not including weapons or pay to US personnel.[59] Under
the agreement, Japan contributed about 100 billion yen.
As the yen appreciated in value, US expenses increased
in terms of dollars expended. Wages were paid to Japanese workers in yen, and it required more and more dollars to meet those obligations. These personnel costs
amounted to $400 million. As an immediate measure, the
Japan government decided to bear a new share of 6.1
billion yen towards social insurance and welfare costs
for US Forces Japan employees.[60]

The opposition parties criticized this move as a
deviation from the SOFA. Their criticism was muted by
the consideration that if the government did not help in
meeting employee costs, the US bases might have been
forced to dismiss some employees. The government also
agreed to build certain facilities for the US bases,

such as sound-proof walls for engine tests.[61]   These
arrangements, although reasonable, were seen as distor-
ting the legal provisions of the SOFA.   In the judgment
of _Mainichi Shinbun_, the agreement had been virtually
nullified, because there was the possibility of unlimited Japanese facility construction for USFJ under the
government's new interpretations.[62]

US forces in Japan were using 120 facilities, with
a total of 341 square kilometers, in addition to ten
facilities (141 square kilometers) under SDF management
which were rented by USFJ.[63]   When SOFA was negotiated
in 1960, Japan's GNP was only 9% of the US's.[64]   With
economic problems in the US in the later 1970s and Japan's rapidly rising output, earlier economic assumptions
were no longer valid.

Government leaders hoped to retain Japan's constitutional and peace oriented structure in the face of US
pressures and Soviet threats.   Prewar militarism and the
efficacy of peaceful economic development had convinced
many Japanese that their course was correct. Rather than
pursue rapid rearmament which could divert resources
from civilian endeavors or raise anxieties among allies,
trading partners, and the USSR, there was a strong consensus for Japan to work for world peace and prosperity.
This could be accomplished by providing greater economic
aid to ASEAN, continued domestic economic growth, and
improvement of aid to developing nations.

US-Japanese defense consultations were held periodically. These consisted of top-level civilians from both
countries to work out coordination of policies.   A major
topic of discussion at the 1978 meeting was the guide-
line for defense cooperation, which was formulated by
the Defense Cooperation Subcommittee.   In addition, occasional consultations between the US secretary of defense and the JDA director general were carried out.   The
first such talks were in 1975, and the Brown-Yamashita
talks were the fourth (August 1979). Through such talks,
consultations and exchanges, the US and Japan have been
able to work out difficulties, and understand mutual
viewpoints.   These meetings have kept mutual friction on
defense matters to a minimum.   Moreover, they have provided ceremonial occasions to remind the Japanese public
of the close security relationship between the two countries - perhaps sometimes to the point that the Japanese
public has been lulled into acquiescence about defense
matters.

ON JAPAN'S DEFENSE, CONSTITUTION, AND THE SECURITY
TREATY

The central concept of the modern state is sovereignty. This refers to the ability of a political system
to maintain its separateness and independence from other
states, and its power to carry out its commands inter-

208

nally. Under this concept is subsumed the diplomatic, legislative, and defense capabilities of the state.

Thus, the issues of Japan's diplomacy and military policy are recent manifestations of the perennial question of sovereignty in the state. In Japan there are two major, irreconcilable schools of opinion regarding the preservation of Japanese sovereignty. In the interest of abbreviation, I will refer to the two persuasions as "pacifism" and "pragmatism." Pacifism refers to a loose collection of assumptions about the nature of the postwar Japanese state. In general, these are:

(1) The destruction of the Japanese homeland which occurred in world war two was the result of unbridled militarism and its capitalist allies. This militarism was reinforced by isolation from other countries' culture, the emperor cult, the fusion of state and shinto, a highly centralized educational and police system, and the zaibatsu.

(2) The defeat of the militarists and their allies, and the sweeping away of the old system was a major positive contribution by the US occupation after the war. The American-inspired constitution, with its peace clause, the legalization of labour unions, land reform, abolition of the zaibatsu, and other reforms were introduced during the US occupation, and provided a foundation for the postwar state which must be preserved. This foundation has ensured Japanese economic prosperity, and has allowed development of a stable democratic polity unparalleled in East Asia.

(3) Any revival of military institutions must be opposed. The JSP and the JCP consider the SDF unconstitutional, while the Komeito proposes a scaled down version of the SDF for national defense. Unilateral disarmament is not always advocated, but pacifists claim that the existence of the present SDF provides the core for future militarism and involvement in foreign wars, and therefore must be dissolved.

(4) Japanese pacifism opposes the US-Japan Security Treaty because it involves Japan in American global strategy. US forces in Japan participate in annual maneuvers with South Korean forces, and thus Japan is seen as a staging ground for further ground wars in Asia. In a major war, US bases would be prime targets for Soviet ICBM'S.

(5) Pacifism finds further validation for its premises in Japan's postwar prosperity. By concentrating Japan's skilled labor force and scarce resources into civilian production, the nation's economy has attained phenomenal success. Any diversion into military spending will detract from productivity, and further weaken lagging welfare spending.

The strength of Japan's postwar pacifism has been due to several factors:

(1)   the wartime experiences of death, destruction and postwar hardships, intensified by the nuclear holocausts in Nagasaki and Hiroshima which had personalized pacifism for many people;

(2)   the existence of Article Nine in the constitution as a specific limitation on the war-making power of the state; and

(3)   an international environment in East Asia where wars and the threat of wars were constantly present, making it imperative for Japan to remain disengaged from any action which could eventually involve the nation in war.

The major opposition to pacifism in contemporary Japan cannot be correctly termed "militarism," although some writers see this as a case. The benefits of 35 years of peace have been too obvious to most Japanese to be discarded for any discredited ultra-nationalism or nationalist doctrines. Rather, the main doubts about the arguments of pacifism are raised by pragmatists, who recognize a changing international environment which requires modification of Japan's attitudes. In general, the pragmatist position can be summarized as follows:

(1)   The postwar reforms, subsequent democratization, and economic development have produced major benefits to the Japanese people. There is consensus that the institutions, including the peace constitution, which produced these benefits, must be maintained.

(2)   However, the pacifists vastly overestimate the ability of Japan to maintain those institutions without some US guarantees for Japan's security. That is, Japan has been able to pursue its experiment in military minimalism because the US carried much of Japan's defense burden for a long time. The presence of US forces in Japan, resented and opposed by pacifists, has not involved Japan in wars in Asia. On the contrary, US forces have helped to insulate the country from external tensions and have provided a symbolic continuity in the postwar period. Without the US presence, it is possible that the SDF would have developed much faster than it did, with the result of significant political cleavages. The US presence has inhibited the revival of domestic militarism, by shielding the country from external threats and making major Japanese defense efforts unnecessary.

(3)   As Japan became a major economic power in the world, there are demands that it take up responsibilities commensurate with that power. To NATO and the US, this has meant greater defense spending. China and ASEAN do not oppose moderate expansion of Japan's defense capability. To the other industrial nations of Europe and North America, Japan's foreign aid to developing countries is too small in proportion to GNP.[65] Simultaneous with Japan's economic achievements, the US economy has been stagnating, resulting in US irritation over Japan's

free ride in defense. The pragmatic persuasion in Japan suggests that defense and foreign aid be augmented significantly.

(4)   In the 1970s, as the US concentrated military efforts in Vietnam, then withdrew, and appeared ready to disengage from East Asia, the USSR was steadily building up its own military forces. Japan's tilt toward the PRC antagonized the Soviet Union further, while the US has become more distracted in the Middle East. The result has been to increase Japan's vulnerability to Soviet pressures. Pragmatists thus argue for greater defense capabilities to resist those pressures and to indicate Japan's resolve to resist any incursions. The alternative is inability to defend the islands, for Japan cannot depend on the permanent altruism of the US to defend Japan if Japan is unwilling to make larger contributions.

(5)   Until recent years, Soviet and Chinese threats to Japan were distant. The USSR's main forces and modern weapons were either in the European theater or along the Chinese border region. As for the Chinese, their main preoccupation has been continental, or directed against Taiwan. The Korean war raged for three years without involving Japan, and any renewal of the conflict would probably be contained. In the 1970s, however, the USSR started deploying its most recent long-range weapons in the Far East. The buildup in the Sea of Okhotsk and the northern islands off Japan has brought the country into a situation of possible direct confrontation with the USSR.

The increasing threat of Soviet air and naval forces have a profound effect on Japan's defense planning. Pragmatists, supported by US defense experts, say that Japan has a major role to play in this new situation. An attack against Japanese shipping lanes would be as serious as direct invasion of the country. Can the concept of self-defense be expanded to cover this possibility? Pragmatists argue that it should. Such preparation for naval and air defense will raise numerous strategic and political problems. For example, it is argued that protection of Japanese shipping lanes from the Persian Gulf is vital to Japan's defense because of essential oil imports. Under these new conditions and interpretations, the notion of self-defense as the ability to repulse small-scale limited invasion attempts is insufficient.

(6)   With regard to the domestic threat of remilitarized Japan, the new focus on naval and air forces carries little potential for imposing military rule on Japan of prewar type. The Ground Self-Defense Forces of Japan have been relegated to an inferior role in comparison to the maritime and air forces.

The pragmatist solution on the defense question recignizes that the basic assumptions of a pacifist Japan had a certain validity under conditions that existed in the prewar period. However, the situation of unconditional US defense commitments to Japan, and remoteness of Soviet military power no longer holds, so modification of pacifism is necessary. These modifications are presently seen as budgetary and psychological, and possibly legal and constitutional.

The pacifist persuasion fears that accommodation to pragmatist arguments will weaken fundamental pacifism. Increasing the defense budget, loosening restrictions on the SDF, and breaking various taboos are viewed as weakening the postwar barriers against revived militarism in Japan. If the pragmatist arguments are translated into policy, more hawkish sentiments may next be legitimized. Conscription and nuclear weapons lurk in the background as politically explosive issues in the future.

The pragmastists argue that adherence to pure pacifism is unrealistic under present conditions. Japan's endorsement of China's anti-hegemony compromised Tokyo's neutrality in the Sino-Soviet conflict. Meanwhile, the close relation between Japan and the US raises both benefits and problems for Japan. The two countries are major trading partners, and American civilization has had a major role as model for Japan's political, economic, technological, and educational modernization. In a period of US difficulties, both in global military commitments and economic problems, Japan should recognize the obligation to assist its longtime friend.

The constitution remains perhaps the most important guarantee of postwar pacifism. The constitution has been interpreted to meet changing conditions. The pacifist persuasion leans toward the belief that the existence of a military establishment is the cause of war. Yet it may also be argued that the absence of a sufficiently strong military force can be the source of war in inviting attack.

Until the Carter years, a delicate equilibrium of forces was maintained in East Asia. The Soviet buildup, the end of US-PRC tensions, the intention to withdraw from South Korea, and US problems in the Mideast indicated that the US was no longer willing or able to maintain the balance of power in the region. A hasty US-PRC accommodation was worked out in 1978 which seemed to assert a new balance. The US has also been calling on Japan to take up a larger share of the defense burden.

The international conditions for Japan's defense increases have become prominent. Past patterns indicate that expansion of defense forces and budget will be difficult and takes place within constitutional parameters. But what about the Security Treaty? Should it be abandoned as the socialists and communists demand, revised to give Japan greater equality, or merely renewed as it stands? Unlike the constitution, the treaty must be renewed every ten years. But similar to the constitution, it has become increasingly accepted in Japan as an integral part of the defense system's definition.

Perhaps another way of looking at the treaty is to see it as making the ideals of Article Nine realizable in Japan. That is, insofar as the forces of pacifism and legal restrictions prevent the expansion of Japan's defense forces, the presence and credibility of US forces have made up for most weaknesses in Japan's security. The treaty gives Japan the best of several worlds. It delivers security benefits without mutual obligation - Japan has no obligation to come to the aid of the US if the US is attacked. The treaty has probably helped Japan to keep its military establishment at a minimum, and thus avoid the budgetary and political problems faced by so many nations.

Rather than viewing Article Nine and the Security Treaty as contradictory, they should be seen as complementary. To understand this, we need only ask, what would happen if the US adopted a constitutional amendment of its own, with wording exactly the same as Japan's? Deployment of US forces abroad would become illegal, and US bases in Japan would have to be closed down. US forces - army, navy, air, and advisors - would have to be pulled out of South Korea back to Hawaii or various US territories. Any capacity for offensive warfare would have to be dismantled. Such a scenario would probably lead to major global disorder.

The purpose of envisaging such a possibility is to underline that Japanese pacifism can be valid only under the rather specific conditions which occurred in postwar Japan. The global position of the US, which includes the Security Treaty and the deployment of US forces in South Korea and Japan, is a precondition to the realization of the peace constitution. This is not to dismiss the inherent dangers of pro-US alignment, but rather to indicate that it has been a major factor in supporting peace, pacifism and prosperity.

To be sure, there is a measure of reduced sovereignty as a result of the Security Treaty. US bases and cooperation in US foreign policy aims have narrowed the options available to the Japanese government. However, Japan continues to control its own destiny in most important affairs. The greater threat would be to be cut off from the special relationship with the US. With no credible military forces under those circumstances, Japan would be at the mercy of the PRC and USSR. With a credible military force, Japan would be seen as a potential threat by its trading partners in Asia. Complete independence from the US would likely produce more serious problems than it would solve.

Japan's defense dilemma can be summarized as follows: The nation depends on the US for a major part of its security. To maintain this situation entails reduced sovereignty as well as implication in US defense

strategy in the Pacific region. To reduce this dependence will involve increased armaments, or Finlandization.[65] In the next and final chapter, we will examine
how the defense debate sees the options available to
Japan.

Footnotes

1. JTW, 6 August 1977, p. 2.
2. Former JDA Director-General Mihara Asao addressed the need for greater Japanese efforts in the alliance between Japan and the US. "Japan-US Alliance at a
Turning Point in History," conference speech at "U.S.-
Japan Mutual Security – the Next Twenty Years." Conference held at Tokyo Prince Hotel, 29-30 August 1980.
3. YS, 2 July 1978, p. 1.
4. YS, 10 November 1978, pp. 1-2.
5. NK, 19 November 1978, p. 2.
6. NK, 14 May 1979, p. 3.
7. YS, 17 May 1979, p. 2.
8. MS, 20 May 1979, p. 1.
9. AS, 2 June 1979, p. 1.
10. AS, 29 July 1979, p. 2.
11. AS, 21 October 1979, p. 2.
12. TS, 27 October 1979, p. 5.
13. YS, 4 February 1978, p. 2.
14. TS, 4 May 1978, p. 3.
15. SK, 22 May 1978, p. 4.
16. NK, 16 May 1978, p. 2.
17. NK, 14 May 1979, p. 3.
18. AS, 20 December 1978, p. 4.
19. Ibid. According to figures provided by the
JDA, the following numbers of SDF personnel received
training in the US.

	GSDF	MSDF	ASDF
1975	1010	2640	760
1976	830	2320	780
1977	770	2690	760
1978	790	2970	800
1979	790	3140	800

20. YS, 1 June 1979, p. 2.
21. SK, 28 September 1979, p. 1.
22. TS, 22 October 1979, p. 5.
23. NK, 20 October 1979, p. 1.

214

24. TS, 27 October 1979, p. 5.
25. NK, 3 February 1980, p. 5.
26. MS, 2 February 1980, p. 2.
27. AS, 2 February 1980, p. 2.
28. YS, 1 February 1980, p. 5.
29. MS, 8 March 1978, p. 5.
30. YS, 24 September 1979, p. 2.
31. MS, 29 November 1979, pp. 1-2.
32. YS, 18 December 1979, p. 3.
33. YS, 26 October 1979, p. .
34. AS, 2 December 1979, p. 1.
35. AS, 7 November 1979, p. 4.
36. YS, 18 December 1979, p. 3.
37. AS, 29 December 1979, p. 5.
38. TS, 26 February 1980, p. 7.
39. AS, 2 December 1979, p. 1.
40. SK, 14 March 1980, p. 1.
41. MS, 16 August 1979, p. 5.
42. MS, 2 September 1979, p. 1.
43. YS, 11 February 1978, p. 7.
44. YS, 11 February 1978, p. 2.
45. YS, 2 November 1978, p. 5 .
46. TS, 16 November 1978, p. 2.
47. Ibid.
48. Ibid.
49. NK, 19 November 1978, p. 2.
50. NK, 4 June 1979, p. 13.
51. See Ezra F. Vogel, Japan as Number One (Tokyo: Tuttle, 1979).
52. SK, 10 March 1980, p. 2.
53. Ibid., p. 1.
54. NK, 31 January 1980, p. 2.
55. YS, 17 February 1980, p. 1.
56. Washington Post, 3 March 1980, p. A20.
57. TS, 2 May 1980, p. 1.
58. AS, 2 May 1980, p. 2.
59. NK, 20 February 1978, p. 2.
60. TS, 28 April 1978, p. 4.
61. NK, 9 November 1978, p. 1.
62. MS, 9 November 1978, p. 1.
63. AS, 26 November 1978, p. 1.
64. YS, 10 August 1979, p. 5.
65. On "Finlandization," see H. Peter Krosby, "Finland After Kekkonen," Current History, December 1982, pp. 381-3.

10
Defense and the Japanese State

The policy and practice of the Russian government have always been to push forward its encroachments as fast and as far as the apathy or want of firmness of other governments would allow it to go, but always to stop and retire when it met with decided resistance and then to wait for the most favorable opportunity to make another spring on its intended victim.[1] (Lord Palmerston, 1784-1865)

By 1902, the Anglo-Japanese alliance was forged to prevent Russian expansion in Manchuria and Korea. In the decades following the Russo-Japan war, Japanese military and imperial policy justified expansion as necessary steps to thwart tsarist, and later, Bolshevik expansionism. Thus, twentieth century Japanese militarism was intimately tied to Russophobic attitudes.

After word war two, the US occupation authorities under General Douglas MacArthur rewrote the Japanese constitution so that the state could not engage in war again. This radical reordering of the state was reinforced by popular sentiments and institutional arrangements. In less than two years, souring of US and Soviet relations, accompanied by communist success in China, prompted second thoughts about Japan's non-belligerence. MacArthur's offhand remark that Japan could become an Asian Switzerland was seized by pacifists as a worthy national goal given the imprimatur by the reforming preconsul.

The outbreak of the Korean war and continued tensions in East Asia reordered US priorities in the region. From a conquered, humbled enemy, Japan became a strategic support case for American forces and a showplace of capitalism and democracy in a continent threatened by revolutionary communism. To many American leaders, the two roles of Japan - as strategic base and showcase - were perfectly compatible. Therefore, it might be feasible to add a third role - that of ally in the region so that the Japanese could taken on more of

215

their own self-defense, and lighten some of the US burden.

Japan had made a break with the militarist past in the 1947 constitution, and American expectations about an expanded defense role for the country appeared to contradict the spirit of postwar reforms. Nowhere was this sentiment more evident than in the popular movement to prevent signing the US-Japan Security Treaty in 1960. It was feared that the close alignment of US and Japan would determine Japan's foreign policy, making the enemies and friends of America into the enemies and friends of Japan. In addition, Chinese and Soviet weapons would bring war to Japan as well as to the US if hostilities broke out. This was too high a cost for millions of Japanese who had suffered the horrors of war a decade and a half before.

The US policy of détente and pursuit of SALT with the USSR, followed by US withdrawal from Vietnam in 1975, were welcomed by most Japanese. But the further reduction of US presence in Asia, represented by Carter's policy of withdrawal from South Korea, was a more ambivalent move from Japan's standpoint. With decreased US commitment to security of the Seoul regime, could Tokyo be far behind? This, as we have seen, made the PFT more attractive than previously, despite the antihegemony clause, because it could facilitate dialogue with China over the Korean peninsula.

While protesting that the PFT had nothing to do with the USSR, the Fukuda government continued to lean towards Beijing in outlook. Sino-American rapprochement eclipsed the Sino-Japanese connection, but gave it an added anti-Soviet significance. The Soviet buildup in the Far East, initially prompted by Sino-Soviet tensions, assumed new meaning in the late 1970s. The Self Defense Agency interpreted the Soviet military buildup as a threat to Japan, at a time when renewed American suspicion of the USSR had emerged.

The situation is particularly critical for Japan because it contains the possibility of negating at least part of the postwar gains of peace and prosperity. There is a large body of opinion in Japan which recognizes the Soviet threat and there has been growing support for the SDF, although neither factor gives a green light for re-arming on a large scale.[2]   US pressures and Chinese gestures of support for enlarged military capacity further serve to establish an environment conducive to rearming.

Those who had predicted and feared Japanese rearmament are confounded over the sequence of events in past years. Greater pressure for rearming has occurred, but not from the directions anticipated. Axelbank, for example, described the radical right in Japan as the major pressure for rearming, with abetting from the US.[3] Halliday and McCormack predicted revived Japanese imperialism as a consequence of monopoly capitalism.[4]   While

Soviet ideology echoes the same themes, it is also more
likely that rearmament logic is strengthened by Soviet
expansionism, the declining US presence in East Asia,
and China's united front strategy, rather than simple
domestic forces. In fact, domestic opinion and institutions may be the most effective inhibitions to revived
militarism.

With regard to Japan's security relationship to the
international environment, three possible situations can
be identified. First is neutrality, in which the government maintains equidistance in foreign relations, including with the US. Until 1978, Japan maintained a quali-
fied neutrality, which consisted of equidistance from
major powers except the US. With the 1978 PFT, Japanese
neutrality was further compromised as the country tilted
towards the PRC, and relations with the USSR cooled.

The second situation can be described as "defense
equilibrium," where Japan maintains sizable forces for
self-defense only, and depends on the US for a nuclear
umbrella and long-term defense. Ideally, from Japan's
perspective, the defense budget and SDF remain at a minimum, while American guarantees remain permanent and
open-ended. This enables Japan to concentrate on economic growth and avoid creating military anxieties among
Asian trade partners.

Third is the situation of rearmament. This condition is assumed to be a repeat of past experiences, with
accompanying external expansion, military control of the
state, and a defeat for the commercial democratic polity
which exists today.

Today, at the beginning of the 1980s, Japan has
nearly abandoned the neutrality which existed in the
postwar period. To critics of the Japanese state, the
present defense equilibrium appears unstable. Soviet
threats, and pressures from the US, PRC and domestic
hawks could produce a reluctant rearmament of Japan, if
the vectors of international politics and strategy were
the sole criteria of national defense policy. However,
Japan seems neither psychologically, nor economically,
nor institutionally prepared to take on major rearmament
combined with an anti-Soviet posture. Japanese public
opinion, commercial orientation, and state institutions
appear to preclude a rapid shift to rearmament - or back
to neutrality - from the situation of defense equilibrium.

Psychologically, the Soviet threat is distant and
abstract. The LDP attempt to generate popular sentiment
for reversion of the northern territories is more a dis-
traction, rather than a focus of mass expectation. Also,
while the limited SDF is becoming acceptable to a majority of Japanese, this overcoming of past anti-militarism
can not be interpreted as support for rearmament. There
is widespread realization that Japan's low defense budget has made economic success and a high standard of

living possible.

Economically, Japan's status as an economic super-power is more fragile than often realized. Japan must trade or die. The absence or paucity of most vital re-sources in a sophisticated economy makes the nation highly vulnerable to vagaries of the world economy and to interdiction in time of war. Prewar Japan could draw on the resources of its colonies in Korea and Taiwan, while today, long shipping lanes from its trading part-ners make revived belligerence all but unthinkable.

Institutionally, the peace constitution remains in place, and inhibits expansion of the SDF. The opposition parties further restrict movement towards remilitariza-tion, and the factional structure of the ruling LDP ren-ders concerted action difficult. The mass media and other elements of a democratic state may inhibit major growth of the defense establishment.

In addition to these internal inhibitions to a rearmed Japan, there is the consideration that even a doubling of defense expenditures would not necessarily provide a net increase in security. The Soviets would undoubtedly meet a Japanese buildup with further coun-termoves against potential threats to Soviet interests in the Far East.

SECURITY AND THE JAPANESE STATE

The question of Japanese defense policy is broadly related to two major factors: the nature of the inter-national system and of the Japanese state. By state, I refer here to the institutions of government, the inter-connection of social and economic institutions, and sov-ereign territory. Defense policy is "made" by govern-ment, which consists of individuals acting within the institutional constraints of law, party, factions, Cabi-net, and the Diet. That is, one subset of the state's institutions, called government, is responsible for for-mulating and executing policies which aim at preserving the entire state from external and internal enemies.

The state exists in a world environment of other states. Since world war two, the US and USSR have emer-ged as superstates whose relations vitally affect not only each other, but Japan and all other nations as well. Because of the overwhelming influence these two superpowers hold over the international system's direc-tion of peace or war, we can postulate three sets of conditions to describe their respective power: US domi-nance, parity and Soviet dominance. These conditions are central in considering strategic weapons, and the "bal-ance of terror." But they can also indicate balance or imbalance at a regional level such as East Asia. At the regional level, conventional weapons, geopolitical place-ment, alliances, and the will to act may be as important as numbers or destructive power of strategic weapons.

For the moment, we can consider Japanese defense policy as a function of Japan's perceptions of the international system - i.e., the regional balance of the US and USSR -and leave aside the intervening variable of the Japanese state. From 1945 through 1975, the US held air and naval dominance over most of the Pacific region. This was reinforced by land bases on the periphery of East Asia -from Thailand to South Korea. The withdrawal from Vietnam and other points, as well as rapprochement between the US and the PRC, meant that American presence in the region declined because communist China was no longer perceived as a threat to states in the region. It also meant that American military superiority declined as the Soviets increased their weaponry, first along the Sino-Soviet border, and then into the East Asian region and Vietnam.

In terms of superstate relations, the region was moving towards the second condition, parity, especially as Japanese and others expressed doubts about the US administration's will to use its military forces. By 1978, the third condition - Soviet dominance - was becoming a possibility. Although the Soviet buildup was primarily directed against the PRC, and secondly against the US, this did not alter the potential threat against US dominance and Japan's security.

If Japan's defense policy was merely a matter of adjusting to the international environment, we might expect the following policy outcomes: Under condition one (US dominance), Japan's defense posture could be minimal. The SDF need only be large enogh for local self-defense and expensive enough to minimize US criticism of the free ride in defense. While pacifists and leftists will complain about any US presence in Japan, or criticize any expenditure on the SDF, it may be a small price to pay for US good will and the defense umbrella.

Under condition two, with US-Soviet regional military parity, Japanese defense policy becomes more problematic. The US pressures Japan to take up more responsibility for its own defense, while to do so, could create further antagonism from the USSR. Moreover, Japan would risk further confrontations with the Soviet Union at a time when the US defense umbrella was springing leaks, so to speak. Under this condition, government recognition of declining defense guarantees, and popular insecurity could be expected to result in a higher Japanese defense posture.

With Soviet dominance in the region, where the US could be expected to back down in challenges from the Soviet military, condition three could affect Japanese defense policy in one of two ways: US defense guarantees would no longer be credible, so rather than risk war, Japan might adopt a variation of "Finlandization" - pacifism, with the only option of surrender if the USSR threatened blockade or invasion. The other option would be significant rearmament, in the hope of reestablishing a balance of forces in the region, in coordination with the US. Along with rearmament, old taboos would be abandoned, including arming with nuclear weapons and dispatching Japanese forces to other countries. Collective security agreements might also be concluded under the third condition if the Japanese government so chose.

In examining the above options and international conditions, however, we have purposely omitted one key intervening variable for the sake of simplicity. Therefore, let us consider the Japanese state as an intervening variable: The postwar state has been described as a "pacifist commercial democracy"[5] or a "welfare state." The antiwar constitution of 1947 made the Japanese state unique among nations. The question today is whether or not, as conditions which brought about that state recede, the same degree of pacifism can be maintained. Until the early 1970s the situation described as condition one prevailed. Democratic opposition to the Security Treaty in 1960 was in part generated out of fear that the presence of US forces in Japanese could compromise the pacifist state.

Nevertheless, it was that very presence which had contributed to the formation of the pacifist state in Japan, and which allowed Japan to rebuild the economy. Critics rebutted that this was part of the US global strategy to integrate the country into its chain of military bases around the perimeter of China. The dilemma for Japan was that a crucial element of sovereignty – the right of self-defense – seemed to have been surrendered under Article Nine of the constitution.[6] It did not prevent formation of the SDF, but each expansion of its size and role has been bitterly opposed by the pacifist sector of opinion. As a result, the SDF has been characterized as an "illegitimate child."[7]

The prevailing condition one led to a situation in which the Japanese people looked upon their national security as something akin to a natural phenomenon – it was free and entailed no obligation.[8] With the American defense umbrella, and the absence of rivals in the Pacific region, this popular notion was not far from the truth. But as American strength waned during the 1970s, Japanese security was becoming more questionable. A government study group on Comprehensive National Security reported in 1979:

> In considering the question of Japan's security, the most fundamental change in the international situation that took place in the 1970s is the termination of clear American supremacy in both military and economic spheres.

Militarily, the military balance between the United States and the Soviet Union has changed globally and regionally as the United States has held back on strengthening its military arsenals since the mid-1960s while the Soviet Union has continued to build up its military force. As a result, U.S. military power is no longer able to provide its allies and friends with nearly full security.[9]

Thus, condition two of the regional system is expected to prevail during the 1980s, or even deteriorate to condition three. For Japan, the central question has become one of whether the pacifist state can survive in this less secure environment. Pacifists argue that the constitution has already been stretched too far to accommodate the law establishing the SDF. Inoki Masamichi, chairman of the Comprehensive National Security Group, argues that the constitution can and should be amended to fully legalize the SDF.[10] Unless this is done, a contradictory situation will emerge, with a pacifist constitution on the one hand, and growing pressure to expand Japanese military forces on the other. Such a situation can only nurture cynicism about the whole constitution and eventually undermine Japanese democracy.

This intimate relation between defense and the state acts as a brake on any arms buildup in Japan. Defense is not an affair of narrow policy choices - of selecting among various weapons systems, or increasing the JDA's share of the national budget. The constitutional and political parameters, established under condition one of the international system, are at odds with condition two, as the Japanese state finds its security less guaranteed by the US.

A major readjustment of the state is required as the wartime generation retires, and as the US defense umbrella decays.[11] Shimizu Ikutaro had been an opponent of the US-Japan Security Treaty in 1960. In 1980, however, he argued that Japan had lost its condition of being a state because of Article Nine.[12] It was a punishment far greater than the scale of "crimes" committed in wartime when Japan, he argued, was merely following the example of advanced Western nations in expansion.[13] This condition of lacking a central requisite of a state - autonomous defense - was not only acceptable, but desirable, to pacifist thinking. Likewise, the Japanese trust in the UN was based on a belief that the general security organization would protect Japan, even though Japan could not take part in any military sanctions. In this respect, Shimizu wrote that Japan seeks UN protection without making any contribution. If Japan really wants neutrality, the example of Switzerland should have been followed, and membership in the world organization not sought.[14]

222

Japanese have accepted peace as pleasant tranquility - seeing only its bright and happy side after the
war.[15] But there is a dark side to peace as well - the
postwar balance of other states which could be upset by
war at any time. Because there are no suprastate laws
to punish acts of aggression, nor authority above individual states, the only foundation of peace is balance
between selfish interests of various states. Even the
introduction of nuclear weapons has not made war unthinkable, as postwar history amply demonstrates. Thus, the
condition of peace is fragile, and Shimizu wants his
country to take positive steps to preserve it.

This can only be accomplished by retrieving Japan's
lost "stateness." After the war, he maintains, Japan
ceased to be a true state.[16] Empty terms as "cultural
state," "peace-loving state," and "welfare state" have
disguised this transformation. Japan has become a society, and without military strength, cannot be considered a state. The essence of a society is economic
activity, based on self-interest. The quality of loyalty
and dedication which once characterized Japanese nationalism has been transferred to corporations and other
subnational units of social activity at the expense of
loyalty to the state.

Corporations, which are in a perpetual state of
war, are microcosms of the state. These economic bodies
demand loyalty from workers, and in return, workers gain
material remuneration and spiritual sustenance.[17] Corporations provide a deep sense of identity and gratify
the workers' sense of loyalty with symbols, collective
activity beyond the workplace, and lifetime employment.
The corporation had coopted the state in this sense.
While this redirection of loyalty has fueled Japan's
engine of economic development, the nation has little
leverage in international affairs. National influence
ultimately derives from military strength, and Japan's
status as an economic giant carries little weight in international affairs. It is a vulnerable giant, depending
on imports of food, fuel, and many vital resources.[18]
Unable even to defend vital sea lanes, the nation must
rely on the US. With the Americans now losing their
military edge, Japan the society (non-state) will be
threatened.[19]

The constitution "imposed" on Japan by the occupation troops cannot be valid forever.[20] The postwar disarmament was purely in American self-interest, and this
policy was reserved in October 1948.[21] The nation had
the opportunity to create a military force during the
Korean War, but the consensus of intellectual circles,
the press, and educators has been that the military is
dangerous and "unclean." This fear and loathing has resulted in continued Japanese powerlessness in international affairs.

In an age when the world has entered proliferation

of nuclear weapons, Japan still thinks that it will be spared because the nation was the first and only victim. In reality, a nation without nuclear weapons is vulnerable to blackmail and intimidation. Japan's three non-nuclear principles are merely a confession of weakness. Without physical force, the free and democratic society of Japan cannot be defended. But in Japan, the members of the SDF are scorned as subhuman, and face discrimination in local communities.[22]

Finally, Shimizu examines the US-Japan Security Treaty, which he considers a part of US global strategy, and consistent with Japanese interests in many parts. However, the treaty is meaningful only if Japan can guarantee its own defense. If Japan fails to work for its own security, the US may abandon the country - just as Japan abandoned the peace treaty with Taiwan in 1972 when relations with Beijing were normalized. A postwar age has arrived. The former US military superiority has been eclipsed by Soviet buildups. Even NATO can not completely depend on US aid in an emergency. How can Japan, with more tenuous ties to the US, continue to rely on the Americans in an emergency? For Shimizu, Japan must rely on the Japanese people and its own military preparations.

Shimizu's rearmament thesis was denounced by Inoki, who wrote that military strength was no guarantee of security.[23] Japan can best maintain security by "making as many friends and as few enemies as possible," and "make it clear that Japan will never again become a military giant."[24] Inoki also attacked Shimizu's argument that Japan had been disarmed by Article Nine because of American interests. Rather, "Japan had fought rashly against the world, and so was disarmed after defeat."[25] The constitution does not prohibit Japan from developing military potential, but it does prevent it from becoming a military giant.[26] Most dangerous in Shimizu's essay is the tendency to urge Japan to become a military superpower. This would be accomplished by eliminating Article Nine, removing civilian control over the military, and propagating the myth that Japan's forces had not been defeated in the second world war but were stabbed in the back and forced to surrender because of the emperor's proclamation.[27] Inoki fears that if Japan opts for nuclear weapons, the US-Japan treaty structure would collapse and place Japanese security in jeopardy: "This is because the major assumption underlying the security treaty is that Japan will rely on US for deterrence, based on strategic nuclear weapons, while Japan concentrates on building up its capacity for resistance. The collapse of the security treaty could be followed by a Sino-Soviet rapprochement and the ensuing encirclement of Japan in the Far East."[28]

Professor Kataoka Tetsuya offers another critique of the present Japanese state as inappropriate to changing international conditions. The current defense posture, adopted in 1976, claims to have the international environment as its point of departure. But to Kataoka, Japan's defense posture has almost nothing to do with the international environment, however defined.[29] Rather, the 1976 National Defense Program Outline was tailored to suit Japan's domestic politics.[30]

The premise of the present defense force is a domestic political decision to hold defense spending within 1% of GNP. So the government plans defense on the basis of the potential enemy's intent, rather than capability, within the budget ceiling of 1% - an attitude he characterizes as "waiting for Pearl Harbor."[31] If Japan is to protect itself against future external crisis, "it will have to amend the Constitution first, and that in turn will create a new regime to supersede the present postwar Japanese state."[32] He calls the present state the "First Republic," which is essentially a pacifist commercial democracy. This is characterized by an excess of democracy, and by private interests taking precedence over public interests. This Japanese democracy is also designed in such a way that it could survive "only on condition that someone else protects Japan."[33] It could become a nation which has no higher goal than "doubling national income." At present, Japan is content merely to survive, willing to exchange autonomy for security, regardless of the price.

In the search for material well-being, the Japanese First Republic has reached its logical conclusion, and now searches for a new goal. Kataoka urges his country to become the state he calls the Second Republic, which would not weaken democracy of the first. The new regime would cease to depend wholly on other countries for defense, and would establish its own security autonomy. This regime would need a force de frappe, including nuclear weapons. Japanese Gaullism would shift away from pure democracy, and adapt the Aristotelian aristocratic element to government which has been lacking. In international affairs, Japan will adopt a bolder political posture, and end the single-minded pursuit of economism.[35]

Autonomy in national defense does not mean the revival of militarism. If it did, it means that Japan has no alternative to war with the US, or becoming dependent on the US.[36] The Second Republic cannot come into being as long as LDP power is excessively dispersed. A stronger party president is needed. Nakasone suggested popular election of the prime minister every four years to overcome the lack of concentrated power in the government.[37] Japan's weak diplomatic and defense policies can be overcome only by reducing the excessive aggregation of local interests and pressures.[38]

Nixon was the first to suggest a Gaullist Japan in his concept of a pentagonal world, with five autonomous poles of power. This was impossible as long as the world was still divided into two ideological camps. With the emergence of China as an independent "sub-superpower," the bipolar division has broken down. If Japan acquires an autonomous defense capability, a condition of multipolarity will be more likely.

Kataoka is satisfied that Japan's integration with the free market economies of the world insures that democracy and capitalism will be preserved in Japan. Autonomous defense does not equate with militarism, as many Japanese think. It is an attitude which sees the Japanese people as either economic animals or military animals. If US leaders fear an authoritarian or militaristic Japan, there are sufficient trade levers available to influence events. [39]

To Kataoka and Shimizu, questions of defense transcend the realm of mere policy choices. Defense goes to the heart of the nature of the state, its sovereignty, and its very survival. Japan must possess strategic nuclear weapons to counter Soviet nuclear blackmail. [40] Japan must have a full range of conventional weapons, but without nuclear weapons, there will still be dependency on the US. Nuclear weaponry is the capstone to autonomy, and represents self-reliance in the world. Without nuclear weapons, Japan has no deterrent to free itself from involvement in a US war against the USSR. Possession of nuclear status will preserve Japan's neutrality in future wars. [41]

The concept of the state has largely slipped out of Anglo-American political discourse. In part, this is because of the liberal tradition which stresses voluntarism and private interest as the foundation of political order. The state, with its monopoly of force, represents the dark side of political order which is best kept at a distance or in the closet. Lenin and his followers exaggerated the coercive element of the state by labelling all states as dictatorships, thus giving their own "proletarian dictatorship" justification by claiming that it was organized force against a counter-revolutionary minority. The military, the police and the prisons represent this coercive aspect of the state. Historical Anglo-American suspicion of authority finds expression in the delimitation of military capacity. The current US "all-volunteer" armed forces are the latest manifestation of the sentiment that people should not be forced to do anything, even to defend their country. [42]

The liberal state was, ironically, imposed on the Japanese after the war. While few would deny that this democratic experiment has been successful, nevertheless its foreign origins continue to trouble many individuals The peace constitution was imposed on Japan, although at least one alternative draft was available. [43] Pacifists argue that, on the contrary, the peace constitution was the logical continuation of previous tendencies, made

possible by popular disgust over the excesses of militarists. A disarmed Japan, Kamashima Jiro argued, was the
culmination of centuries of reducing numbers of individuals who had the right to bear arms.[44] In 1588, Hideyoshi disarmed the common people with his sword hunt.
Arms possession was restricted to the samurai only. The
Meiji government took this privilege away in the nineteenth century. Today, individual possession of weapons
is tightly restricted, with a high level of public
peace: "Some people deem it to be unhealthy that many
Japanese believe that security, like air, is free, but
we must give due credit to the nation's historical legacy in preparing a climate conducive to this belief."[45]
Therefore, the retention of Article Nine must be understood in light "...of natural progression from the traditional disarmament of the people to the postwar demilitarization of the state. Because of this corres-
pondence with tradition, the people willingly accepted
the state's demilitarization and have faithfully guarded
the antiwar provisions in the constitution."[46]

Although this concept of the demilitarized state
was a source of satisfaction to the pacifist persuasion,
it had two major flaws in the existing world: First, it
required the indulgence of other states which guaranteed
Japan's security or which refrained from attacking Japan. Second, it distorted the nature of the political
community in a way which drained citizenship of its traditional meaning.

Force was a fundamental condition of the state, as
Hobbes described in his Leviathan. If sovereign force
was necessary to bring about order in domestic society,
how could it be avoided or ignored in international society, which has been as anarchic as the state of nature
described by Hobbes. The price to be paid for peace,
stability, and order is the state as the sole arbiter of
justice and law.[47]

Because of a congenial environment, the existence
of the Japanese state has not been subjected to the intense scrutiny it has in the West. According to Katsuda
Kichitaro, the Japanese people treat the state as if it
had fallen as a gift from heaven.[48] Social unity is
accepted as a natural phenomenon.

The emperor has stood at the center of the Japanese
state. On the two occasions when national unity faced
crisis, in 1853 and 1945, the institution of the emperor
served to avert state collapse and turmoil. To General
MacArthur, the emperor was worth ten army divisions,[49]
since his proclamation to surrender had allowed the landing of US occupation forces without resistance.

Having had good fortune in past crises does not
guarantee maintenance of social order in a future emergency. The present constitution contains no provisions
to deal with national emergency, reflecting the belief
that social unity is a spontaneous phenomenon.[50] Rejec-

ting the various emergency provisions of the Meiji constitution, postwar Japanese tend to believe that it is
undemocratic to prepare for emergency. West Germany and
Italy allow extraordinary powers to government in their
constitutions, but no such concern about the collapse of
government has affected Japan.

Katsuda is disturbed that the Japanese people and
their leaders believe the state and social unity are
similar to natural phenomena - requiring little or no
effort to sustain. In reality, the state is an artifice,
and can dissolve if neglected.[51] The notion of citizenship has been corrupted by so-called progressive forces,
and the media which treat citizenship and the state as
antagonistic concepts. To sing the national anthem, or
hang the national flag, or to speak of public duties and
sacrifice is to invite accusations of fascism, writes
Katsuda.[52]

Since the war, the state has receded from popular
consciousness. The state is considered evil in the views
of Marxist radicals and various anarchist groups. Instead of representing the public good, to be sustained
through sacrifice, the state in contemporary Japan represents "public goods" to be distributed through the
agencies of the "welfare state." The state becomes the
satisfier of public needs and citizens hope to become
the beneficiaries of the state.[53] It is a development
which Katsuda terms the "womanly state." The state looks
after its charges with care, and is regarded as an enti-
ty with gentle features prepared to accept whatever task
is asked.

Such thinking obscures the truth that force is the
ultima ratio of the state. When hijackers seized a
Japan Air Lines plane, the government gave in to demands
of the Red Army.[54] The use of physical force was shun-
ned, in contrast to West Germany and Israel which refuse
negotiations with hijackers. Thus, if Japanese want a
state that can be relied on, there must be acknowledgement that coercive force is part of its essence. The
central issue in the defense debate is not the proportion of GNP spent on the SDF, or whether the US is a
reliable ally: It is "whether the people are prepared
to accept death to protect Japan's independence and to
uphold law and order."[55]

A major difference between a pacifist view such as
Kamashima's, and the pragmatist Katsuda is that the former tends to stress Japanese uniqueness - Japan is different because of past rampant militarism, its victimi-
zation by nuclear weapons, and its present peace constitution. The Japanese state is sui generis and must be
preserved. In contrast, Katsuda takes Japan's special
characteristics as evidence of a lack of realism, and
wants the country to understand the notion of the state
as an important part of world development. Millions of
Japanese watched the demise of the South Vietnamese

state in 1975 on their terebi (televisions), and should realize the terrible consequences of losing a state. Because the state possesses a monopoly of force, this does not place it in antagonism to justice In ancient Greece, the state was "sacred," according to Katsuda, and the individual was an integral part. In modern society, the state is seen as a mere convenience for the protection of property and lives - the state is expected to be a docile servant of civil society.[56] In Japan, the state has become a kind of profit-seeking community which serves the true core communities - the corporations. Because the state does not appear to embody any higher values and has no claim to individual sacrifice, it seems that there is no dishonor for the state to surrender whenever lives and property are threatened. But if surrender in event of attack is the preferred option of the postwar Japanese state, then any defense spending is wasted money, since the SDF will be ordered to give up rather than resist. The only possible justification for the SDF then is for natural disaster relief, and for this, it does not need advanced weapons and combat training. Or, 0.9% of the GNP is a small price to pay to humor the Americans so that they will not desert Japan too early, or inflict trade restrictions in retaliation for the "cheap ride" in defense. This seems to be the ironic logic of the minimalist, pacifist Japanese state.

Katsuda prefers the Burkean notion of the state as a partnership of the living, the dead, and the yet unborn. The present generation pursues material gratification, forgetting the sacrifices of the wartime generation.[57] The liberal utilitarian state is a corruption of the spiritual dimension of liberal thought, which recognized the individual as a human being with rights of dignity, freedom and property. The state does have a core of physical force and brute power, but coercion alone does not make a state.[58] Without ethical and legal justification, the state's possession and use of force is mere violence, and the state is merely St. Augustine's "band of thieves." The state must be deserving of the contributions, sacrifice, and obligations of its citizens. If not, even the most powerful of armies will not prevent its disintegration.[59]

The debates of intellectuals will not solve the profound questions of state and defense, but they are bound to influence future developments. There is recognition that the postwar conditions of US military dominance have ended in the region, and that Japan's peace and security are no longer "natural phenomena." Some intellectuals and a growing number of politicians realize the changes, and are moving to inform the public. In democratic Japan, however, nobody wants to be the messenger of bad news for fear of risking blame for the new situation. The government, media and political parties continue to take the pulse of the electorate through public opinion polls, but no leader grasped the nettle.

COMPREHENSIVE NATIONAL SECURITY

On 2 April 1979, Prime Minister Ohira appointed a Comprehensive National Security Study Group to examine all aspects of the security question, and report its recommendations. The group consisted of twenty members and was chaired by Inoki Masamichi, president of the Research Institute for Peace and Security. The group's report was completed and presented to Acting Prime Minister Masayoshi Ito on 2 July 1980.

The notion of "comprehensive security" referred to the fact that national security policy, at least for Japan, was much more than defense preparations. It included ideas such as "a true security policy aims to create a peaceful world."[60] Military power alone could not guarantee the existence of the state: "However much wealth a nation may consume to acquire a powerful military capability, it cannot gain security if it continues to take actions which make many or almost all countries its enemies in international society. This was how Japan failed before World War II."[61]

The Report criticized Japan's failure to make sufficient security efforts:

...precisely because ours is an imperfect world marred by confrontation and conflict, security efforts are required.

...to preach a peaceful world and to put hope in it only means to depend on others. Japan has tended to act in this manner since World War II...Since the international order that has come into being.. is imperfect, each nation's self-reliant efforts are required, and the order itself presumes this self-reliance as an essential factor of its composition.[62]

Japan's security policy, both in a narrow sense and in the broader economic context, requires efforts to maintain a peaceful interdependent international order, and demands efforts to achieve greater self-reliance. There must be a balance between these efforts.[63] Prior to the oil crisis of 1973, Japan's security question was concerned largely with military threat or natural disaster. Subsequently, questions of energy and food have become vital in Japan's comprehensive security picture.

The inclusion of other areas of concern under comprehensive security does not reduce the importance of military security, since "military capability is a major factor governing the foreign policy of each country... Weaknesses in the field of economic resources are offset

with strengths in the field of military resources, and
vice versa."[64] The fundamental assumption of the Report
is that the world has changed in one important aspect:

> The most fundamental fact in the changing interna-
> tional situation in the 1970s is the termination of
> clear American supremacy in both military and eco-
> nomic spheres. Until the end of the 1960s, the
> United States had been the "policeman of the world"
> and at the same time the "banker of the world" as
> the main pillar of the IMF and GATT system, which
> covered most of the earth. That is not the case
> any longer. (Author's emphasis)[65]

The balance of military power shifted from the US to the
USSR: US military expenditures declined from 9% to 5%
of GNP, while the USSR kept its military expenditures at
11-14%. In nuclear weapons, the Soviets have achieved
rough parity. Also, the USSR has expanded its naval
forces and airlift capacity so that it can exert its
power in remote places. In addition to geopolitical
advantages because of control of the Eurasian heartland,
the Soviets now have the capacity for long-distance
intervention.

The US, in contrast, has shifted from a 2.5 war to
a 1.5 war strategy, with the result that,

> The allies and friends of the United States were
> given nearly full security by American military
> power in the past. However, this is not the case
> anymore...The credibility of the nuclear umbrella
> was high while the United States had superiority
> over the Soviet Union in strategic nuclear weapons,
> but now that a "parity" in nuclear forces has been
> achieved, the credibility of the nuclear umbrella
> cannot be maintained for allies and friends who do
> not have a close relationship with the United Sta-
> tes.[66]

There was also a change in American will:

> As a result of the failure in the Vietnam War, the
> American people have grown skeptical about inter-
> vention as illustrated by the fact that they have
> watched in silence the Soviet indirect intervention
> in Angola and Ethiopia.[67]

The new position is that the US will help in defense only where it makes a real difference and where it
is considered in its interests. In the past, when the US
maintained nuclear superiority, and the Soviet navy was
not dangerous, Japan was completely safe. Now, "the United States is no longer able to provide a high degree of
security."[68] Therefore, Japan must consider self-reliant

defense measures for the first time since world war two:
"More than just retaining overall friendly relations
with the United States, it has become necessary for
Japan to prepare for well-functioning military relations
with America as well."[69]

In addition, the US is playing a delicate diplomatic game in which Japan will also be affected. The
change in US policy towards China conforms to the need
to "exploit Sino-Soviet confrontation to cope with Soviet expansion." Normalization has thus had a double
meaning: "On the one hand, it normalized and stabilized
the political order in the Asia-Pacific region; on the
other, since it served as a means of restraining the
Soviet Union, to some extent it aroused the Soviets."[70]
The Report also acknowledges that Japan's friendship
with China and the USSR involves power politics.[71]

In contrast to remarkable progress of Sino-Japanese
relations during the 1970s, there was little change in
Japanese-Soviet relations, according to the Report. As
described in previous chapters of the present study, the
Report also noted Soviet concerns over the direction of
Japan's foreign policy:

> The primary reason for the Soviet Union's apprehen-
> sion over the progress in Japan-China relations is
> that the two-way economic exchange will contribute
> to China's modernization and thereby make China
> stronger. The Soviet Union is particularly sensi-
> tive to economic exchange that may lead to the
> strengthening of China's military power. Beyond
> that, the Soviet Union seems to hold the view that
> the existence of the Japan-US Security Treaty, the
> conclusion of the Japan-China treaty, and the nor-
> malization of Sino-American relations might lead
> these countries - the United States, China and
> Japan - toward a tripartite alliance, and further,
> that taking into consideration NATO as another
> element, a net to encircle the Soviet Union is
> taking shape.
>
> The Soviet reaction is excessive but not en-
> tirely groundless.[72] (Author's emphasis)

These developments cannot fail to affect Japan's security policy:

> If the vicious circle of better Japan-China rela-
> tions and negative Soviet reactions is left unat-
> tended, thus greatly aggravating Japanese-Soviet
> relations, Japan's national security will be affec-
> ted in an extremely adverse way. This is because
> the Soviet Union, at least for the time being, is
> the only potential threat to Japan.[73]

The strengthening of Japan's self-defense capability will not pose a threat to the USSR, and thus would not obstruct better relations. It is necessary for Japan to consolidate its defense forces in order to maintain diplomatic credibility. "The present task throughout the world is to demonstrate that the strengthening of Soviet military power will not bear fruit."[74]

The Comprehensive Security Group recommended to the prime minister that, in order to consolidate national defense, the government's own "National Defense Program Outline" be implemented. This had been adopted by the National Defense Council and Cabinet on 29 October 1976. The Group pointed out that much can be done within the existing constitutional structure, the 1976 Outline, and a defense budget of around 1% of GNP. For example, they note that only 1% of defense expenditures is allotted for research and development, in contrast to about 10% in other industrialized countries. Also, air bases and radar sites have little survivability in event of attack. Changes in these and other areas would considerably enhance the nation's self-defense capacity.

The Report provides a thoughtful evaluation of Japan's present situation in the world, and denies that the democratic state should be changed:

We are living in an age when Pax Americana is nearing an end without any substitution order taking its place. This change has transformed the scope of the security issue from a limited one to a comprehensive one and made the issue pressing. When an order is shaken, danger is great...

Japan's national security efforts thus far, however, have been deplorable indeed. Over the thirty-odd years since the end of World War II, Japan has firmly established an internal political system resting on the foundation of freedom and democracy, and it has also achieved great success in developing its national economy...

Not until the Japanese people become clearly aware that their state and society are irreplaceable and must be defended will the security issue become a national task. Such an awareness is steadily increasing according to recent opinion surveys, but it leaves much to be desired; the Self-Defense Forces are not sufficiently appreciated and concern about national defense is largely absent in the people's mind.[75]

The Japanese people and state have adapted to new situations before, and the Comprehensive Security Group recommends that certain policy directions be followed - within the scope of existing institutions.

Since the issuance of the report, the American decline may have been arrested. The election of a conservative president and a shift in the US public mood away from support for the withdrawal syndrome in foreign affairs may provide Japan with a justification to pursue past policies. That is, the turnaround in US defense and foreign policy posture could mark a reversal in Soviet-US parity in the East Asian region back to earlier US dominance. Certainly, Soviet problems in Afghanistan and Poland indicate USSR expansion may have been over-extended.

It would be a serious mistake, however, for Japan's leadership to rely too heavily on Reagan restorationism as a loophole to avoid heavier self-reliance in defense. His near-assassination in March 1981 was a reminder that leadership is a tenuous and mortal quality. This does not mean that reliance on the US defense guarantees is folly, but rather that the modest proposals of the Comprehensive National Security Group are prudent and probably workable.

Politicians in Japan - as elsewhere - have sometimes sought for dramatic symbols or programs or breakthroughs in order to capture public imagination and consolidate their positions. Tanaka's program for reconstructing the Japan archipelago, or Fukuda's PFT with China, or Suzuki's Japanese-US alliance are examples that come to mind. But as we have seen in the case of the PFT, the settlement of one issue generates problems in other areas. The 1978 PFT settled an anomalous situation between China and Japan, and may have helped stabilize the Korean peninsula. But it was also an event in power politics of the region which Sonoda and Fukuda would not admit. It was a catalyst in cooling relations between Japan and the USSR, and possibly increased the likelihood of faster Soviet-Vietnam links.

Many Japanese feel that the status of economic giant requires a higher military posture. The notion of Comprehensive Security, however, should remind them of the fragility of Japan's position and the necessity of avoiding defense buildups which could upset the fragility of the system. Likewise, the lesson of the PFT should be that autonomous diplomacy cannot be lightly undertaken by Japan.

Footnotes

1. Quoted in Denis and Peggy Warner, The Tide at Sunrise (New York: Charterhouse, 1974), p. 557.

2. In a 1979 public opinion survey, 86% of the respondents answered that the SDF was necessary - an increase from 77% in 1975. Negative responses dropped from 8% to 5%. However, a slight majority considered that the present scale of defense forces was sufficient,

234

while those favoring increase were a higher proportion than those calling for reduction. Prime Minister's Secretariat, Public Relations Office. Public Opinion Survey on Self-Defense Force and Defense, February 1979.

3. Albert Axelbank, Black Star Over Japan (New York: Hill and Wang, 1972).

4. Jon Halliday and Gavan McCormack, Japanese Imperialism Today (Middlesex, England: Penguin Books, 1973).

5. Kataoka Tetsuya, "The Concept of the Japanese Second Republic," Japan Echo 7:1 (1980), p. 87.

6. Inoki Masamichi, "From Utopian Pacifism to Utopian Militarism," Japan Echo 7:4 (1980), p. 94.

7. Fukuda Tsuneari, "A Critique of Opinions on Defense," Japan Echo 7:1 (1980), p. 71.

8. Kamishima Jiro, "The Tradition and Realism of Demilitarization," Japan Echo 7:3 (1980), p. 26.

9. Report on Comprehensive National Security (Translation) (Tokyo: no publisher, 1980), p. 7.

10. Inoki, ibid., p. 96.

11. Shimizu Ikutari, "The Nuclear Option: Japan, Be a State," Japan Echo 7:3 (1980), p. 34.

12. Ibid., p. 35.

13. Ibid., p. 37.

14. Ibid., p. 38.

15. Ibid., p. 39.

16. Ibid., p. 40.

17. Ibid.

18. Yagisawa Mitsuo, "America's Four Umbrellas: Both Sides of the Japan-U.S. Security System," Japan Quarterly 28:2 (1981), pp. 161-174.

19. Shimizu, p. 41.

20. Ibid., p. 42.

21. Ibid.

22. Ibid., p. 44.

23. Inoki, p. 88.

24. Ibid.

25. Ibid., p. 94.

26. Ibid., p. 96.

27. Ibid., pp. 89,97.

28. Ibid., p. 97.

29. Kataoka, p. 85.

30. Defense of Japan 1977, pp. 143-150.

31. Kataoka, p. 87.

32. Ibid.

33. Ibid., p. 88.

34. Ibid., p. 89.

35. Ibid., p. 88.

36. Ibid., p. 91.

37. Ibid., p. 92.

38. Ibid.

39. Ibid., p. 95.

40. Ibid., p. 96.

41. Ibid., p. 97.
42. James Fallows, "The Civilianization of the Army," The Atlantic 247:4 (April 1981), pp. 98-108.
43. Shimizu, p. 34.
44. Kamishima, p. 26.
45. Ibid.
46. Ibid.
47. Katsuda Kichitaro, "In Defense of the State," Japan Echo 7:2 (1980), p. 81.
48. Ibid., p. 82.
49. Ibid., p. 83.
50. Ibid.
51. Ibid., p. 86.
52. Ibid, pp. 85-86.
53. Ibid., p. 87.
54. On details of the hijacking, and Japan's payment of the $6 million ransom, see JTW, 8 October 1977, pp. 1-2.
55. Katsuda, p. 88.
56. Ibid.
57. See Yoshida Mitsuru, "Proxies for the War Dead," Japan Echo 7:2 (1980), pp. 75-80.
58. Katsuda, p. 91.
59. Ibid., p. 92.
60. Report on Comprehensive Security, p. 19.
61. Ibid.
62. Ibid., p. 20.
63. Ibid., p. 22.
64. Ibid., p. 23.
65. Ibid., p. 25.
66. Ibid., p. 27.
67. Ibid.
68. Ibid., p. 28.
69. Ibid.
70. Ibid.
71. Ibid., p. 29.
72. Ibid., p. 50.
73. Ibid., p. 52.
74. Ibid., p. 53.
75. Ibid., pp. 34-35.

Selected Bibliography

Serials (with abbreviations used in footnotes)

Mainichi Shimbun (MS)
Nihon Keizai (NK)
Asahi Shimbun (AS)
Yomiuri Shimbun (YS)
Sankei (SK)
Tokyo Shimbun (TS)
Korea Herald
China Quarterly
New York Times
Christian Science Monitor
Japan Times Weekly (JTW)
Daily Report: China (DR:China)
Japan Quarterly
Beijing Review (Peking Review)
Nikkan Kogyo
Nihon Kogyo
Daily Report: USSR (DR:USSR)
Daily Report: Asia and the Pacific (DR:AP)
Globe and Mail (Toronto)
Daily Summary of the Japan Press
Washington Post

Books

Agawa, Hiroyuki. The Reluctant Admiral; Yamamoto and
      the Imperial Navy. Tokyo: Kodansha, 1979.
Asian Security (Annual). Tokyo: Research Institute for
      Peace and Security.
Axelbank, Albert. Black Star Over Japan. Toronto:
      Hill and Wang, 1972
Barnds, William J., ed. Japan and the United States.
      New York: New York University, 1979.
Black, Cyril E. et. al. The Modernization of Japan and
      Russia: A Comparative Study. New York: Free
      Press, 1975.
Blaker, Michael. Japanese International Negotiating
      Style. New York: Columbia University Press,
      1977.
Buck, James H., ed. The Modern Japanese Military
      System. Beverley Hills: Sage, 1975.
Clough, Ralph N. East Asia and U.S. Security.
      Washington, D.C.: The Brookings Institution, 1975.

238

Comprehensive National Security Study Group. Report on
    Comprehensive National Security. Tokyo: (no
    publisher cited), 1980.
Craig, Albert M., ed. Japan: A Comparative View.
    Princeton: Princeton University Press, 1979.
Emmerson, John K. and Leonard A. Humphreys. Will Japan
    Rearm? A Study in Attitudes. Stanford: Hoover
    Institute, 1973.
Feulner, Edwin J. Jr. and Hideaki Kase, ed., U.S. Japan
    Mutual Security. Washington, D.C.: The Heritage
    Foundation, 1981.
Gibney, Frank. Japan: The Fragile Superpower. New
    York: Norton, 1975.
Halliday, Jon. A Political History of Japanese
    Capitalism. New York: Pantheon, 1975.
Hasegawa, Sukehiro. Japanese Foreign Aid: Policy and
    Practice. New York: Praeger, 1975.
Hellmann, Donald C. Japan and East Asia: The New
    International Order. London: Pall Mall Press,
    1972.
Houn, Franklin. Chinese Political Traditions.
    Washington, D.C.: Public Affairs Press, 1965.
Ienaga, Saburo. The Pacific War. New York: Pantheon
    Press, 1978.
Iriye, Akira, ed. The Chinese and the Japanese: Essays
    in Political and Cultural Interactions. Princeton:
    Princeton University Press. 1969.
Jansen, Marius B. Japan and China: From War to Peace,
    1894-1972. Chicago: Rand McNally, 1975.
Johnson, Stuart E., with Joseph A. Yager. The Military
    Equation in Northeast Asia. Washington, D.C.: The
    Brookings Institution, 1979.
Kahn, Herman. The Emerging Japanese Superstate.
    Engelwood Cliffs, N.J: Prentice-Hall, 1970.
Kajima Institute of International Peace. Japan in the
    World. Tokyo: Japan Times, 1976.
Kataoka, Tetsuya. Waiting for a "Pearl Harbor": Japan
    Debates Defense. Stanford: Hoover Institute,
    1980.
Langdon, Frank C. Japan's Foreign Policy. Vancouver:
    University of British Columbia Press, 1973.
Lee, Chae-Jin. Japan Faces China. Baltimore: Johns
    Hopkins University Press, 1967.
Mendl, Wolf. Issues in Japan's China Policy. New York:
    Oxford University Press, 1978.
Morley, James W., ed. Forecast for Japan: Security in
    the 1970s. Princeton: Princeton University Press,
    1972.
Mueller, Peter G. and Douglas A. Ross. China and Japan
    - Emerging Global Powers. New York: Praeger,
    1975.
Okazaki, Hisahiko. A Japanese View of Détente.
    Lexington, Mass.: Lexington Books, 1974.

Reischauer, Edwin O. The Japanese. Cambridge: Harvard
    University Press, 1978.
Sansom, George. A History of Japan to 1334. Stanford:
    Stanford University Press, 1950.
Scalapino, Robert A., ed. The Foreign Policy of Modern
    Japan. Berkeley: University of California Press,
    1977.
Singer, Kurt. Mirror, Sword and Jewel. Tokyo:
    Kodansha, 1973.
Stephan, John J. The Kuril Islands. Oxford: Clarendon
    Press, 1974.
Swearingen, Rodger. The Soviet Union and Postwar Japan.
    Stanford, CA.: Hoover Institution, 1978.
Thayer, Nathaniel B. How the Conservatives Rule Japan.
    Princeton: Princeton University Press, 1969.
Vasey, Lloyd R. Pacific Asia and U.S. Policies: A
    Political-Economic-Strategic Assessment. Honolulu:
    Pacific Forum, 1978.
Vogel, Ezra F. Japan as Number One. Tokyo: Tuttle,
    1979.
Warner, Denis and Peggy. The Tide at Sunrise. New
    York: Charterhouse, 1974.
Weinstein, Franklin B., ed. U.S.-Japan Relations and
    the Security of the Far East. Boulder: Westview
    Press, 1978.

Articles

Bedeski, Robert. E. "China's Options in Relations with
    Japan." International Journal 34:4 (1979), pp.
    680-89.
Beloff, Nora. "Escape from Boredom: A Defector's
    Story." Atlantic Monthly 246:5 (1980),pp.42+61.
Curtis, Gerald L. "Japanese Security Policies and the
    United States." Foreign Affairs 59:4 (1981), pp.
    852-874.
Falkenheim, Peggy L. "The Impact of the Peace and
    Friendship Treaty on Soviet Japanese Relations."
    Asian Survey 19:12 (1979), pp. 1209-1223.
Fukuda, Tsuneari. "A Critique of Opinions on Defense."
    Japan Echo 7:1 (1980), pp. 69-84.
Fukushima, Shingo. "Japan's Wavering Defense Plan, The
    New Moves Toward Strengthening Defense Power."
    Japan Quarterly 25:4 (1978), pp. 399-406.
Gordon, Bernard K. "Japan, the United States and
    Southeast Asia." Foreign Affairs 56:3 (1978), pp.
    579-600.
Ha, Joseph M. "Moscow's Policy Toward Japan." Problems
    of Communism 26:5 (1977), pp. 61-72.

240

——, "Japanese Rearmament: Fukuda's Legacy, Ohira's Choice." Asian Perspective 3:2 (1979), pp. 230-251.

Han, Sungjoo. "South Korea 1978: The Growing Security Dilemma. Asian Survey 19:1 (1979), pp. 41-50.

Inoki, Masamichi. "From Utopian Pacifism to Utopian Militarism." Japan Echo 7:4 (1980), pp. 87-98.

Ishida, Takeshi. "A Look at the New China." Japan Echo, Volume 8, special issue (1981), pp. 55-62.

Kamishima, Jiro. The Tradition and Realism of Demilitarization." Japan Echo 7:3 (1980), pp. 24-32.

Kataoka, Tetsuya. "The Concept of the Japanese Second Republic." Japan Echo 7:1 (1980), pp. 85-97.

Katsuda, Kichitaro. "In Defense of the State." Japan Echo 7:2 (1980), pp. 81-92.

Kimura, Hiroshi. "Soviet Strategy in Northeast Asia." Problems of Communism 30:5 (1981), pp. 71-76.

Klein, Donald W. "Japan 1978: The Consensus Continues." Asian Survey 19:1 (1979), pp. 30-40.

Luttwak, Edward N. "Against the China Card." Commentary 66:4 (1978), pp. 37-43.

Mendl, Wolf. "The Security Debate in Japan." International Affairs (Autumn 1980), pp. 607-621.

Nakagawa, Yatsuhiro. "Why Japan Should Let Nuclear Arms in." Japan Echo 7:4 (1980), pp. 99-110.

Nakajima, Mineo. "Diplomacy as Defense Strategy." Japan Echo 6:1 (1979), pp. 54-63.

Oksenberg, Michel. "China Policy for the 1980s." Foreign Affairs 59:2 (1980) pp. 304-322.

Pi, Ying-hsien. "Impasse in the Proposed Peiping-Tokyo Treaty of Peace and Friendship and the Anti-Hegemony Clause." Issues and Studies 14:3 (1978), pp. 73-85.

Porter, Gareth. "The Great Power Triangle in Southeast Asia." Current History, Vol. 79, No. 461 (1980), pp. 161-164.

Sakanaka, Tomohisa. "Japan's Military Capability: Present and Future." Japan Quarterly 25:4 (1978), pp. 413-421.

Shimizu, Ikutaro. "The Nuclear Option: Japan Be a State!" Japan Echo 7:3 (1980), pp. 33-45.

Simon, Sheldon W. "Japan's Foreign Policy: Adjustments to a Changing Environment." Asian Survey 18:7 (1978), pp. 666-686.

Tretiak, Daniel. "The Sino-Japanese Treaty of 1978: The Senkaku Incident Prelude." Asian Survey 18:11 (1978), pp. 1235-1249.

Weinstein, Franklin B. "United States-Japan Relations and the Fallacies of Burden-Sharing." Pacific Community 9:1 (1977), pp. 1-16.

Yagisawa, Mitsuo. "America's Four Umbrellas: Both
    Sides of the Japan-U.S. Security System." _Japan
    Quarterly_ 28:2 (1981), pp. 161-174.
Yoshida, Mitsuru. "Proxies for the War Dead." _Japan
    Echo_ 7:2 (1980), pp. 75-80.
Zumwalt, Elmo R. "Gorshkov and His Navy." _Orbis_ 24:3
    (1980), pp. 491-510.

Government Documents

US Department of Defense. _Annual Report._
_The Eleventh National Congress of the Communist Party of
    China (Documents)._ Peking: Foreign Languages
    Press, 1977.
_Documents of the First Session of the Fifth National
    People's Congress of the People's Republic of
    China._ Peking: Foreign Languages Press, 1978.
Japan, Ministry of Foreign Affairs. _Diplomatic
    Bluebook._ 1980.
_____, _Japan's Northern Territories._ 1981.
Japan, Defense Agency. _Defense of Japan._ Annual.

Index